RELATING TO JANE

*Studies on the Life and Novels of
Jane Austen with a Life of her Niece
Elizabeth Austen/Knight*

M.C. Hammond

MINERVA PRESS

LONDON
ATLANTA   MONTREUX   SYDNEY

RELATING TO JANE: *Studies on the Life and Novels of Jane Austen with a Life of her Niece Elizabeth Austen/Knight*
Copyright © M.C. Hammond 1998

All Rights Reserved

ISBN 0 75410 060 X

First Published 1998 by
MINERVA PRESS
195 Knightsbridge
London SW7 1RE

Printed in Great Britain for Minerva Press

RELATING TO JANE
*Studies on the Life and Novels of
Jane Austen with a Life of her Niece
Elizabeth Austen/Knight*

To my husband Nicholas, without whose help and support this book would not exist; and to Henry Rice, the 'fons et origo' of the whole of the second part of this work, and a most encouraging supporter.

Contents

BOOK ONE

Partial and Prejudiced:
Essays on Jane Austen and her Work

Here was a woman about the year 1800 writing without hate, without bitterness, without fear, without protest, without preaching. That was how Shakespeare wrote, I thought... and when people compare Shakespeare and Jane Austen, they may mean that the minds of both had consumed all impediments; and for that reason we do not know Jane Austen and we do not know Shakespeare, and for that reason Jane Austen pervades every word that she wrote, and so does Shakespeare.

Virginia Woolf on Jane Austen,
A Room of One's Own

Edward Austen/Knight = Elizabeth Brid
1767–1852   1774–1808

Henry Rice = (1776) Sarah Samson
1743–1797   1755–1841

and ten other children

Henry = Lucy Lefroy   John   Edward Royds = Elizabeth
1776–1860   1773–1799   1789–1878   1800–1884

Edward Bridges = (1864) Cecilia Harcourt   Henry   John Morland = (1863) Caroline York
1819–1902   1821–1848   1823–1897
       Henry   unm.   no children   Elizabeth Louisa
Earl of Winchilsea (1850) Fanny Margaretta   1824–1916
                          1820–1909   unm.

3 sons, 1 daughter

Marianne Sophia = (1857) Emilius (Derby) Bruce   Charles Augustus = (1875) Adela M.M. Knight
1825–1909   (later Laurie)   1828–1905
       4 or 5 children   3 daughters   (i) Frances Napier = (1866) Cecil = (ii) L
                                 George William   1831–1917   Sey
                                 1827–1853
                                 unm.   5 sons, 4 daughters

Caroline Cassandra   Arthur   Florence May = (1862) John Wright
1835–1923   1838–1863   1841–1910   (later Osmaston)
unm.   unm.   11 children, 4 stepchildren
       Walter Brook   Eleanor Murray = (18   nel Knig
       1837–1892   1844–192
unm.   (i) Laura York = (1868) Ernest = (ii) Fanny Gunning   no children
                                1840–1910
       1 son, 2 daughters

Who was Jane Austen?

Jane Austen has suffered from misrepresentation at the hands of critics, reviewers and readers more than most novelists; partly because, a woman, she wrote at a time when women wrote novels (and quite a number of women did) of a certain kind, and it was not immediately apparent that hers were of a different kind. She has too, a curious sleight of hand whereby she herself conveys one impression to an unobservant reader, while meaning something very different. This can be exemplified by her friend Mrs Charles Cage's opinion of *Emma*, which she concluded was 'so very comfortable', ignoring the more devastating aspects of that remarkable book. The 'Janeites' and the 'anti-Janeites' love her or abhor her for similar, and at least partly mistaken reasons – the loveable, innocuous, gently humorous Jane, with her impeccable taste, her unruffled urbanity. The false assumptions that have been made have varied from one period to another; at first they were mainly concerned with contemporary notions of the general function of the novel, later they were more concerned with misconceptions about Jane Austen herself.

Her novels were something entirely new when they appeared in the early years of the nineteenth century; whatever she owed in her literary heritage to Samuel Richardson or Samuel Johnson, to Crabbe or Fanny Burney, she was in fact the founder of the modern novel, which depicts, not *la belle nature*, that is, nature in her most sentimental, refined and idealistic condition, but the day-to-day activities in ordinary, not to say commonplace surroundings. Sir Walter Scott was amongst the first to perceive this, and to regard it as laudable; but even he felt the need to apologise for her failure to set her novels in a higher rank of society:

> In adventuring upon this task (i.e., the representation of that which is daily taking place around him) ...the author makes obvious sacrifices and encounters peculiar difficulty.

The novels of Jane Austen, he continued:

> have a great deal of nature in them – nature in ordinary and middle life to be sure, but valuable. They do not, it is true, get above the middle class of society, but there she is inimitable.

He felt this to be a limitation, and his tone is condescending.

Another early presumption concerned the moral purpose of literature, the insistence that literature, and especially the novel, should reinforce the moral standards of the day; not only must virtue triumph and vice be punished, but vice must only be referred to in the most generalised terms. It was a paradox that the popular romantic novels of the period should deal with crimes and viciousness of the most exaggerated nature, but so unspecified that the 'frissons' experienced would be delicious rather than disgusting. With the advent of the 'modern' type of realistic novel, immoral behaviour became more difficult to handle, in proportion as it became more conceivable. It was more important than ever that vice or frailty should meet with its due reward. In 1853, Mrs

Gaskell's novel *Ruth*, in which the heroine, though seduced in her youth, is depicted as a saintly character, was denounced as immoral in its tendency, and was burnt publicly by several indignant fathers lest their daughters should fall under its pernicious influence. *Lizzie Leigh* was a story on the same theme, and in spite of its highly moral emphasis on repentance and forgiveness, which makes it almost unreadable nowadays, so earnestly does Mrs Gaskell eschew anything like the condonation of sin, it met with similar strictures. Archbishop Whateley, in an admirable review of Jane Austen's two posthumously published works, still emphasised that the importance of her work lay in the implicitly moral and Christian tone: '...it guides the judgement, and supplies a kind of artificial experience.'

Most of the early commendations of Jane Austen's novels referred to the unexceptional moral tone in less subtle terms; *Sense and Sensibility* was described as a 'genteel, well-written novel, from which both amusement and instruction can be drawn,' – it had 'an unexceptionable tendency'. *Emma* came in for similar treatment, being damned with faint praise in such notices as that in the *Gentleman's Magazine* of September 1816 which begins '*Dulce est desipere in loco*' and concludes 'it is amusing, if not instructive, and has no tendency to deteriorate the heart.' The reading of novels at this time was regarded almost entirely as a rather disreputable leisure activity of idle young women[1] – many reviews refer to 'the fair reader', implying that men never read that form of literature, and the flood of rubbishy

[1] As in Sheridan's *The Rivals*, where Lydia makes such a to-do about hiding her forbidden literature, or indeed in Jane Austen's own *Northanger Abbey*, where over-indulgence in novel-reading of a sensational nature is a characteristic of the empty-headed Isabella, and leads to some sadly foolish notions on the part of Catherine. The Austen family, however, were avid and unrepentant novel readers, and it will be remembered that it is in *Northanger Abbey* that the author makes her strong plea in favour of the novel.

fiction of a melodramatic or highly sentimental kind certainly justified somewhat the refusal of critics to take the form seriously. A more perceptive critic in May 1812 however, declared of *Sense and Sensibility*: 'We think so favourably of this performance that it is with some reluctance we decline inserting it among our principal articles...' To have done so no doubt would have been like the *Times Literary Supplement* devoting its leading article to the latest book from the house of Mills and Boon.

Jane Austen has also suffered not only in being admired for doing what she had no particular intention of doing, but in being criticised for failing to do what she never attempted. Her limited range (in a physical sense) has made her particularly vulnerable in this respect. Her 'two or three families, gathered together in a village', with the action confined to visiting, gossiping and courtship have laid her open to critical comment ranging from condescension to abuse; and the general misapprehension that a circumscribed, everyday scene must lead to a limited and commonplace achievement. More serious still are the assaults on her emotional range, like the attacks by Charlotte Brontë, which tell us perhaps more about Charlotte Brontë than about Jane Austen. In 1847, G.H. Lewes wrote in *Fraser's Magazine* that Jane Austen was, with Fielding, the greatest novelist in the language, a 'prose Shakespeare' in her dramatic power and delineation of character. Poor Charlotte Brontë, in her northern hermitage, her innate misanthropy and lack of humour intensified by the appalling tragedies of her domestic life, her predilection for romantic melodrama increased by isolation and deprivation, was puzzled and uncomprehending. It was unfortunate, perhaps, that the one novel she should seize upon to investigate this prodigy should be *Pride and Prejudice*, which Jane Austen laughingly confessed was almost too 'light and bright and sparkling'. As it was,

Charlotte Brontë could not appreciate the humour, she found the exuberance no substitute for passion, and she failed entirely to penetrate beneath the surface glitter to the serious treatment of values and social predicaments that Jane Austen was concerned with.

'I got the book,' she wrote,

> and what did I find? An accurate daguerro-typed portrait of a commonplace face! A carefully fenced, highly cultivated garden, with neat borders and delicate flowers; but no glance of a bright, vivid physiognomy, no open country, no fresh air, no blue hill, no bonny beck. I should hardly like to live with her ladies and gentlemen in their elegant and confined houses.

In fact, Charlotte Brontë's 'bright, vivid physiognomy' etc. brings to mind so compulsively a picture of Elizabeth Bennet hastening indecorously through the countryside to the sickbed of her sister at Netherfield, where her muddied skirts, her disordered hair and her eyes and cheeks brightened by the exercise aroused caustic comments from the ladies and secret admiration from the gentlemen, that one wonders if that very picture may not have remained in Charlotte Brontë's mind as she wrote. But in fairness, such an open-air physically strenuous picture is relatively rare in the novels, and the bleak elemental scene at Haworth was indeed a world away from the milder climate of rural Hampshire. Charlotte Brontë's comments on *Emma* were even more acid and self-revealing; she insisted that Jane Austen's work entirely lacked sentiment and poetry, and that no artist could be called great without poetry. Jane Austen she found 'only shrewd and observant, without profundity.'

I have likewise read one of Miss Austen's works – *Emma* – read it with interest and with just the degree of admiration which Miss Austen herself would have thought sensible and suitable – anything like warmth or enthusiasm; anything energetic, poignant, heartfelt, is utterly out of place in commending these works; all such demonstration the authoress would have met with a well-bred sneer, would have calmly scorned as outré or extravagant. She does her business of delineating the surface of the lives of genteel English people curiously well; there is a Chinese fidelity, a miniature delicacy in the painting; she ruffles her reader by nothing vehement, disturbs him by nothing profound; the Passions are perfectly unknown to her; she rejects even a speaking acquaintance with that stormy Sisterhood; even to the feelings she vouchsafes no more than an occasional graceful but distant recognition; too frequent converse with them would ruffle the smooth elegance of her progress. Her business is not half so much with the human heart as with the human eyes, mouth, hands and feet; what sees keenly, speaks aptly, moves flexibly, it suits her to study, but what throbs fast and full, though hidden, what the blood rushes through, what is the unseen seat of life and the sentient target of Death, *this* Miss Austen ignores;… Jane Austen was a complete and most sensible Lady, but a very incomplete and rather insensible (not senseless) Woman…

This was a judgement based on strong temperamental antipathy, even a little jealousy towards a rival who could arouse such unaccountable enthusiasm from her own reviewer and admired acquaintance. And her judgement is endorsed, though with blind approval, by the band of 'Janeites' who have found her such very comfortable reading; J.I.M. Stewart points out:

> No novels can touch Miss Austen's when it comes to straight solace and refreshment. They must have been read and read again in convalescence... This is a very great achievement... If we are minded to establish a sort of Top Ten from the most delightful books in the language, all six of the novels have a claim. It is a staggering triumph on Miss Austen's part. How is it to be explained?
>
> The simplest answer comes from her detractors – or from those of them who assert, in effect, that the books represent a perfectly achieved invalid cookery.

Her appeal, they say, lies in the fact that there are no extremes of death or passion or violence, indigence or suffering; there are no political or social problems – indeed, 'no sort of general ideas exist so we have no occasion to reflect on how inadequate our own particular brains are for perpending them.' From this mindless sort of approval it is a short step to the hero-worship or 'Janeolatry' of Kipling's lines:

> Jane lies in Winchester – blessed be her shade!
> Praise the Lord for making her, and her for
>   all she made!
> And while the stones of Winchester, or

> Milsom Street remain,
> Glory, love and honour unto England's Jane!

The Janeites have been influenced by the pious tone of the earliest biographical notices of Jane Austen, that by her brother Henry in the posthumously published volume of *Persuasion* and *Northanger Abbey* of 1817, and the much fuller *Memoir* by her nephew James Edward Austen-Leigh, published in 1870, invaluable for their unique biographical information, but written in a tone of family pride and devotion which leaves no room for dispassionate critical appraisal. The emphasis is on the sweetness of her nature, the 'perfect placidity of temper'. (A.C. Bradley, very much later, referred to her as 'exceptionally peaceful reading'.) Henry Austen's brief memoir is a mixture of solid information,[2] turgid grandiloquence, and genuine feeling ('until the Spring of this present year, those who knew their happiness to be involved in her existence could not endure to despair'), but not surprisingly, there is little attempt at dispassionate literary judgement. The perfection of her personality had to be made clear to the public.

> Though the frailties, foibles and follies of others could not escape her immediate detection, yet even on their vices did she never trust herself to comment with unkindness. The affectation of candour is not uncommon; but she had no affectation. Faultless herself, as near as human nature can be, she always sought, in the faults of others, something to

---

[2] Some of Henry Austen's statements might have received more attention from speculating critics, for example, 'Her power of inventing characters seems to have been intuitive and almost unlimited. She drew from nature, but, whatever may have been surmised to the contrary, never from individuals.'

excuse, to forgive, or forget. Where extenuation was impossible, she had a sure refuge in
silence. She never uttered either a hasty, a silly
or a severe expression.

From such bland family adulation it is salutary to turn to a
more critical contemporary judgement, no doubt equally
prejudiced, and certainly not based as assuredly on personal
experience, that of Miss Mitford, whose grandfather, the
Rev. Mr Russell, had been Rector of Ashe, a parish adjoining Steventon, and whose mother in consequence knew the
family in Jane's childhood. From her evidently sprang Miss
Mitford's report of Jane Austen in her youth as 'the
prettiest, silliest, most affected husband-hunting butterfly';
from a friend (whose family at the time were at law with
Jane's brother Edward), Miss Mitford reported a description of Jane Austen in about 1815, when she was forty years
old:

> ...a friend of mine, who visits her now, says
> she has stiffened into the most perpendicular,
> precise, taciturn piece of single blessedness
> that ever existed, and that, till *Pride and
> Prejudice* showed what a precious gem was
> hidden in that unbending case, she was no
> more regarded in society than a poker or a
> fire-screen, or any other thin, upright piece of
> wood or iron that fills its corner in peace and
> quietness. The case is very different now; she
> is still a poker – but a poker of whom every-
> one is afraid. It must be confessed that this
> silent observation from an observer is rather
> formidable – a wit, a delineator of character,
> who does not talk, is terrific indeed!

Following on the 'sweet St Jane' myth is the delusion about the spontaneous upsurging of natural genius, artless and effortless; of Jane Austen as the inspired amateur. Henry James, while condemning the myth of 'our dear, everybody's dear Jane' as a 'beguiled infatuation, a sentimentalised vision' took the view that her art was of a gossamer nature that defied analysis, a view equally dangerous in its belittling and sentimentalising tendency. Examination of the facts proves otherwise. From Henry Austen's statement in the *Biographical Notice* that:

> some of these novels had been the gradual performance of her previous life; for though in composition she was equally rapid and correct, yet an invincible distrust of her own judgement induced her to withhold her works from the public till time and many perusals had satisfied her that the charm of recent composition was dissolved,

through the evidence in her letters and of family report that her books were worked over, transformed, revised, pruned and polished over very long periods of time, and through the research and scholarly assumptions of critics like Q.E. Leavis, all show that she was very much a professional in her approach to her work.

Personal idiosyncrasies of taste must be allowed for in literary judgements, and Jane Austen has suffered her fair share of prejudice in dislike as well as unthinking adulation. Incomprehension was one of the milder reactions. Joseph Conrad wrote to H.G. Wells, 'What *is* all this about Jane Austen? What is there *in* her? What is it all about?' Mme de Stael's dismissal of her with the single word, 'Vulgaire!' and Mary Russell Mitford's criticism on similar grounds reflect the fashion of the period for novels set in a high rank of society, with heroines of unblemished nobility of character breathing the pure air of unreality; the realism of Jane Austen and her satiric tone was too uncomfortable, her flawed and all too human heroines shocking. 'The want of elegance is almost the only want in Miss Austen,' wrote Miss Mitford,

> it is impossible not to feel in every line of *Pride and Prejudice* in every word of Elizabeth, the entire want of taste which could produce so pert, so worldly a heroine as the beloved of such a man as Darcy. Wickham is equally bad. Oh! they were just fit for each other, and I cannot forgive the delightful Darcy for parting them, Darcy should have married Jane. He is of all the admirable characters the best de-signed and the best sustained. Miss Austen ...wants nothing but the *'beau ideal'* of the fe-male character to be a perfect novel writer.

The 'animal repulsion' felt by Mark Twain is even more extreme, though his antipathy was shared by several American writers. Twain, reporting on the absence of any of her works in a ship's library, went on to say, 'Just that one omission alone would make a fairly good library out of a library that hadn't a book in it.' This view, echoed by Professor Garrod in his *Depreciation*, represents the male rejection of a view exclusively female, which is evasive of the sexual element in what is, after all, the main theme of all the works, namely matrimony; and an aversion towards the image conjured up, however unreasonably, of a middle-aged, satirical spinster in whom the wellsprings of animal vitality have dried. Emerson's attitude is similar in its violence, though it is not inspired by a physical antipathy, but a more profound disquiet.

> I am at a loss to understand why people hold
> Miss Austen's novels at so high a rate, which
> seem to me vulgar in tone, sterile in artistic in-
> vention, imprisoned in the wretched
> conventions of English society, without gen-
> ius, wit, or knowledge of the world. Never
> was life so pinched and narrow. The one
> problem in the mind of the writer …is mar-
> riageableness. All that interests in any
> character introduced is still this one, has he (or
> she) the money to marry with, and conditions
> conforming? 'Tis the 'nympholepsy of a fond
> despair', say rather, of an English boarding-
> house. Suicide is more respectable.

Emerson failed to understand that what concerned Jane
Austen was what concerns all novelists worthy of the name,
the human condition, whose problems are much the same
in an English village, on a Colonial farm, a battlefield, a
ballroom, or a bar. But the way of life which was all that
Jane Austen knew or cared to write about and which she
accepted (though not uncritically) and which formed the
background to her exploration of the human condition, was
utterly alien to Americans of that time, particularly to
writers like Emerson, with his philosophical and idealistic
outlook. The charge of a calculating materialism is often
levelled at Jane Austen, summed up amusingly by W.H.
Auden in *Letter to Byron:*

> You could not shock her more than she shocks
>   me;
> Beside her Joyce seems innocent as grass,
> It makes me feel uncomfortable to see
> An English spinster of the middle-class

> Describe the amorous effects of 'brass',
> Reveal so frankly and with such sobriety
> The economic basis of society.

Certainly the fundamental importance of economic matters in her world is reflected in her language, her imagery and her tone, as well as forming the basis of her plot structure. It could not well be otherwise, given her themes and the nature of a society where a young woman of the middle class without an income was faced with the limited choices of matrimony, governessing or dependence on the charity of her relatives. Everyone in Jane Austen's books is labelled by the extent of their fortune or their expectations, and such information is speedily supplied as being of prime general interest and importance. But the ironic attitude is everywhere sustained; it is only the vulgar, the worldly, the self-seeking who eagerly assess the value of the marital 'goods' in terms of cash; though the rejection of worldly advantage is now and then deplored by 'good' characters, as in the surprised disappointment felt by Sir Thomas Bertram and Edmund at Fanny Price's rejection of Henry Crawford. A realistic idealism as portrayed in Elinor Dashwood, Anne Elliot and Elizabeth Bennet is Jane Austen's own attitude, and is clearly seen in her letters to Fanny Knight – the attitude that it is wicked to marry for money, but folly to marry without it.

What, then, are we to make of Jane Austen? Who was she, of all these characters that the generations of readers, critics and commentators have paraded before us? There was the adored Aunt Jane, beloved sister, devoted daughter, but she does not really concern us; there is saintly Jane, Kipling's Jane who tides you over in any tricky situation, even in the trenches, and always has the apt remark, like the Bible or Shakespeare; she is akin to the medicinal Jane, the soother of fevered brows and sleepless pillows. There is genteel Miss Austen, very correct and conventional, rather prim, morally sound and in the practice of her religion above reproach (though *not* very profound, according to Cardinal Newnan, 'What vile creatures her parsons are! She has not a dream of the high Catholic 'ethos'); there is the vulgarian, with her ill-bred heroines, there is the repressed spinster, there is the passionless, unpoetical Lady with the eye of a hawk and a heart of stone. There is Miss Austen the wit, the sceptic, the shrewd observer and the secret critic of her own society. It is a very strange thing that this middle-aged, middle-class country gentlewoman whose personality on all the evidence was of the most delightful and amiable sort, should arouse so many varied reactions. But it is the works that one must be judging, and it is perhaps a measure of their greatness that they arouse such varied responses. Although one cannot agree with some of his premises, Marvin Mudrick sums up and as it were accounts for much of what has been said of Jane Austen when he writes:

> We may not like Jane Austen's defects of personality, we may even refuse to recognise them; but the artist, or rather the art, is here to be judged. The fact remains that close observation without sympathy, common-sense without tenderness, densely imagined representation without passion may not limit the comic novelist at all, may indeed be the ideal instruments for penetrating the polished surface of the bourgeois world to its unyielding material base... She will prove that these instruments, far from limiting her to a

Burneyian reflection of manners, can reconstitute the whole cold, anxious atmosphere in which the middle class lives and breathes.

Jane Austen and the Young

Before the publication of Jane Austen's letters, which reveal, in a way that the early memoirs and biographies cannot do, the precise tone of family relationships and her own attitude of intense interest and affectionate preoccupation with all her relatives and connections, there were early critics who denied to Jane Austen any interest or affection for children. This is no doubt because children play a very minor role in the novels; in some cases, it is true, the role has a function of some importance, as in *Persuasion*, but their value is often a nuisance value. Even in those cases, however, it is usually not the children whom Jane Austen criticises, but the foolish, indulgent or misguided treatment of them; they serve to emphasise the characteristics of the adults involved with them, as well as furthering the action or complicating the plot by their demands. Such is the case, for example, in *Persuasion* when Anne Elliot's first meeting with Captain Wentworth is delayed on account of the accident to Mary and Charles Musgrove's little boy; it indicates too Mary's indifference to the care of her child when there is an exciting social occasion in view; and more importantly, Anne's calm and competent handling of the crisis is a prelude to the more significant scene later in the book when Louisa falls on the Cob at Lyme and Anne on that occasion is the only member of the party not to lose her head. Lady Middleton in *Sense and Sensibility* is a notable example of a foolish and doting mother, and here again, the children are used as a device to further the plot; Lucy

Steele, condemned to pass her evening finishing a 'filigree basket' for the spoilt Annamarie, is thereby enabled to have an important confidential talk with Elinor.

It is interesting too that Jane Austen, revealed in her correspondence as an amused, loving and sympathetic observer of adolescence, does not interest herself in that particular period of life in her characters; certainly many of her young girls – Harriet Smith, Fanny Price, or the younger Bennet girls – are still in their teens, but they are not portrayed as fledglings as it were, but as complete young women. Harriet's characteristics, for example, her chronic indecisiveness, her facile emotions and her mind-less susceptibility, are endemic traits rather than the result of immaturity and lack of experience. In a letter to her niece Anna, commenting on Anna's attempts at a novel, Jane Austen wrote, 'till the heroine grows up the fun must be imperfect... One does not care for girls until they are grown-up...' Catherine Morland, the heroine of *Northanger Abbey*, is probably the only example in Jane Austen's work of a study in developing adolescence; characters like Elizabeth Bennet or Emma are reformed or modified by experience, but Catherine has to learn and mature, in fact to grow up.

The evidence in the letters and the recorded recollec-tions of her nephews and nieces all emphasise, not the intellectual distinction and literary accomplishment of their aunt, but her exceptional qualities as an aunt (a role she declared she valued), her humour, her interest, which made visits to Chawton an invariable joy, and rendered then, after her death, a disappointment. Mary Augusta Austen-Leigh says in her *Personal Aspects of Jane Austen*, 'On no point is the family testimony more unanimous than on the unfailing love and kindness she bestowed on them, together with the warm love they felt for her in return.' Ironic as she so often was in her attitude to the people of her world and their

behaviour, ironic and self-deprecatory in her overt attitude
to herself (an attitude characteristic of people who are
sensitive and reserved in their nature), good-naturedly
ironic sometimes in her remarks about children, she never
seems to have taken this tone *towards* them, instinctively
aware no doubt of a child's mistrust and incomprehension
of such an attitude. She had the rare gift of meeting them at
their own level, without condescension, whether it was the
toddler clinging to her skirts, the schoolboy approaching
manhood, or the young girl seeking sympathetic advice on
suitors or her first literary efforts. Her niece Caroline
wrote:

> As a very little girl, I was always creeping up to
> her, and following her whenever I could, in
> the house and out of it – I might not have re-
> membered this, but for the recollection of my
> mother's telling me privately, I must not be
> troublesome... Her charm to children was
> great sweetness of manner – she seemed to
> love you, and you loved her naturally in re-
> turn. *Everything* she could make amusing to a
> child, she would tell us the most delightful
> stories, chiefly of Fairyland, and her fairies had
> all characters of their own...

Aunt Jane seems to have been the favourite aunt (in
Hampshire at least, though at Godmersham where
Cassandra was perhaps the more frequent visitor, that
might not have been the case). 'Of the two,' continued
Caroline Austen,

> Aunt Jane was by far the favourite – I did not
> *dislike* Aunt Cassandra – but if my visit had at
> any time chanced to fall out during *her* ab-

sence, I don't think I should have missed her – whereas, *not* to have found Aunt Jane at Chawton *would* have been a blank indeed.

James Austen's son, James Edward, echoed this sentence in his *Memoir* when he recalled how disappointing his visits to Chawton were after the death of Aunt Jane, 'for he could not help expecting to feel particularly happy at Chawton and never till he got there, could he fully realise to himself how all its peculiar pleasures were gone.'

There is an emphasis on the atmosphere of happiness which Jane Austen seemed to create for children – not that she was more kind or indulgent – she was probably rather firm with regard to their behaviour – but that it was a positive joy to be in her company; that she was a friend, a companion, and a playmate. There is no doubt that children have an unerring instinctive knowledge concerning the genuineness of adult interest in them or warmth towards them; this is not to say that they are good instinctive judges of character, which they are not, any more than dogs are. Jane Austen evidently evoked this response in her young relations to an exceptional degree, and however stringent her remarks might be in letters or novels about spoilt or unruly children, her warm and sympathetic attitude to children is undeniable, even when allowance is made for the rosy-tinted recollections of loving relatives. Talking of local friends and neighbours, Caroline Austen recalls, 'they sometimes served for her amusement, but it was her own nonsense that gave zest to the gossip – she never turned them into ridicule... she was as far as possible from being either censorious or satirical...' We may find this hard to credit, recalling many tart comments in the letters, but this was how her Aunt Jane appeared to a child. There are occasions indeed, when Jane Austen felt almost apologetic for her indulgent attitude. 'Though the children are very noisy,' she wrote near the end of her life, after a visit to a lively family of nephews and nieces, 'and not under such order as they ought and easily might [be], I cannot help liking them, or even loving them, which I hope may be not wholly inexcusable in their and your affectionate Aunt J.A.'

The early letters are not concerned at any length with children, although James at Overton was raising his small family, and Edward and Elizabeth in Kent were producing children at the rate almost of one every year until the unfortunate Elizabeth succumbed after the birth in 1808 of the eleventh; Jane and Cassandra were frequent visitors in both houses. Jane showed a considerable interest in the pregnancy, lying-in and early parenthood of Mary (née Lloyd), James' second wife, who gave birth to Jane's future biographer James Edward in November 1798. She wrote in the same letter which subsequently, in a postscript, announced the baby's arrival '...Mary, who... is still plagued with the rheumatism, which she would be very glad to get rid of, and still more glad to get rid of her child, of which she is heartily tired... Mrs Coulthard and Anne, late of Manydown, are both dead, and both died in childbed. We have not regaled Mary with this news.' In December, a week or two after James Edward's birth, Jane Austen wrote again to Cassandra:

> Mary does not manage matters in such a way as to make me want to lay in myself. She is not tidy enough in her appearance; she has no dressing-gown to sit up in; her curtains are all too thin, and things are not in that comfort and style about her which are necessary to make such a situation an enviable one. Elizabeth was really a pretty object with her

nice clean cap put on so tidily and her dress so
uniformly white and orderly.

These are the remarks of an observant young woman very
much absorbed in the bearing of relatives in a role which
very likely will be hers in the future. As time went by, her
comments on the subject lead one to suspect that in spite of
her interest and affection as an aunt, it is a role she is not
unhappy to have escaped. 'Poor woman!' she exclaimed of a
Mrs Tilson (who ultimately had five sons and seven
daughters) 'how can she be honestly breeding again?' and in
1817, in a letter to her niece Fanny Knight, affected perhaps
by her own fatal illness, her tone is almost despairing, as she
considers the fate of the married woman: 'Anna has not a
chance of escape; (Anna Austen, now Anna Lefroy, mother
of two little girls born within a year) poor animal, she will
be worn out before she is thirty – I am very sorry for her.
Mrs Clement too is in that way again. I am quite tired of so
many children – Mrs Benn has a thirteenth.'

In an earlier letter to the same niece, full of wise and
witty advice on the young woman's matrimonial problems,
she wrote, 'by not beginning the business of Mothering
quite so early in life, you will be young in Constitution,
Spirits, figure and countenance, while Mrs Wm Hammond
is growing old by confinements and nursing.' Apart from
postponing matrimony, she realistically recommended also
'the simple regimen of separate rooms.'

Yet in spite of Jane Austen's strong feelings about the
tyranny of recurring motherhood, as well as its dangers and
tediums, the references to individual children scattered
throughout the letters speak always of a gay and affectionate
involvement. She was not sentimental, and saw them as
they were. Anna, eldest daughter of James, came to spend
the day with the Cooper cousins, Caroline and Edward in
1796 – she was then not quite three – '…but she does not

much take to them, or anything about them, except Caroline's spinning wheel.'

'Little Edward [Knight, aged two],' she wrote from her brother Edward's home, 'was breeched yesterday for good and all, and was whipped, into the bargain.' She mocked gently at maternal foibles. 'Mary,' she wrote, 'grows rather more reasonable about her child's beauty, and says she does not think him really handsome; but I suspect her moderation…' Yet she had her favourites amongst the infant relatives; George, Edward's second son, was evidently a great favourite at one time, and was mentioned repeatedly in the autumn of 1798, when he would have been three years old.

> I flatter myself that 'itty Geordie will not forget me at least under a week. Kiss him for me.

And again,

> My dear 'itty Geordie's remembrance of me is very pleasing to me, foolishly pleasing, because I know it will be over so soon. My attachment to him will be more durable. I shall think with tenderness and delight on his beautiful and smiling countenance and interesting manners till a few years have turned him into an ungovernable, ungracious fellow.

She took some trouble to amuse him, as she did throughout her life in divers ways on behalf of other nephews and nieces. 'I hope George was pleased with my designs. Perhaps they would have suited him as well had they been less elaborately finished, but an artist cannot do anything slovenly. …I shall send George another picture when I write next.' (George was then three years old.) In October

1808, when Edward and Charles Austen (Knight), aged fourteen and thirteen, were spending a few days at Southampton with Jane and Mrs Austen after the death of their mother, Jane introduced them to the game of Speculation, and 'it was so much approved that we hardly know how to leave off.' A month or two later, she wrote to Cassandra, who was at Godmersham:

> The preference of Brag over Speculation does not greatly surprise me, because I feel the same myself; but it mortifies me deeply, because Speculation was under my patronage; and after all, what is so delightful in a pair royal of Braggers? It is but three nines or three knaves, or a mixture of them. When one comes to reason upon it, it cannot stand its ground against Speculation – of which I hope Edward is now convinced. Give my love to him if he is.

She rounded off the mock controversy in a following letter:

> I have just received some verses in an unknown hand [her own, of course] and am desired to forward them to my nephew Edward at Godmersham,
>
> Alas! poor Brag, thou boastful game!
> What now avails thine empty name?
> Where now thy more distinguish'd fame?
> My day is o'er, and thine the same –
> For thou, like me, art thrown aside,
> At Godmersham, this Christmastide,
> And now, across the table wide,
> Each game save Brag or Spec. is tried.

Such is the mild Ejaculation
Of tender-hearted Speculation.

Some years later, while staying with the Knights at
Godmersham, she described playing Battledore and
Shuttlecock with William, aged six or seven; '...he and I
have practiced together two mornings, and improve a little;
we have frequently kept it up *three* times, and once or twice
six.' She was then thirty-three years old, quite an old maid
by the standards of the day, but she was evidently still adept
at many of the minor sports beloved of small children. Her
niece Caroline, who was only twelve at the time of Jane
Austen's death, recalls that 'General handiness and neatness
were among her characteristics – she could throw the
spillikins for us, better than anyone else, and she was
wonderfully successful at cup and ball.' She delighted in
children behaving like children: 'In the evening we took a
quiet walk round the Farm, with George and Henry [eight
and ten] to animate us by their races and merriment.'

By 1817 Jane Austen was an aunt twenty-four times
over, and already twice a great-aunt. Her family was a
prolific one as well as very close and affectionate. Henry,
although married twice, was destined to be childless;
neither Jane nor Cassandra married, James was twice
married and had three children, Edward's wife Elizabeth
produced eleven children in their seventeen years of
marriage, a pattern that was exactly repeated by Frank
Austen and his wife Mary, though their last four children
were not born until after Jane's death. The youngest
brother, Charles, had three daughters by his first wife
Frances Palmer, and four more children by his second wife,
Frances' sister Harriet, but this second marriage did not
take place until after Jane Austen had been dead some years.
These large numbers were perhaps not as surprising as the
high survival rate; one hears only of one infant who failed

to survive (of those born during Jane Austen's lifetime), Mrs Charles Austen's fourth baby, whose birth was fatal to her also. There may of course have been others stillborn or miscarried which were not referred to. The survival rate of the mothers was not so satisfactory. The first Mrs Charles Austen, Mrs Edward Austen, and the first Mrs Francis Austen all died in childbirth.

It is not surprising, therefore, that Jane Austen's letters to her sister, devoted as they were to domestic and personal trivia, contain frequent references to infants and juvenile relations; and in her remarks, she does not manifest any marked maternal traits; there is a great interest in appearance and disposition, particularly the latter. To Fanny Knight she wrote in March 1817, of Anna Lefroy's two little girls (aged eighteen and six months!):

> How soon the difference of temper in Children appears! ...Jemima has a veritable bad temper (her Mother says so) – and Julia a very sweet one, always pleased and happy. I hope as Anna is so early sensible of its defects, that she will give Jemima's disposition the early and steady attention it must require.

Little Cassandra Austen, eldest daughter of Charles, came in for some fairly critical comment from an early age; in the summer of 1813, she and her little sister were at Chawton for a month, aged then four and a half and three and a half, and were thought to have derived much benefit from their stay, 'Harriet in health, Cassy in manners,' Jane Austen continued, 'the latter *ought* to be a very nice child – Nature has done enough for her – but Method has been wanting; ...she will really be a very pleasing child, if they will only exert themselves a little...' In October, Jane Austen at Godmersham reported on the arrival of Charles' family;

anticipating their arrival, she wrote, 'I should be very happy in the idea of seeing little Cassy again too, did not I fear she would disappoint me by some immediate disagreeableness.' But later in the same letter, when the belated and weary party had arrived, her natural sympathy and affection were aroused: 'Cassy was too tired and bewildered just at first to seem to know anybody – we met them in the Hall – but before we reached the Library she kissed me very affectionately…' 'Poor little love,' she added, 'I wish she were not so very Palmer-y.' (Her mother's family.)

Everything points to a child who has suffered from the vicissitudes of the life of a naval officer's family, periods on shipboard, where she preferred to endure sea-sickness rather than the pangs of separation, long visits to relatives, and constantly changing 'homes' on shore – shy, temperamental and 'difficult'. Jane Austen was not unaware of these difficulties: 'Cassy… agrees pretty well with her cousins, but is not quite happy among them; they are too many and too boisterous for her – she… did not look as if the idea of going to Chawton again was a pleasant one…' 'Do not force poor Cassy to stay if she hates it,' she advised her sister in a later letter. A year later, from London, she called on the Charles Austens where they were living in Keppel Street in Russell Square – 'that puss Cassy,' she observed, 'did not shew more pleasure in seeing me than her sisters, but I expected no better; she does not shine in the tender feelings,' and added, having, as was customary, made several excursions to the London theatres, 'she will never be a Miss O'Neill – more in the Mrs Siddons line.' As her mother had died in childbirth in the September of that year, perhaps the child's reticence was understandable.

Thenceforward Charles's children were often at Chawton, and evidently Cassy felt more at home and more responsive; she worked a doll's quilt for her cousin Caroline at Steventon, which her Aunt Jane despatched, and showed an unusual degree of feeling upon the receipt of a book from her married cousin Anna. 'I do not know,' Jane Austen commented, 'when I have seen her so much struck by anybody's kindness as on this occasion. Her sensibility seems to be opening to the perception of great actions!' When Cassy had returned to Keppel Street, Jane Austen, already unwell at the onset of her final illness, wrote her an affectionate note in mirror-writing. These rather sparse scraps of information we thus obtain about Jane's attitude and her relationship with just one of her many nieces are nevertheless enlightening; she has the novelist's keen and impersonal observation of character from the earliest stages of its development, and an ironic humour in her comments upon it, but at the same time a loving and sympathetic way of behaving towards the small object of her rather devastating scrutiny. One can envisage, for example, the scene in the big hall at Godmersham, the aunt taking the tired little girl by the hand and leading her to the warm Library, the gentle voice trying to draw out the shy and sullen child, the sudden response and recognition, and the child's warm hug; or the serious aunty interest in the child's 'work' and discussion as to its best use – 'Cassy has had great pleasure in working *this* – whatever it may be – for you, I believe she rather fancied it might do for a quilt for your little wax doll, but you will find a use for it if you can I am sure…'

Jane Austen enjoyed watching her nephews and nieces grow up, and she found real pleasure and benefit in the companionship of the more senior of them. The boys, James Edward at Steventon and a regular stream of Knight sons, would be in and out of the house at Chawton constantly from Winchester, where they were at school. 'We shall rejoice in being so near Winchester when Edward belongs to it,' she wrote, 'and can never have our spare bed filled more to our satisfaction than by him.' In December

1816 she remarked, 'Charles Knight and his companions passed through Chawton about 9 this morning; …Uncle Henry and I had a glimpse of his handsome face, looking all health and good humour.'

When Elizabeth Knight died, leaving her eleven children, Jane Austen's tender heart went out in sympathy to the bereaved family, and writing to Cassandra she envisaged all the degrees and varieties of grief, the stricken husband and Fanny quite overcome but struggling to exert herself to support her father; and little Elizabeth, the second daughter – 'Poor child!' exclaimed Jane, 'one must hope the impression *will* be strong, and yet one's heart aches for a dejected mind of eight years old.' It was proper that under such circumstances one's immediate reaction of grief should be violent, and should be seen to be so. Her anxiety to be active in comforting the bereaved was at first frustrated; Cassandra was of course at Godmersham, where she had been attending her sister-in-law's confinement; 'the poor boys' (Edward and George from Winchester) were at Steventon with their Uncle James and Aunt Mary – 'I own myself disappointed at the arrangement; I should have loved to have them with me at such a time.' Later however, Edward and George came to Southampton, where the Austen ladies were then living, and their Aunt Jane had the satisfaction of devoting several days to entertaining them, cheering them as well as she could, caring for them and observing them. 'They behave extremely well in every respect, showing quite as much feeling as one wishes to see,' she reported. 'George sobbed aloud, Edward's tears do not flow so easily, but as far as I can judge, they are both very properly impressed by what has happened. …George [her "itty Geordie' of earlier days] is almost a new acquaintance to me, and I find him in a different way as engaging as Edward.'

'We do not want amusement,' she continued, 'bilbocatch, spillikins, paper ships, riddles, conundrums, and cards, with watching the flow and ebb of the river, keep us well employed.' Her time was devoted ungrudgingly to their entertainment, which included walks and water-parties, where the boys rowed up the river and entertained their aunt by the eagerness of their enquiries – George in particular 'reminds me often of his Uncle Henry.'

Jane Austen's interest in the young was not confined to members of her own family. She conjures up a very delightful scene in a letter from Southampton to Cassandra at Godmersham in February 1807, when she received a visit from the daughter of a Captain Foote RN, a little girl of nine called Catherine: '...our little visitor... is now talking away at my side and examining the treasures of my Writing-desk drawer; very happy, I believe, not at all shy, of course... What is become of all the shyness in the World?' Later she added:

> Evening; our little visitor has just left us, and left us highly pleased with her; she is a nice, natural, open-hearted, affectionate girl, with all the ready civility which one sees in the best Children in the present day – so unlike anything that I was myself at her age, that I am often all astonishment and shame. Half her time here was spent at Spillikins, which I consider a very valuable part of our Household furniture, and as not the least important Benefaction from the family of Knight to that of Austen.

No doubt Jane Austen 'threw the Spillikins' for Catherine as skilfully as she was reported to do for her niece Caroline.

With her two senior nieces and with her eldest nephew, and to a lesser extent with his sister Caroline Austen, Jane Austen developed a relationship which went a long way beyond the general amiability of an aunt to her young relatives. To Fanny Knight she seems to have been uncritically devoted, and allowed herself a good deal more than auntly licence in her later letters, not refraining from critical remarks on other members of the family, and letting her mind run on in the contemplation of her young friend's problems, sometimes serious, sometimes frivolous, but never condescending. In October 1808, when Fanny was fifteen years old, Jane Austen wrote to her sister, 'I found her... almost another sister, and could not have supposed that a niece would ever have been so much to me. She is quite after one's own heart.' By the time Fanny was eighteen, she was beginning to appreciate her aunt's style and wit:

> I am gratified by her having pleasure in what I write – but I wish the knowledge of my being exposed to her discerning Criticism, may not hurt my Stile, by inducing too great a solicitude. I begin already to weigh my words and sentences more than I did, and am looking about for a Sentiment, an illustration, or a metaphor in every corner of the room.

She added, with the inconsequence which makes her letters often so delightful, 'Could my ideas flow as fast as the rain in the Store closet, it would be charming...'

Fanny was a girl of equable and amiable temperament, well-brought-up, friendly and lively. She was early mature and responsible, as the eldest member of a large family left motherless when she was only fifteen – a great burden to a girl situated even as comfortably as were the Edward

Austens; for she would be expected to shoulder the responsibilities of running the household and acting as comforter and hostess to her father. Fanny in her early twenties provided her aunt with a companionship which was almost as free, intimate and affectionate as her real sister's, and evoked some of her most interesting and entertaining letters. Fanny was a pretty and popular girl, a very good 'match', and evidently had many beaux whose merits and demerits were discussed at length with Aunt Jane. One can imagine many tête-à-têtes at Godmersham or at Henrietta Street or Hans Place in London, the homes of Uncle Henry Austen which Fanny visited at the same time as Jane in 1814 and 1815.

The first serious young man we hear about is John Plumptre, the son of a Kentish neighbour, and very serious he was. Jane Austen's first reaction to him was 'a handsome young Man certainly... sensible rather than brilliant.' And she added with the consciousness of her thirty-seven years, 'there is nobody Brilliant nowadays'. A week or two later she mentioned him again as having left Godmersham for another country house, Norton Court, the home of the Lushington family. 'I like him very much; he gives me the Idea of a very amiable young man, only too diffident to be as agreeable as he might be.' Diffident he may have been, but certainly attentive, for we next find him calling at Henrietta Street with his friend Mr Wildman, when Fanny and her aunt were staying there; he found the ladies out, but persevered, for a few days later he had secured a box for the theatre, and an invitation to dinner from Henry Austen. The play, *The Farmer's Wife* – 'a musical thing' – did not greatly impress Jane Austen or her brother, but 'Fanny and Mr John Plumptre are delighted'. After the departure of Fanny and her father to Kent, Henry commented that he saw 'decided attachment between her and her new acquaintance.'

Fanny and Mr Plumptre danced together at a Canterbury Ball that August – he 'was her second on Thursday, but he did not dance with her any more. This will content you for the present.' Cassandra's interest in her niece's affairs was as keen as Jane's. By 18th November, 1814 however, matters had gone a good deal further, as is clear from a letter Jane Austen wrote to Fanny on that day. Mr Plumptre and Fanny had *almost* reached the stage of having an understanding between them, but Fanny was now having serious second thoughts. The liaison was not news to Jane Austen, who had been in Fanny's confidence throughout. '...with all my heart,' she wrote, 'I wish I had cautioned you... when first you spoke to me.' Her letter on this occasion is an admirable letter in many different ways, a model of how to handle a notoriously difficult subject – advice on someone else's love affairs. She is warm, wise, diffident and humorous by turns. She is aware of the dangerous responsibility of proffering advice that may be acted upon. 'You frighten me out of my wits by your reference,' she said in a second letter of 30th November, '...indeed, you must not let anything depend on my opinion. Your own feelings, and none but your own, should determine such an important point.' Jane Austen thought very well of the young man herself, as well as feeling confident that Fanny had a strong attachment to him, and this made her thoughts veer this way and that way, not vacillating, but balancing one aspect against another. 'I am feeling differently every moment, and shall not be able to suggest a single thing that can assist your mind.'

At first she pleaded his cause with vehemence, urging his 'uncommonly amiable mind, strict principles, just notions, good habits, superior Abilities – he is, I dare say, such a scholar as your agreeable idle brothers would ill bear a comparison with... Oh, my dear Fanny,' she exclaimed half-humorously, 'the more I write about him... the more strongly I feel the sterling worth of such a young Man and the desirableness of your growing in love with him again.' She went on to emphasise his suitability as the eldest son of a wealthy man, 'belonging to your own county... His only fault indeed seems Modesty.' Mr Plumptre was evidently almost too good for Fanny, and probably appeared gauche and stiff in comparison with the easy manners and ready humour of her own family. He reminds one very much of Jane Austen's own Edward Ferrars, and had the latter not pre-dated him by several years, one would be tempted to think that he had been the prototype. Jane Austen concluded her eulogy, 'Wisdom is better than wit, and in the long run will certainly have the laugh on her side; and don't be frightened by the idea of his acting more strictly up to the precepts of the New Testament than others.' Here we see the Jane Austen of *Mansfield Park*, which had been published in May of that year, 1814. But she finally concluded by urging Fanny to follow the dictates of her own heart. On the essential points she was clear, firm and practical. 'Anything is to be preferred or endured rather than marrying without Affection.' She was emphatic that Fanny must 'resolve upon one or the other course', and give him up at once if 'his deficiencies of Manner strike you more than all his good qualities... I have no doubt of his suffering a good deal for a time,' she asserted, 'but it is no creed of mine, as you must be well aware, that such sorts of Disappointments kill anybody.' In her next letter, in reply to another indecisive one from Fanny, Jane Austen was more emphatic. Were Fanny and Mr Plumptre able to marry immediately, 'with all his worth you would soon love him enough for the happiness of both.' But evidently there was no prospect of an immediate marriage – 'Years may pass before he is independent.' No doubt the young man had to wait to step into dead men's shoes. Jane Austen finished by saying, 'You like him well enough to marry, but not well enough to wait.'

She had argued on the young man's behalf in realistic, though not purely worldly grounds, perceiving his many qualities, and knowing how rare they were, but in the last analysis realised that this was not enough, compatible neither with Fanny's safety nor her integrity. 'I cannot wish you with your very cool feelings to devote yourself in honour to him.' Fanny had met very few young men, and would be capable of 'being really in love' in the next six or seven years – 'it is the very period of life for the *strongest* attachments to be formed.' On Friday, 18th November she had written:

> there *are* such beings in the World perhaps,
> one in a thousand, as the Creature you and I
> think Perfection, where Grace and Spirit are
> united to Worth, where the Manners are equal
> to the Heart and Understanding but such a
> Person may not come in your way...

She continued the theme later – 'It is very true that you never may attach a Man his equal altogether, but if that other Man has the power of attaching you *more*, he will be in your eyes the most perfect.' The shift in her focus is from *his* qualities to *her* feelings, and incidentally from an abstract to a direct style; and it caused her to reiterate her former advice: 'nothing can be compared to the misery of being bound *without* love, bound to one and preferring another.'

Fanny decided against Mr Plumptre,[1] but not without some regrets and heart-searchings. As late as February 1817,

---

[1] Mr Plumptre. John Pemberton Plumptre (1791–1864) married in 1818 Catherine Mathilda Methuen of Corsham, Wilts (died in 1886). They had three daughters and lived at Fredville in Kent. They were near

more than two years after this earlier exchange of letters, Jane Austen was writing, 'Why should you be living in dread of his marrying somebody else? ...You did not chuse to have him yourself; why not allow him to take comfort where he can?' Partly serious and partly playful, she went on,

> My dearest Fanny, I cannot bear you should be unhappy about him. Think of his Principles, think of his father's objection, of want of Money, of a coarse Mother, of Brothers and Sisters like Horses, of sheets sewn across, etc.

As a postscript to the rejected Mr Plumptre, one of Jane's own postscripts might be quoted: 'Your trying to excite your own feelings by a visit to his room amused me excessively. The dirty Shaving-Rag was exquisite! Such a circumstance ought to be in print. Much too good to be lost'. It was not indeed lost, but transformed into the piece of court plaister retrieved by Harriet in *Emma*.

Another flirtation of Fanny's was not such a serious affair. In the autumn of 1815 Jane Austen was in London at Hans Place, staying with her brother Henry in order to correct the proofs of *Emma*; and later nursing her brother through an illness which proved to be serious enough to warrant the frequent attendance of a doctor, Mr Haden, 'the apothecary from the corner of Sloane Street, a young man said to be clever, and he is certainly very attentive.' Fanny joined the household at some point, and Mr Haden's name became more frequently mentioned. 'Tomorrow Mr Haden is to dine with us – There's Happiness! – We really grow so fond of Mr Haden that I do not know what to expect.' He was an entertaining and witty conversationalist, and something of a musician – 'Fanny played, and he sat

---

neighbours and friends of Elizabeth, younger sister of Fanny, and her husband Edward Royds Rice, who lived at Tilmanstone in East Kent.

and listened and suggested improvements.' He had a voice, but refused to sing for the company, 'without a pianoforte accompaniment' and shocked Jane delightfully ('I have been listening to dreadful Insanity!') by asserting, like Shakespeare, that 'a person *not* musical is fit for every sort of wickedness.' She noted with approval, when he was called away to a patient in the course of the evening, 'he never does appear in the least above his Profession, or out of humour with it...' In the next letter, Mr Haden's name figures frequently again, dining and bringing 'good Manners and clever Conversation;' – after dinner, 'Fanny and Mr Haden in two chairs (I *believe* at least they had two chairs) talking together uninterruptedly – Fancy the scene! And what is to be fancied next? Why, that Mr Haden dines here again tomorrow.' Henry was on the mend, but Mr Haden... 'will not let him be well... Perhaps when Fanny is gone, he will be allowed to recover faster.' At this stage did Cassandra sound a warning note about his social eligibility? For in her next letter Jane Austen replies in the most frivolous and high-spirited tone:

> You seem to be under a mistake as to Mr Haden – You call him an apothecary; – he is no Apothecary, he has never been an Apothecary, there is not an Apothecary in this neighbourhood... he is a Haden, nothing but a Haden, a sort of wonderful, nondescript Creature on two legs, between a Man and an Angel – but not the least spice of an Apothecary.

The aunt was as delighted with this clever and conversable young man as was the niece; no doubt she was enormously grateful and relieved that he had brought her favourite brother safely through a serious illness, but more than that, she enjoyed his easy and lively talk, the interests shared in common ('Mr Haden is reading *Mansfield Park* for the first time, and prefers it to *Pride and Prejudice*.') Even after Fanny had been fetched away by her father (a calculated move, perhaps?) Mr Haden must have been a regular visitor, as there is a note in existence from Jane Austen to him of 14th December, 1815, returning some books; the tone is very friendly, and the note concludes, 'we... shall depend upon your giving us some part of this Evening. I leave Town... on Saturday, and must say "Goodbye" to you.'[2]

A Mr Wildman appeared as one of Fanny's suitors too; as his home was Chilham Castle, an estate bordering on Godmersham, be was no doubt more eligible than Mr Haden, the apothecary. He is referred to in spring of 1814 as a companion of Mr Plumptre, and no doubt was an important member of the 'Harrisons and Wildmans' of whom Fanny saw a great deal in Bath at that time. He reappeared much later, in February 1817, in the course of a letter to Fanny from Jane Austen, which is full of exclama-

---

[2]Charles Haden. Winifred Watson, in an article in *The Lady* (27th October 1960), quoted at length in the collected reports of the Jane Austen Society, 1961, gave more details of the life of Charles Thomas Haden. He was the son of a Derby surgeon, educated at Rugby School, qualified as MD at Edinburgh. He joined the staff of the Chelsea and Brompton Dispensary in 1812, where he cared for the poor, in addition to running a private practice. He launched a paper for women, published as one volume in 1827 as *Practical Observations on the Management and Diseases of Children*; he had many sensible ideas on the proper care, cleanliness and health of children and their mothers, advocating fresh air and exercise and regular hours for both. He went so far as to design a sort of babies' battledress, having noticed how irritating to them was the elaborate dressing and undressing which the clothing of that day demanded.

By 1823 he developed signs of tuberculosis and died in Malta in that year at the age of thirty-eight. He had evidently married soon after the 'Austen' period, as he left a son aged six, born 1818, who also became a well-known surgeon, and who married the sister of the artist James Whistler.

tory compliments and lively and affectionate comments on her extravagances and vagaries of mood and feelings. 'You are inimitable, irresistible,' Jane Austen began, 'you are the delight of my life.' But she was suspicious of the attentions of Mr John Wildman, and of his family too, who were cultivating Fanny's acquaintance. 'He will have you,' she warned, in a tone of mock seriousness, 'he must be wishing to attach you.' Not that she had any real objections to the match – 'I have rather taken a fancy to him than not, and like Chilham Castle for you. I only do not like you should marry anybody.' By mid-March however, Jane Austen had dismissed Mr Wildman as a serious threat – 'I have pretty well done with Mr Wildman. By your description, he *cannot* be in love with you, however he may try at it, and I could not wish the match unless there were a great deal of Love on his side.' She concluded this section of this, her last surviving letter to Fanny, with serious and practical advice: 'Do not be in a hurry; depend upon it, the right Man will come at last, …and then, by not beginning the business of Mothering quite so early in Life, you will be young in Constitution, spirits, figure and countenance, while Mrs Wm Hammond is growing old by confinements and nursing.'

These final letters to Fanny in the February and March of 1817, only months before she died, and when she was already suffering much from sickness, languor and fever, are remarkably full of vigour and humour and interest, as though the personality of the recipient, and the liveliness and interest of *her* letters to her aunt evoked such a response. Fanny had been aware for a longer time than most other members of her family how seriously ill her aunt was, and no doubt wrote frequent and lively letters to entertain and distract her as much as possible – indeed, one arrived at Winchester on the day of Jane Austen's death, and was opened and perused; Cassandra wrote to Fanny, 'never shall I forget the proofs of love you gave her during her illness in writing those kind, amusing letters at a time when I know your feelings would have dictated so different a style.' Jane Austen's letters to Fanny, like those to Cassandra, are open and uninhibited; with these two alone she could say anything and knew that all the correct assumptions would be made, the gaps filled in the right way. The sardonic comment, the harsh criticism, the buffoonery, which the outsider may condemn, are taken in the context of what these two most intimate and beloved correspondents knew of the writer's whole outlook and attitude. But with Fanny, communication was more consistently through the medium of letters than it was with Cassandra, with whom all great events and important decisions would be discussed in person; so the letters to Fanny contain more expressions of feelings, and also more gems of wit and wisdom than those rather more common-place letters which were all that Cassandra allowed to survive of the many addressed to her.

Pride and Prejudice:
Distress and Discomfiture

Jane Austen described *Pride and Prejudice* as 'my own darling child – rather too light and bright and sparkling; it wants shade...' Even allowing for the fact that the passage – in a letter to her sister Cassandra in February 1813 – continues in a facetious vein:

> it wants to be stretched out here and there
> with a long chapter of sense, if it could be had;
> if not, of solemn specious nonsense, about
> something unconnected with the story; an es-
> say on writing, a critique of Sir Walter Scott,
> or the history of Buonaparte, or anything that
> would form a contrast, and bring the reader
> with increased delight to the playfulness and
> epigrammatism of the general style.

this was at the time and still is the general opinion of *Pride and Prejudice*. The lively and ironic tone, the brilliance and charm of Elizabeth, ('as delightful a creature as ever appeared in print' declared her creator with perfect justice), the witty, subtle dialogue, and the array of entertaining characters have all concealed the serious and sometimes bitter assessments Jane Austen makes of the contemporary scene.

Jane Austen was neither reformer nor rebel; she raised no banners, and she waved no flags. But she observed and she recorded the scene before her, in the class and the period and the place in which she was situated, herself an integrated element within it; she saw the pressures and the prejudices exerted by the social, economic and moral laws of the day, and used her only available weapon to comment and pass judgement – her ironic genius. The surface is deceptively bland; but 'I do not write,' she misquoted Scott to Cassandra, 'for such dull elves As have not a great deal of ingenuity themselves.'

Her books have been prescribed in convalescence, read as a relaxation by bishops and prime ministers at times of crisis, cherished as a comfort and a solace in war; this most astringent of writers has been used as a universal balm. But, as E.M. Forster says, 'The devout Janeites, like all regular church-goers …scarcely notice what is being said.'

D.W. Harding has emphasised this in his essay entitled *Regulated Hatred*, where he shows Jane Austen using some surprising expressions – the 'neighbourhood of voluntary spies' in *Northanger Abbey*, and the description of Miss Bates in *Emma*, who had 'no intellectual superiority to …frighten those who might hate her'. It is interesting to note in this regard the strength and vigour of Elizabeth Bennet's language throughout *Pride and Prejudice*, and the actual words she uses; words such as 'disgust', 'contempt', 'despicable', 'hate' and 'despair'.

There is plenty to discomfit in *Pride and Prejudice*, to shake the complacency of those for whom she chiefly wrote, with their settled acceptance of the rightness and the inevitability of the social order. In the first place, the whole social stratification is a shifting and ambiguous one, both in respect of background and of behaviour; the wealthy and eligible Charles Bingley, with his snobbish and arrogant sisters, has a fortune founded on trade in the north of England; Mr Darcy's aunt, Lady Catherine de Burgh, of unimpeachable aristocracy, is guilty time and again of thoroughly ill-bred behaviour and remarks, rarely, indeed, does she behave otherwise. On her first dinner-visit to Rosings, Elizabeth Bennet resists some of her more offensive personal enquiries, and suspects herself 'to be the first creature who had ever dared to trifle with so much dignified impertinence'. On a later occasion, her nephew Darcy has the grace to look 'a little ashamed of his aunt's ill-breeding'. Even Mr Darcy himself behaves very ill at the Assembly ball, not only in being disobligingly unsociable, but in making an offensive remark about an innocent guest within her hearing: 'She is ...not handsome enough to tempt *me*; and I am in no humour at present to give consequence to young ladies who are slighted by other men...' No amount of self-justification or explanation – '...I am ill-qualified to recommend myself to strangers' he explained in extenuation, and 'I certainly have not the talent which some people possess of conversing easily with those I have never seen before' – can excuse the unpleasantness of the remark, which, however, was a necessary device to give Elizabeth grounds for her initial strong aversion to him. But one must bear in mind that members of the aristocracy in the eighteenth and nineteenth centuries claimed for themselves quite extraordinary privileges and exemptions from the codes of behaviour laid down for ordinary mortals, and were accorded a degree of respect an account of their rank which we would find sycophantic. Mr Collins observed with approval that 'she [Lady Catherine] likes to have the distinction of rank preserved.'

Mrs Bennet's father had been an attorney in Meryton, a profession which at that time ranked in the social scale, along with surgeon–apothecaries, above tradesmen but well below the landed gentry. Mrs Bennet herself is a thoroughly vulgar-minded woman, 'a woman of mean understanding, little information, and uncertain temper'. Her sister Mrs Phillips is no worse than a cheerful, gossiping, sociable nonentity; but their brother and his wife, Mr and Mrs Gardiner, are portrayed as very much more than 'respectable'; they possess intelligence uncluttered by any false sense of position or pride of breeding. Finally, there is Sir William Lucas, a foolish man innocently dazzled by his elevation to a knighthood and his brief glimpse of the court; a man who made his fortune as a local tradesman and has aspired to a higher rank in society. He is saved from unpleasant pretentiousness by a nature 'inoffensive, friendly and obliging', and a desire to be 'civil to all the world'.

The behaviour of the different members of the Bennet family is the result more of individual character and propensities than of background and breeding. They have, after all, been exposed alike to the same training and influences, benefiting from their opportunities little or much according to their inclination and intelligence, as Elizabeth explained to the astonished Lady Catherine, 'such of us as wished to learn, never wanted the means. We were always encouraged to read, and had all the masters that were necessary. Those who chose to be idle certainly might.'

There is more that a suspicion of neglect here, or lack of discipline, between the indolent, disillusioned father and the silly and indulgent mother, with her preoccupation with the trivial and the superficial. Yet she had the energy her husband lacked, and could run a household with the genteel and elegant appearance which was lamentably lacking in her own behaviour; the household has nothing in common with the Portsmouth home of the slatternly Mrs Price in *Mansfield Park*. What humiliates Elizabeth in the behaviour of her family is more deeply rooted, being based on an inherent triviality of mind, a lack of any real propriety in the behaviour of so many of its members, an absence of moral discrimination which is far more damaging than a mere neglect or ignorance of proper forms. The fact that her mother, her cousin Collins, and her sisters Lydia, Kitty and Mary are contemptible on more fundamental grounds than those of birth and breeding makes the situation more unendurable for Elizabeth, and more impossible for Mr Darcy to overlook. Jane is preserved from the worst effects of this by a natural saintliness, that 'candour' which meant in Jane Austen's day the determination to see only the good in everyone, and by a sensitivity and perception of behaviour in others far inferior to Elizabeth's. Her sweet nature, her patience to endure and her determination never to see evil makes her one of Jane Austen's most perfect minor heroines, but a dull one; there is no mystery, no development, little depth; she only becomes engagingly comical through Elizabeth's affectionate teasing, as she is an object of our pity mainly through Elizabeth's distress and grief on her behalf. One is not moved by her predicament as one is by the similar plight of Marianne in *Sense and Sensibility*.

Mr Bennet has long since retired from the arena, and does nothing either to moderate the follies of his family, which serve for his entertainment, or to alleviate them by making any social contribution himself – with the single exception of his curtailment of Mary's musical exhibition of herself at the Netherfield ball by a cutting remark which even Elizabeth a little regrets: 'That will do extremely well, child. You have delighted us long enough. Let the other young ladies have time to exhibit.'

Mr Bennet's action after the elopement of Lydia and George Wickham arises from the only moments of self-examination and self-criticism he ever allows himself: 'Who should suffer but myself?' he exclaims in this unique moment of truth, 'it has been my own doing, and I ought to feel it.'

'You must not be too severe upon yourself,' replied Elizabeth.

'You may well warn me against such an evil. Human nature is so prone to fall into it! No, Lizzie, let me once in my life feel how much I have been to blame. I am not afraid of being overpowered by the impression. It will pass away soon enough.'

Pass away it does, and by the time the newly wedded couple arrive at Longbourn, he is fully restored to his cynical enjoyment of the impertinence of his son-in-law and the folly of his youngest daughter.

How much Elizabeth takes after him, and how easily, as an older woman, with a few disappointments or miscalculations behind her, she could become like him, is indicated in one or two of her exchanges with her congenial aunt, Mrs Gardiner, and in a conversation with Jane.

'Oh,' she declares to her aunt,

'...I have a very poor opinion of young men who live in Derbyshire; and their intimate friends who live in Hertfordshire are not much better. I am sick of them all. Thank Heaven! I am going tomorrow where I shall find a man who has not one agreeable quality, who has neither manner nor sense to recommend him. Stupid men are the only ones worth knowing, after all.'

To which her aunt replies: 'Take care, Lizzy; that speech savours strongly of disappointment.'

In her disillusionment over her friend Charlotte's engagement to Mr Collins, and over Charles Bingley's cruel defection, she exclaims to Jane:

'Do not be afraid of my running into any excess, of my encroachment on your privilege of
universal good-will. You need not. There are
few people whom I really love, and still fewer
of whom I think well. The more I see of the
world, the more am I dissatisfied with it; and
every day confirms my belief of the inconsistency of all human characters, and of the little
dependence that can be placed on the appearance of either merit or sense.'

These two speeches are strong meat indeed, and are a hint
of the sort of facade that an intelligent and brilliant character like Elizabeth (and like Jane Austen herself) must put up
to conceal her awareness of the cruel and dangerous
position of young unmarried and dowerless females of her
class of society. Gay, witty and cheerful as Elizabeth is, she
is far more intelligent than almost anyone else in her
immediate circle, and her perceptive laughter at the follies
and foibles of those around her turns to frustration and
despair when their behaviour threatens her happiness or
more especially Jane's.

Elizabeth in fact reacts both to her mother and her sister
Lydia with either an unresponsive silence or a wincing
sensitivity and apprehensiveness that is usually justified by
events. When Mrs Bennet arrives at Netherfield to visit her
daughters during their enforced stay which she has rather
disgracefully contrived herself, her social brashness consists
mainly of a touchy unawareness of what is really being
discussed, and a rudeness to Darcy which makes Elizabeth
'tremble lest her mother should be exposing herself yet
again'. But the ball at Netherfield is the greatest test of
Elizabeth's composure, a penance to endure without relief
except for the pleasure of seeing Jane happy and oblivious
in the company of Charles Bingley. Her new friend George

Wickham is not present, as a result, she learns, of Mr Darcy's presence, which deprives her of expected pleasure and does nothing to improve her feelings towards Darcy; she is irritated with herself for being surprised into accepting him as a partner; and Sir William Lucas causes her distress and opens Darcy's eyes by his heavy-handed insinuations of the impending engagement between her sister and Mr Bingley; she goes on to quarrel with Caroline Bingley over Mr Wickham.

> 'Insolent girl!' said Elizabeth to herself. 'You are much mistaken if you expect to influence me by such a paltry attack as this. I see nothing in it but your own wilful ignorance and the malice of Mr Darcy.'

It is an added touch of irony that with very little more information to go on, Caroline Bingley had made a more correct assessment (of the Wickham situation) than Elizabeth; although what confirms Miss Bingley in her own opinion is the humble and inferior origins of Wickham – 'really, considering his descent, one could not expect much better.'

Mr Collins' presumption in presenting himself to Mr Darcy as a neighbour and protégé of his aunt does not now strike us as a very glaring example of ill manners; indeed, in the course of this episode, Mr Collins utters one of his very few respectable remarks, when he says to Elizabeth, 'I consider the clerical office as equal in point of dignity with the highest rank in the kingdom.' But in Jane Austen's time it was a breach of etiquette to address a 'superior in consequence' without a formal introduction; and Mr Collins' obsequious and pompous mode of doing so gave added distress to Elizabeth as she watched him exposing himself in all his imbecility to Darcy's astonishment and scorn. The greatest exposure, with the greatest distress, was to come when the company sat down to supper, and Elizabeth had to listen to her mother expatiating to Lady Lucas in a very loud whisper on all the expected felicities of Jane's imminent marriage to Mr Bingley.

> In vain did Elizabeth endeavour to check …her mother's words. …for to her inexpressible vexation, she could perceive that the chief of it was overheard by Mr Darcy…
>
> 'What is Mr Darcy to me, pray, that I should be afraid of him? I am sure we owe him no particular civility as to be obliged to say nothing he may not like to hear.'
>
> 'For Heaven's sake, madam, speak lower… What advantage can it be to you to offend Mr Darcy? You will never recommend yourself to his friend by so doing.'

Nothing that she could say, however, had any influence: 'Elizabeth blushed and blushed again with shame and vexation.'

Even now her trials were not yet over, for she had to face her sister Mary exposing herself to the derision of the company by her singing with more eagerness than talent; and to her cousin Mr Collins making a fool of himself before all the company with a more than usually pompous and asinine speech.

> To Elizabeth it appeared, that had her family made an agreement to expose themselves as much as they could during the evening, it would have been impossible for them to play their parts with more spirit, or finer success; happy did she think it for Bingley and her sis-

ter that some of the exhibition had escaped his
notice, and that his feelings were not of a sort
to be much distressed by the folly which he
must have witnessed. That his two sisters and
Mr Darcy, however, should have such an opportunity of ridiculing her relations was bad
enough, and she could not determine whether
the silent contempt of the gentleman, or the
insolent smiles of the ladies, were more intolerable.

This is the vein of the highest comedy, but for Elizabeth
there is real suffering. Her shame and humiliation are
justified by the real gracelessness of her family's behaviour.
(Were it not so, Elizabeth would be guilty of a rather
disagreeable disloyalty to her family, but Jane Austen
manages to avoid this impression by a narrow margin.) It is
not enough for her to say with her mother, 'What is Mr
Darcy to me, pray?' – their behaviour would have shamed
her in any company, but the particular relationship established between her and Darcy – of conscious dislike and
subconscious attraction – makes exposure particularly
humiliating. The extent to which her family disgrace
themselves in his eyes by so much diminishes her right and
capacity to hate him for his pride, incivility and apparent
injustice. The scorn and derision so flauntingly displayed
by the Bingley sisters angers Elizabeth, but cannot injure
her in the way that Darcy's grave disapprobation does.

The whole issue of Charlotte Lucas's marriage to Mr
Collins, and her own and Elizabeth's attitude to marriage is
explored very seriously in *Pride and Prejudice*. It is not a
subject for Jane Austen's high-spirited mockery, and
Elizabeth herself does not look upon it in an ironic light.
Although the whole episode is impregnated with the
author's satiric tone, Elizabeth's reaction is one of shock

and loss – she 'felt persuaded that no real confidence could ever subsist between them again.' It is not only a serious disillusionment, but the first revelation of an error of judgement on her part in the assessment of character on which she prides herself, the first of many such revelations that she will have to face. Charlotte Lucas is the only friend in Elizabeth's neighbourhood, apart from her sister Jane, who is at all her equal in intelligence; in background a little inferior, in prospects – financially speaking – very much the same, as the eldest daughter of a large family not very well-endowed with wealth; conscious, however, of lacking attraction and beauty, which has created, not jealousy and antagonism, but a practical eye to the main chance. Elizabeth's real disillusion and unhappiness at her friend's cynical acceptance of half-a-loaf is not so much that she has been influenced by material considerations in accepting a husband who is a fool to whom she can give neither respect nor affection for the sake of an establishment, but that she has betrayed principles of integrity in personal relationships which Elizabeth had hitherto believed they had shared. Jane tries to persuade her that the match is after all a respectable one; but Elizabeth will have none of it:

'...were I persuaded,' she cries,

> 'that Charlotte had any regard for him, I should only think worse of her understanding than I do now of her heart. My dear Jane, Mr Collins is a conceited, pompous, narrow-minded, silly man; you know he is, as well as I do, and you must feel, as well as I do, that the woman who marries him, cannot have a proper way of thinking. You shall not defend her... You shall not, for the sake of one individual, change the meaning of principle and integrity, nor endeavour to persuade yourself,

> or me, that selfishness is prudence, and insen-
> sibility of danger, security for happiness.'

But Elizabeth has been blind to Charlotte's character, as she is blind to Wickham's and to Darcy's; she sees what she expects, or hopes to see, and endows Charlotte with the same sort of self-mocking humour and the same principles of conduct that she has herself. In the dialogue where Charlotte (wisely, as it turns out) warns Elizabeth of the danger of Jane's restraint and composure which conceals her growing love for Charles Bingley, the two girls are viewing the situation from very different angles; Elizabeth is contemplating a developing mutual regard, and Charlotte a potential catch which must not be allowed to escape.

'...it is sometimes a disadvantage,' Charlotte points out, 'to be so very guarded.

> 'If a woman conceals her affection... she may
> lose the opportunity of fixing him; ...there is
> so much of gratitude or vanity in almost every
> attachment, that it is not safe to leave any to it-
> self. ...a woman had better show more
> affection than she feels...'
>
> 'Your plan is a good one,' replies Elizabeth
> laughingly, 'where nothing is in question but
> the desire of being well married.'

Ironically, everything goes as Charlotte suggested, with Jane modest, placid and undemonstrative, Bingley unsure of his power to win her, and suggestible to any advice from his stronger-minded friend. On his unassuming pliability and her apparent composure the romance very nearly founders.

Charlotte insists that a profound knowledge of each other's characters beforehand is as irrelevant to a happy marriage as a deep affection.

'Happiness in marriage is entirely a matter of chance… If the dispositions of the parties are ever so well known to each other, or ever so similar beforehand, it does not advance their felicity in the least. They always continue to grow sufficiently unlike afterwards to have their share of vexation; and it is better to know as little as possible of the defects of the person with whom you are to pass your life.'

'You make me laugh, Charlotte, but it is not sound. You know it is not sound, and that you would never act in this way yourself.'

But alas for Elizabeth's confidence, Charlotte feels it is sound, for herself at least, and within a very short space of time, does act in that way herself, by making a successful bid for Elizabeth's rejected suitor; the announcement finds Elizabeth quite unprepared.

She had always felt that Charlotte's opinion of matrimony was not exactly like her own, but she could not have supposed it possible that when *called into action* she would have sacrificed every better feeling to worldly advantage. Charlotte the wife of Mr Collins, was a most humiliating picture! – and to the pang of a friend disgracing herself and sunk in her esteem, was added the distressing conviction that it was impossible for that friend to be tolerably happy in the lot she had chosen.

Elizabeth could scarcely have expressed herself more strongly had she been describing Lydia's elopement. Jane Austen describes the courtship in her most high-spirited vein:

The stupidity with which he was favoured by nature must guard his courtship from any charm that could make a woman wish for its continuance; and Miss Lucas, who accepted him solely from the pure and disinterested desire of an establishment, cared not how soon that establishment were gained.

But Elizabeth's reaction to it is sad disillusionment. Charlotte's solution to her marriage problems, as Elizabeth later observes, consists in a deliberate blunting of her own sensibility, and an ability physically to avoid (by choosing a less attractive room for her sitting room than that used by her husband, and by encouraging him in his gardening enthusiasm) and mentally to forget as much as possible the provider of her worldly comforts. One has to admire Charlotte's cool, practical, and cheerful handling of a situation which she had engaged in deliberately and with her eyes wide open.

Elizabeth's greatest distress is always on behalf of her beloved sister Jane, for whom alone she manifests any feelings of tenderness (brilliance, light, clarity typify Elizabeth, but not warmth). Her mother's clamorous and damaging advocacy of the match (between Jane and Charles Bingley) in the first place, which was the chief cause of its frustration by Charles's friend, followed by her selfish and imperceptive complaints when the suitor failed to return to claim his bride, are almost intolerable for both sisters.

'Oh!' cries Jane when Mrs Bennet has been more trying than usual, 'that my dear mother had more command over herself; she can have no idea of the pain she gives me by her continual reflections on him.' Jane's generous and uncritical attitude towards Charles Bingley, and her patience in her disappointment call forth all Elizabeth's tenderness. 'My dear Jane! – you are too good! I do not know what to say to you. I feel as if I had never done you justice, or loved you as you deserved.' When Elizabeth is at Hunsford with Charlotte, she eagerly reads and re-reads Jane's letters from London for signs of flagging spirits, and such signs are not wanting. When she hears from Colonel Fitzwilliam how instrumental Darcy has been in separating his friend from her sister, she is angered to bitter tears: '*he* was the cause – he had ruined every hope of happiness for the most affectionate, generous heart in the world; and no one could say how lasting an evil he might have inflicted.' When, fast on the heels of this upsetting revelation, Darcy makes his declaration of love, her loyalty to her sister lends a savagery to her words:

> 'Had not my own feelings decided against you, had they been indifferent, or had they even been favourable, do you think that any consideration would tempt me to accept the man, who has been the means of ruining, perhaps for ever, the happiness of a most beloved sister? I have every reason in the world to think ill of you. No motive can excuse the unjust and ungenerous part you acted *there*. You dare not, you cannot deny that you have been the principal, if not the only means of dividing them from each other, of exposing one to the censure of the world for caprice and instability, the other to its derision for disappointed hopes, and involving them both in misery of the acutest kind.'

But behind all this rage against Darcy is the shameful knowledge of how much wretchedness was owed to 'the contempt which had thus been self-attracted by the rest of her family.' And as 'she considered that Jane's disappointment had in fact been the work of her nearest relations, and reflected how materially the credit of both [herself and Jane] must be hurt by such impropriety of conduct, she felt depressed beyond anything she had ever known before.'

This is even before Lydia's catastrophic elopement from Brighton with George Wickham. Jane Austen's portrayal of Lydia is brilliantly entertaining, but Elizabeth, unlike her father, is not amused. The episode when Kitty and Lydia meet Jane and Elizabeth with Maria Lucas on their road home from their visits exemplifies Lydia's incorrigible frivolity and Elizabeth's impatient scorn; there is not a hint of tolerant affection or amusement at Lydia's prattle of escapades and gossip – some of it no more than harmlessly silly – 'Elizabeth listened as little as she could' and her comments are all ironic, much in her father's vein. She is however, brought up short when Lydia is describing Mary King's escape from the courtship of George Wickham:

> 'I will answer for it he never cared three straws for her. Who *could* about such a nasty little freckled thing?'
> Elizabeth was shocked to think that, however incapable of such coarseness of *expression*, the coarseness of the *sentiment* was little other than her own breast had formerly harboured, and fancied liberal!

Lydia has the vulgarity of mind, reflected in the coarseness of her expressions and the incorrectness of her grammar, which is seen in Lucy Steele and her sister in *Sense and Sensibility*, and like Lucy, though in a different way, she has the power to injure the heroines. Hence Elizabeth's attempts ('detestable as such a step must make her were it known') to persuade her father to refuse his permission for Lydia to go to Brighton. Her main argument is on the 'very great disadvantage to us all, which must arise from the public notice of Lydia's unguarded and imprudent manner.' She speaks of her sister in terms of absolute contempt:

> 'our respectability in the world must be affected by the wild volatility, the assurance and disdain of all restraint which mark Lydia's character ...a flirt – in the worst and meanest degree of flirtation, without any attraction beyond youth and a tolerable person; and from the ignorance and emptiness of her mind, wholly unable to ward off any portion of that universal contempt which her rage for admiration will excite; – vain, ignorant, idle and absolutely uncontrolled, ...will be censured and despised wherever [she is] known, and ...her sisters will often be involved in her disgrace.'

After the elopement, which is more than even she had anticipated, Elizabeth is still preoccupied with the effect of her behaviour on the rest of the family, rather than Lydia's possible fate at the hands of a selfish and penniless rake '...the humiliation, the misery she was bringing on them all.' The self-reproach that she suffers, that she failed to make known the proofs of Wickham's perfidy and profligacy is only a small part of her anguish; she has not the smallest faith in the strength or integrity of her sister's moral character – 'it does seem, and it is most shocking indeed, ...that a sister's sense of decency and virtue should admit of doubt. But, really, I know not what to say.' Wickham's impudent ease and Lydia's noisy assurance on their wedding visit to Longbourn are equally horrifying to Jane and Elizabeth. 'Elizabeth was disgusted, and even Miss Bennet was shocked. Lydia was Lydia still; untamed, unabashed, wild, noisy and fearless.' To Elizabeth's natural antipathy to a character devoid of grace or intelligence, and without decorum or restraint, is added the bitterness of knowing that Lydia's marriage to Wickham – a necessary conclusion to a disastrous escapade, will preclude the possibility of her own to Darcy, which she is just beginning to realise is what she most wishes for. She:

> began now to comprehend that he was exactly the man who, in disposition and talents, would most suit her ...but no such happy marriage could now teach the admiring multi-tudes what connubial felicity really was. ...but how little of permanent happiness could be-long to a couple who were only brought together because their passions were stronger than their virtue, she could easily conjecture.

She has now suffered every variety of mortification, that arising from family disgrace and that from self-deception; but there is a note of complacency as well as jealous anger in her feelings at this point, at which the author gently mocks, in the picture of the ideal marriage which should 'teach the admiring multitudes what connubial felicity really was.'

Yet complacency is not a characteristic of Elizabeth, as it is of the equally self-deluding Emma. She is confident and opinionated, but when her opinions are challenged, she reviews the facts with a logical thoroughness which would do credit to a lawyer, weighing the evidence and facing courageously the mortifying conclusion that she has been in error in nearly every particular.

> She grew absolutely ashamed of herself. Of neither Darcy nor Wickham could she think,

without feeling that she had been blind, partial, prejudiced, absurd. 'How despicably have
I acted!' she cried. 'I, who have prided myself
on my discernment! – I, who have often dis-
dained the generous candour of my sister, and
gratified my vanity, in useless or blameable
distrust! – How humiliating is this discovery!
Yet how just a humiliation! Had I been in
love, I could not have been more wretchedly
blind. But vanity, not love, has been my folly.
Pleased with the preference of one, and offended by the neglect of the other, on the very
beginning of our acquaintance, I have courted
prepossession and ignorance, and driven reason away, where either were concerned. Till
this moment, I never knew myself.'

The whole of Elizabeth's complex series of misapprehensions and self-delusions are a single great movement of
dramatic irony, culminating in her exclamation of, 'Had I
been in love, I could not have been more wretchedly blind!'
At a moment of self-revelation, this is a brilliant ironic
stroke; Elizabeth is still deluded as to her own motives; her
elaborate, almost ritual performances with Darcy, those
dialogues loaded with layers of meaning, her obstinate
refusal to like him or to do him justice, are her defences
against the danger of falling in love with him, just as her
relaxed yielding to Wickham's facile charms are an indication that she is in no danger from him. A critic[1] has said,
'The triumph of *Pride and Prejudice* is a rare one, just
because it is so difficult to balance a purely ironic vision
with credible presentation of a man and a woman undergo-

---

[1]Reuben Brewer. *Light and Bright and Sparkling: Irony and Fiction in Pride and Prejudice* from R. Brewer, *The Fields of Light*, pp.164–181, New York, OUP, 1951.

ing a serious change of sentiment.' It was Elizabeth's pride to be an ironic spectator, her penance – and her fulfilment – to find herself the most involved of all the participants; the most involved because the most aware, the most sensitive, and the most discriminating.

Fitzwilliam Darcy

Many critics consider that Fitzwilliam Darcy, the hero of *Pride and Prejudice*, is a failure. Q.D. Leavis[1] regards him as an unrealised stock figure from Fanny Burney's *Cecilia*: 'Darcy is only Delville with the minimum of inside necessary to make plausible his conduct.' Marvin Mudrick[2] sees him too as a 'stiff-jointed Burneyan hero', flat and inconsistent 'she can do nothing more with him than fit him functionally into the plot.' He is not an entire success, and his origins can no doubt be traced to exemplars from Jane Austen's predecessors; but how nearly she succeeds in bringing him to Austenian life, a worthy companion to Mr Knightley and a more many-faceted individual than Colonel Brandon. His fate in the final third of the novel is to act out – unfortunately off-stage, too – the part of the perfect hero, a combination of knight in shining armour and deus ex machina, and in a sense, it does for him. By the time he returns to the stage, mellowed and chastened, he has time only to renew his proposals to Elizabeth and be accepted before the curtain falls. The conventional pattern is in line with the somewhat unrealistic and stylised resolution of the action in this part of the book. It is all rather contrived, the elopement, the pursuit, and the final

---

[1]Q.D. Leavis, *A Critical Theory of Jane Austen's Writings*, 'Scrutiny', No. X, June 1941.

[2]Marvin Mudrick, *Irony as Discrimination; Pride and Prejudice*, In *Jane Austen, A Collection of Critical Essays*, edited by Ian Watt, Prentice-Hall, N.J., 1963.

revelation of the identity of the noble saviour of the family honour. But what is not stagy or contrived is the pattern of development, self-knowledge and change which is woven with all Jane Austen's customary skill and subtlety in the earlier chapters, so that in fact Darcy's change of heart does not come as a surprise. Or rather, not change of heart, Darcy never loses the powerful attraction he feels for Elizabeth from the outset, rather the reformation of his character and his attitude. The plot structure creaks at this stage, but the characters behave as we have been shown that they will behave, as realised human beings, and not as puppets.

In those final scenes, Darcy is still a little stiff – the circumstances, the household, the knowledge of his reputation with them on the one hand and his services to them on the other (unknown except to Elizabeth) would daunt the boldest lover, and Elizabeth has to warn herself not to be too quick to tease – 'he had yet to learn to be laughed at'; in her unrepentant days when she *had* disliked him, she teased him unmercifully, and he will learn to enjoy her more affectionate raillery in the future. His sense of dignity will not tolerate it from many other people, though perhaps he will appreciate Mr Bennet's sardonic humour at other people's expense. He was, for example, a little put out at his friend Charles Bingley's delightful sally, 'I declare I do not know a more aweful object than Darcy… at his own house… of a Sunday evening, when he has nothing to do.'

But Darcy's sense of humour, his quick awareness of the foibles of others is manifest from the outset. He plays his part in the early fencing matches with Elizabeth adroitly, outwardly grave, always polite, but thoroughly aware of what she is about, and revelling in the battle of wits. Dancing with a very reluctant Elizabeth at the Netherfield ball, he makes quite strenuous efforts to overcome her indifference, which she makes little effort to conceal, and only relapses into silence when the subject of George Wickham makes amicable conversation impossible. Elizabeth's lack of response is forbidding enough to deter all but the most assiduous of partners.

'Sir William's interruption has made me forget what we were talking of.'

'I do not think we were speaking at all. Sir William could not have interrupted any two people in the room who had less to say for themselves. We have tried two or three subjects already without success, and what we are to talk of next I cannot imagine.'

'What think you of books?' said he, smiling.

'Books? Oh! no. I am sure we never read the same, or not with the same feelings.'

'I am sorry you think so; but if that be the case, there can at least be no want of subject. We may compare our different opinions.'

'No, – I cannot talk of books in a ballroom; my head is always full of something else.'

'The *present* always occupies you in such scenes – does it?' said he, with a look of doubt.

'Yes, always,' she replied, without knowing what she said.

His exchanges with Caroline Bingley are masterly, outward courtesy concealing a contempt she is too thick-skinned to perceive.

The perpetual commendations of the lady either on his handwriting, or on the evenness of his lines, or on the length of his letter, with the perfect unconcern with which her praises were received, formed a curious dialogue, and was exactly in unison with her (Elizabeth's) opinion of each.

'How delighted Miss Darcy will be to receive such a letter!'

He made no answer.

'You write uncommonly fast.'

'You are mistaken. I write rather slowly.'

'How many letters you must have occasion to write in the course of the year! Letters of business too! How odious I should think them!'

'It is fortunate, then, that they fall to my lot instead of yours.'

'Pray tell your sister that I long to see her.'

'I have already told her so once, at your desire.'

'I am afraid you do not like your pen. Let me mend it for you. I mend pens remarkably well.'

'Thank-you, – but I always mend my own,'

'How can you contrive to write so even?'

He was silent.

'Tell your sister I am delighted to hear of her improvement on the harp, and pray let her know that I am quite in raptures with her beautiful little design for a table—'

'Will you give me leave to defer your raptures till I write again? At present I have not room to do them justice.'

Poor Miss Bingley's efforts to attract Mr Darcy's attention proving fruitless, she then attempted to engage his attention by walking around the room, displaying her elegant figure and graceful movements; but it was only when she had persuaded Elizabeth to join her in her perambulations that Darcy looked up.

In spite of his unpromising first reaction to Elizabeth, Darcy is quick to be captivated by her lively charm, and even exposes himself to Caroline Bingley's jealous raillery:

> 'I have been meditating on the very great pleasure which a pair of fine eyes in the face of a pretty woman can bestow.'
>
> Miss Bingley immediately fixed her eyes on his face, and desired he would tell her what lady had the credit of inspiring such reflections.
>
> 'Miss Elizabeth Bennet.'
>
> 'Miss Elizabeth Bennet!' repeated Miss Bingley. 'I am all astonishment. How long has she been such a favourite? – and pray when am I to wish you joy?'
>
> 'That is exactly the question which I expected you to ask. A lady's imagination is very rapid; it jumps from admiration to love, from love to matrimony in a moment. I knew you would be wishing me joy.'

Darcy rather enjoys his easy victories over Miss Bingley, and seems almost to court exposure to her transparent manoeuvres and her fatuous malice; these passages help to humanise him in the early chapters, showing his behaviour in the company of his friends and social equals; though, apart from Charles Bingley, who treats him with a blend of amusement and respect, the company at Netherfield is pitifully lacking in liveliness or wit.

As he confesses himself, he has to overcome the lifelong tendencies to be selfish, proud and self-regarding, the spoilt only son born to a position of wealth and authority, backed by a natural intelligence and education which reinforces his sense of superiority. He has to learn what is expected *from* him, as well as what is due *to* him. Given his rather unbending disposition and an inbred unawareness of any obligation to be more than formally courteous to 'outsiders', his behaviour in this new environment in Hertfordshire is not unnatural, however much it may have given offence. (At the first introduction of Darcy in the book, Jane Austen states that his manner 'was continually giving offence'.) Some of the behaviour and manners he meets with are deplorable, particularly Mrs Bennet's rude and ignorant irrelevancies. He is equally critical of the folly of his intimates, and he is quick enough to appreciate and warm to the real merits and attractions of Elizabeth and Jane, and later, to their aunt and uncle Gardiner. His forbidding behaviour partly arises from a sensitivity more acute than Charles Bingley's, who is a friend of all the world, and a fastidiousness which his creator remarked on with tenderness when she failed to find his wife's portrait in any of the London exhibitions. (She found Jane without difficulty), 'I am disappointed, for there was nothing like Mrs D. at either. I can only imagine that Mr Darcy prizes any picture of her too much to like it should be exposed to the public eye, – I can imagine he would have that sort of feeling – that mixture of Love, Pride and Delicacy.'

The curious courtship, begun so inauspiciously with active dislike on the lady's part, and reluctant attraction on his, continues more happily when the pair meet at Hunsford; and there the situation is reversed in that Darcy finds himself embarrassed by his aunt's domineering ill-breeding, as Elizabeth had been by her mother's. The relationship however, for a time is much freer and more relaxed – 'Elizabeth laughed heartily' – her shafts less barbed, more high-spirited – 'prepare yourself,' she says to

Colonel Fitzwilliam, a cousin of Darcy's, 'for something very dreadful! …at this ball, what do you think he did? He danced only four dances! I am sorry to pain you – but so it was.' And the conversation concludes – after a hectoring interruption from Lady Catherine – with a downright compliment from Darcy: 'No one admitted to the privilege of hearing you, can think anything wanting. We neither of us perform to strangers,' where it is clear that it is not only Elizabeth's performance as a musician that Darcy is talking about.

It is Darcy's ill-fortune that his feelings drive him to an avowal of love immediately after his cousin Fitzwilliam's disclosure of Darcy's hand in the separation of Charles from Jane. The proposal is almost the only one in the novels that Jane Austen describes in detail, and in direct speech; and even here, much of Darcy's initial declaration is only described – 'the avowal of all that he felt and had long felt for her, immediately followed.' This is no doubt an example of Jane Austen's practice of depicting only those things of which she had some close experience; it is improbable that she had much personal knowledge of how young men behave in the grip of strong sexual attraction, and such knowledge as she might have acquired she may have felt disinclined to make use of. But in spite of the formalism of the style, and the extraordinarily articulate nature of the expressions of both characters, the whole scene is vibrant with passionate feeling. Darcy is in a constant state of motion, pacing the room, leaning against the mantelpiece, his expression and colour changing as he struggles to control the violence and shock of his varying emotions. Elizabeth in contrast is still and unmoving, stunned with surprise in the first instance, stiff with anger and resentment as the interview goes on. Her response, her rejection, begins in a low key, forceful but with at least an effort at civility – 'if I could *feel* gratitude, I would now thank you,' but, under provocation, her tone sharpens, 'I have every reason in the world to think ill of you,' and she uses entirely unequivocal words such as 'dislike', 'selfish disdain' and, most wounding of all, 'ungentlemanlike', concluding with the words, 'I had not known you a month before I felt that you were the last man in the world whom I ever could be prevailed upon to marry.'

Darcy's long explanatory letter has been derided as a stock device, and as a hangover from the original *First Impressions*, which is generally assumed to have been in letter form; it is a stock device of the eighteenth century novel, and Jane Austen makes a good deal of use of it in many of her novels, for example, the equally long letter of Frank Churchill in *Emma*; it is the equivalent of the detailed narrations, equally stylised and unnatural in their copious minuteness, in which Colonel Brandon, Willoughby, Edmund Bertram or Mrs Smith (in *Persuasion*) indulge in order to cast light upon some hidden mystery of the plot, illuminate a character or simply fill in some of the action which has taken place elsewhere. Jane Austen never uses these devices without differentiating them so as to throw into relief the writer or speaker in an ironic or entertaining way. Frank Churchill's letter was indeed written by his very self, the style, vocabulary, tone reflects all we know of him, impulsive, repentant, hopeful; quick and lively feelings which are not, we fear, very profound, but whose charming and affectionate nature will earn him the forgiveness which he always optimistically expects. The style is dramatic, and the words he uses are too colloquial and unrestrained to be used by such a man as Darcy – 'I am mad with anger…', 'I behaved shamefully', 'I raved…' etc. Darcy's letter is expressed in a far more stiff and stilted, dignified tone, as befits a man who has just received personal criticism such as he must have felt inconceivable, and certainly unjustified, from the object of his avowed admiration. It is impossible to imagine that anyone had ever addressed him before with such blunt and uncompromising disapprobation. His intention is self-justification, and he begins with all the grandeur of offended pride:

> Be not alarmed, Madam, on receiving this letter, by the apprehension of its containing any repetition of those sentiments, or renewal of those offers, which were last night so disgusting to you. I write without any intention of paining you, or humbling myself, by dwelling on wishes which, for the happiness of both, cannot be too soon forgotten; and the effort which the formation, and the perusal of this letter must occasion, should have been spared, had not my character required it to be written and read. You must, therefore, pardon the freedom with which I demand your attention; your feelings, I know, will bestow it unwillingly, but I demand it of your justice.

This is magnificently in character, the firm tone, the commanding language; even his sense of deep humiliation and all the pangs of rejected love give way to the demands of self-justification and the reinstatement of his injured pride; in which cause he is even prepared to renew his offence to Elizabeth in condemning the impropriety of her family:

> If, in the explanation of [my actions] *which is due to myself*, I am under the necessity of relating feelings which may be offensive to yours, I can only say that I am sorry. The necessity must be obeyed – and further apology would be absurd.

This is still a proud and self-willed man, who is burning under the sense of ill-usage; it will take longer reflection and self-examination before he takes a different view; to be able to confess that:

> as a child I was taught what was *right*, but I was not taught to correct my temper. I was given good principles, but left to follow them in pride and conceit, …to be selfish and over-bearing, to care for none beyond my own family circle, to think meanly of all the rest of the world, to *wish* at least to think meanly of their sense and worth compared with my own… You showed me how insufficient were all my pretensions to please a woman worthy of being pleased.

Marvin Mudrick[3] agrees with Q.D. Leavis[4] that Darcy is 'derived and wooden' and scolds Jane Austen for first introducing him with an example of out-of-character discourtesy to Elizabeth at the Assembly in Meryton, and then at a later date explaining himself to Elizabeth in a 'thoroughly frank and unreserved letter, which… seems an author's gesture of desperation to weigh the scales in favour of her predetermined hero… Out of inconsistency, Darcy emerges into flatness.' This is to ignore the long series of scenes between these two episodes in which we see his character gradually unfolding in his confrontations with strangers, familiars, those he admires and, rather more numerously, those he despises; and that same character

---

[3]Marvin Mudrick, *Irony as Discrimination; Pride and Prejudice,* In *Jane Austen, A Collection of Critical Essays*, edited by Ian Watt, Prentice-Hall, N.J., 1963.
[4]Q.D. Leavis, *A Critical Theory of Jane Austen's Writings*, 'Scrutiny', No. X, June 1941.

being mellowed and modified under chastening or benign influences.

Even at his most forbidding, he very much relates to his environment and company; he is observant and penetrating, and Jane Austen is at pains to show him not only awkward, austere and withdrawn in uncongenial surroundings, but relaxed and witty and exposed like any other mortal to the banter and teasing of friends in his home circle; and ultimately, through the eyes of his housekeeper at Pemberley ('what praise is more valuable than the praise of an intelligent servant?'): 'He is the best landlord, and the best master,' said she, 'that ever lived... There is not one of his tenants but what will give him a good name. Some people call him proud; but I am sure I never saw anything of it...' When, hotfoot on this account, the master of the house himself unexpectedly appears, his civility and manner of speaking ('which had none of its usual sedateness') makes it evident that resentment is giving place to less self-centred feelings; and the whole of this rather idyllic episode illustrates the fact that a man rarely shows to better advantage than on his own home ground. We leave him at the inn in Lambton with regret, to pursue his conventional course of heroic action off-stage, and after a brief interlude of that glum, grave and silent behaviour which was his usual demeanour formerly in the Bennet household, to receive the due reward for his labours and his love.

'I Cannot Praise a Fugitive and Cloistered Virtue' or Disquiet at Mansfield Park

Let us imagine that we are reading the works of Jane Austen for the first time; we have chuckled over *Northanger Abbey*, sighed a little over *Sense and Sensibility*, laughed and suffered with the heroine over *Pride and Prejudice*, rejoiced and revelled in *Emma* – feeling that here is a writer who is more modern than most Victorians, whose processes of thought and feeling we can understand and find congenial. If we have read any of the letters also, this feeling is reinforced. Then we take up *Mansfield Park*; it opens in the way we have learnt to expect, a survey of a country family, everyone paired off and labelled with a price tag, in a tone of gentle irony whereby the author uncensoriously comments upon the inevitable economic facts: 'there certainly are not so many men of large fortune in the world, as there are pretty women to deserve them.'

But as we continue, we find little to laugh at, very little of the sparkling ironic humour which effervesces in *Emma* and *Pride and Prejudice*; there are plenty of comic characters, to be sure, drawn with the customary skill; Dr Grant and Lady Bertram delight us – Lady Bertram indeed is the glorious consummation of a whole series of vapid and self-indulgent noodles, which include Mrs Allen in *Northanger Abbey*, Mrs Palmer and her sister Lady Middleton in *Sense and Sensibility*, and old Mr Woodhouse in *Emma*. The humiliations and disappointments of Mr Rushworth and the Hon. John Yates cause us wry amusement; but we cannot laugh very much at Mrs Norris, that sadistic figure who combines the characteristics of Cinderella's ugly sisters with *Jane Eyre*'s abominable Aunt Reid. Edmund Bertram, marked down as the hero from the moment when as a schoolboy, he befriends little Fanny weeping on the stairs, grows up to be a dull fellow, with only a very little more humour than Fanny, who has none at all. Fanny seems a very milk-and-water heroine after Elizabeth Bennet and Emma Woodhouse. Her salient characteristics are singularly charmless and unheroic – timidity, moral censoriousness, abject self-abnegation and physical debility. It cannot be denied that she possesses moral courage to a high degree, resisting the persuasions of those she respects or fears and those she loves, as well as those whose opinions she despises. But her firmness too often seems to be obstinacy, her shyness a denial of natural human relationships. The Crawfords, vibrant with vitality, good humour and charm, having been portrayed with a positively loving touch, are eventually thrust into outer darkness with relentless condemnation; Julia and Maria Bertram, equally lively though without the Crawford charm, are tainted with the same worldliness, and are rejected too. The terrible fuss about the theatricals (from an author whose family revelled in such entertainments in her youth) is more or less incomprehensible to us – apart from the liberties taken with the Mansfield Park fittings and furniture, activities not condemned by Lady Bertram and Aunt Norris. Fanny and Edmund engage together in some sanctimonious moralising which we must find repellent, the more so as they are presented to us as admirable and 'right-thinking'. Early in the acquaintance with Mary Crawford, Edmund says:

'Was there nothing in her conversation that struck you, Fanny, as not quite right?'

'Oh! yes, she ought not to have spoken of her uncle as she did. I was quite astonished. An uncle with whom she had been living so many years, and who, whatever his faults may be, is so very fond of her brother... I could not have believed it!'

'And very ungrateful, I think.'

...and so on, greatly to their mutual satisfaction.

Where, we may well ask, is the life-loving spirit of *Pride and Prejudice*, the warm and tolerant tone so understanding of human foibles, of *Emma*, the latent sympathy with ardent and impulsive feeling in *Sense and Sensibility*? Here it seems to be replaced by a forbidding rejection of vitality and passion, a retreat into a safe and strict adherence to a narrow code of social propriety and moral rectitude.

Yet many people consider *Mansfield Park* to be Jane Austen's finest achievement; Lionel Trilling says it is, 'a great novel, its greatness being commensurate with its power to offend.' In her own time it was highly commended as a novel of more power and gravity than its predecessors; it was praised for its 'pure moral tendency' – 'all who think deeply and who feel much will give the preference to *Mansfield Park*,' said a Mrs Carrick, a family friend – approved for its truth to life, its good sense, and its vivid characterisation. While admiring its moral tone, most people in her immediate circle confessed to a preference for *Pride and Prejudice* or even *Sense and Sensibility*, and tended to single out for especial praise the Portsmouth scenes in *Mansfield Park* as the liveliest and most entertaining passages. One warms to Jane Austen's mother for her firm opinion that Fanny was 'insipid', an opinion shared by her granddaughter Anna, who 'could not bear Fanny', and her grandson George Knight, who was interested in nobody but Mary Crawford! On the other hand, there were those who had nothing but praise for the heroine; 'Fanny is a delightful character!' exclaimed Francis Austen, one of the sailor brothers, who however was one of those who preferred *Pride and Prejudice* as a whole. Jane Austen's niece Fanny Knight was 'delighted with Fanny', and only deplored Edmund's lack of love for her; sister Cassandra was 'fond of Fanny', and thought the book 'quite as clever but not as brilliant as *Pride and Prejudice.*'

Jane Austen's family in their comments tended to particularise over one character or another, or over single episodes, rather than giving a judgement on the work as an entity, but the general tenor of critical judgement was that *Mansfield Park* gained in its elevated moral tone more than it lost in liveliness and wit. The elements in the book which disconcert us did not worry them at all; the choices Jane Austen makes and expects us to approve seem to be negative and static ones, whatever their moral validity – safety rather than risk, calm rather than liveliness, sense rather than wit, quiescence rather than movement, and rational compatibility rather than sexual passion. To emphasise the rightness of the choice, all those qualities of life and change and charm and gaiety have to be associated with a failure of integrity and correct thinking, so that they can justifiably be rejected. It is an intriguing reflection that the men to whom, from the evidence in the letters and biographical information, Jane Austen was attracted, and whose company she enjoyed, were people such as her brother Henry, who was lively and unreliable, and Henry's surgeon, Dr Haden, in whose company she delighted as late in her life as 1815, who was far from unreliable, but was certainly lively, musical and intelligent. Her early beau, the nineteen year old Tom Lefroy was probably just such another intelligent and sparkling personality. Yet almost without exception in the novels she endows her 'villains' with those same characteristics of gaiety and charm and intelligence which she enjoyed herself in real life – Willoughby, Crawford, Churchill, Wickham, even Elliot in *Persuasion*, whereas many of her heroes have a much higher percentage of sobriety in their composition, and one or two are downright dull! Henry Tilney is the only hero who sparkles with humour and charm.

Fanny is a Cinderella-like figure, and has much more in common with Jane Eyre than Charlotte Brontë would have cared to admit. She is received into Mansfield Park as a poor relation and is speedily assessed as inferior in person, education and manner. She appears weak, without spirit or animation or particular gifts, except, we are meant to understand, for a thoughtful and sensitive intelligence. She is persecuted by her Aunt Norris, and she nourishes in her bosom a strong obsessive passion for the man of her choice, the only individual who has paid her any attention or been kind to her. Like Jane Eyre, she observes the activities of those around her with a firm sense of her own superiority to them, in mind and morals and feeling. We think of her as plain; though we are told that she 'improves' enormously in the latter part of the book, she has none of that outward assurance that the consciousness of attractiveness gives to a young woman.

Fanny is *never* wrong, in her actions or in her judgement – even Edmund errs, to Fanny's shock and dismay, in action when he agrees to take part in the theatricals, in judgement when he falls in love with Mary Crawford, and when he urges Fanny to accept Henry Crawford. In both actions he is beguiled by his infatuation for Mary, whereas Sir Thomas, also guilty of similar misjudgement over Henry Crawford, is influenced by material considerations in his anger at Fanny for her rejection of such an eligible suitor. Fanny is always the passive, suffering victim, and her strength is in her very inaction; she triumphs in the end by her obstinate refusal to act. One can see her behaviour as a saintly and self-denying adherence to rigid principles, but the other side of the same coin is a tough self-absorbed pursuit of her own goal – Edmund, and secondarily the safety and tranquillity of Mansfield Park. She has for Edmund the devotion of a pupil to a teacher, and also the limpet-like attachment of an adolescent 'crush' – manifested in her eager agreement with his opinions, her shadowy but persistent presence in his courtship of Mary. On the occasions when she has to watch the courtship from a distance, she is consumed with jealousy, although she tries to disguise it to herself, under the cover of more impersonal and high-minded considerations. Mary commandeers her pony, and keeps it beyond the allotted time; Fanny watches the cheerful scene from a nearby slope:

> ...the sound of merriment ascended even to her. It was a sound that did not make *her* cheerful; she wondered that Edmund should forget her, and felt a pang... she began to think it rather hard upon the mare to have such double duty; if she were forgotten, the poor mare should be remembered.

This tone of self-pitying, jealous censoriousness is constantly in evidence; again and again Fanny refuses to participate, pleads physical weakness or moral objections, and then indulges in self-absorbed sulks at being left out and disregarded. The highly symbolic scenes in the grounds of the Rushworth house at Sotherton are a good example of this.

The episode during the planning of the theatricals when Edmund seeks Fanny's advice is full of subtlety, with both Edmund and Fanny only half-aware of their own underlying motives. Fanny has retired to the chilly old schoolroom full of the discarded furnishings 'thought unworthy of being anywhere else', to brood on her refusal to take a part in the play, and thus to oblige those 'to whom she owed the greatest complaisance'; Edmund comes to her for advice, or rather, reassurance, as his decision is already made, and he wants only her approval, which she finds it quite impossible to give. (Fanny has an uncompromising and uncomfortable inability to be socially accommodating, not always because of simple shyness, but because of her rigid adherence to her own code; she can be compared in this respect, if in no other, to Marianne Dashwood, whose sense of her own superior sensibility made it impossible for her to compromise her integrity in the slightest degree for the sake of oiling the wheels of social intercourse.) In spite of his disapproval at the choice of play, and indeed of the whole scheme, Edmund has decided to take a part, to prevent his brother 'riding about the country in quest of anybody who can be persuaded to act', and to save Mary Crawford the embarrassment of having to play love scenes with a stranger:

'Give me your approbation, then, Fanny. I am not comfortable without it.'

'Oh! Cousin...'

'I thought *you* would have entered more into Miss Crawford's feelings.'

'No doubt she will be very glad. It must be a great relief to her,' said Fanny, trying for a greater warmth of manner.

'She never appeared more amiable than in her behaviour to you last night. It gave her a very strong claim on my good-will.'

'She *was* very kind, indeed, and I am glad to have her spared...'

She could not finish the generous effusion. Her conscience stopt her in the middle, but Edmund was satisfied.

His true motive is clear to us, as it is to Fanny – the opportunity to play the part of Mary Crawford's lover is irresistible, especially as it can be cloaked as a defence of her delicacy and an avoidance of impropriety; he is not pre-pared to let an outsider play the role. His brother and sister are not taken in, 'he was to act, and he was driven to it by the force of selfish inclination only. Edmund had de-scended from that moral elevation which he had maintained before…' Fanny's shock and dismay, which she tells herself is due to Edmund's inconsistency and failure of principle, is exacerbated by jealousy:

> Could it be possible? Edmund so inconsistent? Was he not deceiving himself? Alas! it was all Miss Crawford's doing. She had seen her in-fluence in every speech, and was miserable. The doubts and alarms as to her own conduct, which had previously distressed her, and which had all slept while she had listened to him, were become of little consequence now. The deeper anxiety swallowed them up. Things should take their course; she cared not how it ended. Her cousins might attack, but they could hardly tease her. She was beyond their reach; and if at last obliged to yield – no matter – it was all misery now.

This is a real give-away. Her high-principled purpose to refuse to perform is revealed simply as a personal prefer-ence backed by a strong feeling of disapproval at the behaviour of the rest of the party, their dangerous flirtations, their liberties with the sanctities of her uncle's home, reinforced by the joyous sense of her alliance on the subject with Edmund. With the prop of Edmund's support removed, Fanny relapses into a state of jealous misery. She is alone now, except for Julia, sulking in equally miserable jealousy, for whom Fanny spares only a passing sympathy. It is a knife in the wound that it is to Mary herself that she owes her immunity from pressure to co-operate.

> She was safe; but peace and safety were unconnected here. Her mind had never been further from peace. She could not feel that she had done wrong herself, but she was disquieted in every other way. Her heart and her judgement were equally against Edmund's decision; she could not acquit his unsteadiness; and his happiness under it made her wretched. She was full of jealousy and agitation. Miss Crawford came with looks of gaiety which seemed an insult, with friendly expressions towards herself which she could hardly answer calmly. Everybody around her was gay and busy, prosperous and important; each had their object of interest, their part, their dress, their favourite scene, their friends and confederates, all were finding employment in consultations and comparisons, or diversions in the playful conceits they suggested. She alone was sad and insignificant; she had no share in anything; she might go or stay; she might be in the midst of their noise, or retreat from it to the solitude of the East room, without being seen or missed. She could almost think anything would have been preferable to this.

It is hard to imagine that Jane Austen did not know what she was about, and was not gently mocking her saintly heroine, but except for one or two passages, there seems to be a suspension of irony and humour in her approach to Fanny. Such an authorial intrusion as, 'My Fanny indeed at this very time, I have the satisfaction of knowing, must have been happy in spite of everything' is unique in Jane Austen's work in its tone of protective partisanship. She seems to have been unaware, in a very uncharacteristic way, of how often her Fanny's attitudes, lauded as praiseworthy, leave a repulsive impression on the reader's mind; her very happiness in returning to Mansfield Park whose every member is sick or disgraced, disappointed, ashamed or heartbroken is a little macabre, for her joy is achieved by those very disasters. Those who hate or despise her are cast out, and those who remain have at last become dependent upon her; she even rejoices in Edmund's grief. Was Jane Austen aware, for example, of the deplorable impression created in the passage in the penultimate chapter of the book, when the unhappy Edmund, still heartsore at the loss of Mary, has confided to Fanny all the details of his last meeting with her? Having listened to Edmund's recapitulation of 'how she had attached him, and how delightful nature had made her, and how excellent she would have been, had she fallen into good hands earlier,' Fanny feels 'more than justified' in dealing the *coup de grâce* – balm to her irritated feelings, no doubt – by disclosing 'what share his brother's state of health might be supposed to have in her [Mary's] wish for a complete reconciliation. [i.e., that Mary had hoped that Tom might die and that Edmund would succeed to the baronetcy]. This was not an agreeable intimation.' To us it seems both disagreeable and unnecessary, and smacks of malicious and vengeful feelings. But Edmund wins the next round, by concluding to Fanny that his love for Mary, 'was the sort of thing which he never could get entirely the better of; and as to his ever meeting with any other woman who could – it was too impossible to be named but with indignation. Fanny's friendship was all that he had to cling to.'

Jane Austen here wishes us to share her amusement in Edmund's blindness both to his own state of mind and to Fanny's attitude to him, and of her own awareness of the 'cure of unconquerable passions, and the transfer of unchanging attachments'; but our amusement is tempered by the spectacle of such a degree of uncharitableness.

There is a similar note of outraged self-regard in Fanny's reaction to her reception at Portsmouth, though she tries to curb it; she and her brother William arrive to find the house in a turmoil. The *Thrush*, William's ship, which his younger brother is also to join on this voyage as a midshipman, is about to sail, and everything is in a rush and confusion of preparation. Fanny is almost ignored, after the most cursory of greetings:

> ...she had nothing to do, and was glad to have the light screened from her aching head, as she sat in bewildered, broken, sorrowful contemplation.
>
> She was at home. But, alas! it was not such a home, she had not such a welcome, as – she checked herself; she was unreasonable. What right had she to be of importance to her family? – Yet to have so little said or asked about herself – to have scarcely an enquiry made after Mansfield!

One must pity Fanny here, for she had always been something of an outsider, an inferior being, at Mansfield Park, and had clung to the memory of her old home as a place where in former times she had been loved and valued.

The remembrance of all her earliest pleasures, and of what she had suffered in being torn from them, came over her with renewed strength, and it seemed as if to be at home again, would heal every pain that had since grown out of the separation. To be in the centre of such a circle, loved by so many, and more loved by all than she had ever been before, to feel affection without fear or restraint, to feel herself the equal of those who surrounded her – this was a prospect to be dwelt on with a fondness that could but be half-acknowledged.

Poignant indeed is the reality, for she finds herself neither loved nor valued at Portsmouth. Her father disregards her, her mother is too preoccupied with her domestic muddles and her large family – 'she had neither leisure nor affection to bestow on Fanny.' The noise, disorder and total lack of propriety in the household, as well as the cramped quarters and the meanness of the appointments, all come as a horrifying surprise to Fanny, and this, with the realisation that she has no place in the affections of her own family, fixes her once and for all in the world of Mansfield Park, to which she looks back with longing as the haven of perfect happiness. Henceforward Fanny is the conscious, as previously she had been the instinctive champion of Mansfield and all it stands for; this proves to be the result to her of the Portsmouth visit, rather than that which her uncle Sir Thomas had hoped for, to reconcile her to marriage with Henry Crawford, by 'teaching her the value of a good income.'

Critics aver that *Mansfield Park* is a 'Romantic' novel, in an entirely new way; it was written in the first decade of the new century, whose literary giants included Crabbe and

Cowper, Robert Burns, Lord Byron and Sir Walter Scott. While the character of Fanny has elements of the persecuted heroine of the novels of Fanny Burney or Richardson, there is a new feeling evident, embodied chiefly in her. We see her standing solitary by the window, restoring her wounded susceptibilities or taking refuge in the soothing balm of nature.

> The scene without, where all that was solemn
> and soothing and lovely appeared in the brilli-
> ancy of an unclouded night, and the contrast
> of the deep shade of the woods.

To Edmund she can express her rapture, naïve though it may be, confident of a sympathetic ear.

> 'Here's harmony!' said she, 'here's repose!
> Here's what may leave all painting and all
> music behind, and what poetry can only at-
> tempt to describe! Here's what may
> tranquillise every care, and lift the heart to
> rapture! When I look out on such a night as
> this, I feel as if there could be neither wicked-
> ness nor sorrow in the world; and there
> certainly would be less of both if the sublimity
> of Nature were more attended to, and people
> were carried more out of themselves by con-
> templating such a scene.'

This is a different thing from Marianne's exhibition of sensibility in *Sense and Sensibility*. Her response to nature is romantic in the literary sense, finding mystery and glamour in rugged rocks, fallen leaves, tempests, forests and ruined castles. Fanny indeed does indulge in this sort of romanticism when she whispers to Edmund in the chapel at Sotherton:

> 'I am disappointed – this is not my idea of a chapel. There is nothing awful here, nothing melancholy, nothing grand. Here are no aisles, no arches, no inscriptions, no banners. No banners, cousin, to be 'blown by the night wind of Heaven'. No signs that a 'Scottish monarch sleeps below'.

But her attitude to nature is more often a personal one, seeing there a reflection of her own moods – the 'pathetic fallacy' in fact, of the Romantic era. But there is an air of artificiality about it; Fanny's high-minded rhapsodies are being presented in contrast to Mary's declared preference for company, talk and town-life, from which we are intended to infer a criticism of her frivolity and corrupted sophistication. The dialogue between Mary and Fanny in the shrubbery at the Grants' vicarage exemplifies these opposing attitudes, and we are not left in total sympathy with Fanny's point of view.

Mansfield Park was the first of the novels, not counting the discarded *Watsons*, which was entirely the creation of Jane Austen's maturity (Q.D. Leavis relates it closely to *Lady Susan*, but this is a matter of opinion). It was written between 1811 and 1813, and published in 1814, when the author was thirty-nine. She had always, from childhood, written for her family and a close circle of friends, and even now, when her works were reaching a wider public, this narrow circle was her point of reference. In her earlier works she had tilted at aspects of her own world, the world of an accepted and rigid moral order related to an equally inflexible social code, using her powerful weapon of comic irony. Here, in *Mansfield Park*, she discards this weapon, and attempts to affirm, in no equivocal terms, the supremacy, even the moral rightness of a closed and threatened society. She fails in every way because she denies her own nature. If, for example, we examine Mary Crawford in the context of Jane's own surviving letters, the resemblances are remarkable (one can only hazard a guess as to how many more examples one might have found in those letters which Cassandra carefully destroyed in her old age; no doubt there were other passages whose dubious propriety or revealing outspokenness the ageing spinster consigned to the flames, which would remind us of Mary Crawford's iconoclasm, wit and occasional lapses of taste):

> ...the rich are always respectable...

> ...Pictures of perfection make me sick and wicked...

> My preference for Men and Women, always inclines me to attend more to the company than the sight...

> ...I am forced to be abusive for want of a subject, having really nothing to say...

> ...one of the sweet Taxes of Youth [is] to chuse in a hurry and make bad bargains...

> We do not like Mr Cooper's new sermons – they are fuller of Regeneration and Conversion than ever – with the addition of his zeal in the cause of the Bible Society... I do not like the Evangelicals...

She is… the sort of woman who gives me the idea of being determined never to be well – and who likes her spasms and her nervousness and the consequence they give her, better than anything else. – This is an ill-natured sentiment to send all over the Baltic!

Poor Mrs Stent! it has been her lot always to have been in the way; but we must be merciful, for perhaps in time we may come to be Mrs Stents ourselves, unequal to anything and unwelcome to everybody.

…I hope his wife allows herself to be happy on the occasion, and does not give all her thoughts to being nervous.

Mr Husket, Lord Landsdown's painter – domestic painter I should call him, for he lives in the castle. – Domestic chaplains have given way to this more necessary office, and I suppose whenever the Walls want no touching up, he is employed about My Lady's face.

We met not a creature at Mrs L's – and yet were not so very stupid as I expected, which I attribute to my wearing my new bonnet and being in good looks.

…I am proud to say that I have a very good eye at an Adultress – I fixed upon the right one from the first – she was highly rouged, and looked rather quietly and contentedly silly than anything else.

...Mrs Badcock thought herself obliged... to run round the room after her drunken husband. His avoidance, and her pursuit, with the probable intoxication of both, was an amusing scene.

...another stupid party last night – three old *Toughs* came in, ...I respect Mrs Chamberlayne for doing her hair well, but cannot feel a more tender sentiment; Miss Langley is like any other short girl with a broad nose and wide mouth, fashionable dress and exposed bosom; Admiral Stanhope is a gentlemanlike man, but then his legs are too short and his tail too long.

...it is the fashion to think them both very detestable, but they are so civil, and their gowns look so white and nice, that I cannot utterly abhor them, especially as Miss H. owns that she has no taste for music.

...here I am once more in this scene of dissipation and vice, and I begin already to find my morals corrupted...

I am almost afraid to tell you how my Irish friend and I behaved. Imagine to yourself everything most profligate and shocking.

I rather expect to receive an offer from my friend in the course of the evening. I shall refuse him, however, unless he promises to give away his white coat.

> Tell Mary that I make over Mr Heurtley and
> all his estate to her for her sole use and benefit
> in future, and not only him, but all my other
> admirers into the bargain, wherever she can
> find them, even the kiss which C.P. wanted to
> give me, as I mean to confine myself in future
> to Mr Tom Lefroy, for whom I don't care six-
> pence.

> Mrs Hall, of Sherborne, was brought to bed
> yesterday of a dead child, some weeks before
> she expected, owing to a fright. I suppose she
> happened unawares to look at her husband.

Is it Mary speaking in these passages, or Jane? One might
be hard put to it to decide. There is the same animation and
sense of fun, a sort of incorrigible frivolity of manner which
may or may not hide more serious feelings (how much did
Jane Austen feel for Tom Lefroy?) and a high degree of
self-knowledge and self-mockery.

Henry Crawford is nicely in Jane Austen's convention of
the charming scoundrel, a man with many excellent
qualities and a great deal of intelligence. He has a cynically
superficial attitude to young women, who exist, not so
much to be fallen in love with, as to be worked upon to fall
in love with him. Whether it is harder to believe in his
genuinely falling in love with the immaculate Fanny, or in
his abrupt fall from grace when almost on the brink of
success, having, with obvious relish and self-satisfaction,
striven to model himself on the man Fanny could respect
and love – is hard to say. As with Mary, it is necessary for
Henry to show himself rotten at the core, necessary for the
author's design. With Mary's fall from grace one experiences a sense of betrayal, with Henry's no more than slight
incredulity, for Henry's is a more superficial character; he

must be thought of as an actor of roles, which is how he sees himself, and he is an actor of ability. He sees himself as the dramatic performer, – 'in all the riot of his gratifications, it was yet an untasted pleasure' as a preacher, as a lover, of course. He thoroughly enjoys his role vis-à-vis Fanny as a reformed rake and a conscientious landlord, which bids fair to have a longer run than any; but the role he is not prepared to play is the rejected lover where once he was adored – his 'cold-blooded vanity' prompts him to subdue Maria once more, and the disastrous denouement follows.

But Mary is guilty of no crimes; apart from her endearing qualities of wit, vitality and good-humour (no one else in *Mansfield Park* has her sunny disposition), she is truly friendly towards Fanny, who is not only paralysingly unresponsive to her, but sometimes can hardly bring herself to be civil to her. Except in the matter of her feelings for Edmund, Mary is perceptive of Fanny's sufferings and active in alleviating them. We are often made to see Mary through Fanny's disapproving and jealous eyes, and Fanny's judgement, biased though it is by her jealous feelings, is meant to be the final verdict. Edmund, of course, is sublimely unaware of Fanny's real feelings towards Mary, because he is unaware of Fanny's feelings towards himself, and he fondly imagines that the two of them are devoted friends.

> What chiefly surprised Edmund was, that Crawford's sister, the friend and companion, who had been so much to her, should not be more visibly regretted. He wondered that Fanny spoke so seldom of *her* and had so little voluntarily to say of her concern at this separation.

But to Fanny, Mary's absence is a relief to very anxious feelings; she is convinced now that the marriage between her and Edmund is almost inevitable:

> On his side the inclination was stronger, on hers less equivocal. His objections, the scruples of his integrity, seemed all done away – nobody could tell how; and the doubts and hesitations of her ambition were equally got over – and equally without reason. It could only be imputed to increasing attachment. His good and her bad feelings yielded to love, and such love must unite them.

Being without humour or any lightness of touch in her social relationships, Fanny is invariably harsh and often ill-judging in her assessment of Mary's real attitudes. Before her departure for London, and after her brother's proposal to Fanny, Mary calls upon her, and in a tender mood induced by her hopes for a happy future in which they would be united by a double bond, treats her with such affection that even Fanny is not unmoved:

> 'Good, gentle Fanny! when I think of this being the last time of seeing you, for I do not know how long, I feel it quite impossible to do anything but love you.' Fanny was affected… Miss Crawford said, 'I hate to leave you. I shall see no one half as amiable where I am going. Who says we shall not be sisters? I know we shall. I feel that we were born to be connected; and those tears convince me that you feel it too, dear Fanny.'

Fanny's tears indeed, while genuine enough, conveniently mask her inability to utter any response to Mary of an equally affectionate nature.

Mary is not very perceptive about Fanny, but her sincerity is undoubted. The interview continues in a lighter vein, Mary deliberately shaking off the sentimental musings which have overcome her, and putting Fanny more at her ease by chatter about her London friends (of whose characters she has a clear and critical awareness), and some teasing of Fanny about her conquest of Henry. Their parting is affectionate – 'there was no resisting so much *apparent* affection' – is Fanny's carping reaction. Later, brooding on Edmund's attachment, Fanny thus reflects on their meeting:

> In their last conversation, Miss Crawford, in spite of some amiable sensations, and much personal kindness, had still been Miss Crawford, still shewn a mind led astray and bewildered, and without any suspicion of being so; darkened, and yet fancying itself light. She might love, but she did not deserve Edmund by any other sentiment.

These remarks have been made the keystone in some estimations of Mary's character – meretricious, superficial, and led astray by vicious associations and early neglect; but she always shows herself quite aware of the moral deficiencies of these relations and associates, and gives many proofs moreover of the rightness of her judgement of people, and of her capacity for deep feeling. Fanny in fact is struggling to rationalise her invincible antipathy to her rival in love, who is in any case a personality she can never hope to understand or appreciate. Her feelings come right out into the open after she has read Edmund's long and confiding letter to her when she is in Portsmouth – malice, resentment and envy are here nakedly exposed.

> She was almost vexed into displeasure and anger against Edmund. 'There is no good in this delay,' said she, 'why is it not settled? He is blinded and nothing will open his eyes, nothing can, after having had truths before him so long in vain. He will marry her, and be poor and miserable. God grant that her influence will not make him cease to be respectable!' She looked over the letter again. 'So very fond of me! 'tis nonsense all. She loves nobody but herself and her brother. Her friends leading her astray for years! She is quite as likely to have led them astray!…'

Mary shares her brother's rather frenetic love of change, and his mercurial disposition; she is very quickly influenced by her environment. Her attitude to her brother is admirable, loyal and affectionate, but she is not blind to his defects of character; she only takes them a little too light-heartedly. To her sister Mrs Grant she is warm and protective; she sees and resents Dr Grant's selfish tyranny, just as she is aware of the viciousness of her uncle's way of life, and the superficial cold-heartedness of her London circle. But she is an observer, not a reformer – like Jane Austen herself, and moreover, circumstances have made her spoilt and self-indulgent – she likes 'a good time', and is quite happy to compromise with these second-rate standards to achieve it. She values money, knows herself too well not to know how ill she would manage without a good deal of it; she is full of cynical remarks about matrimony, but she is prepared to reject the idea of a wealthy young heir to a baronetcy for the love of his younger brother with no inheritance at all.

Her rooted prejudice against the clergy is not primarily an attack against religion, and only partly a repugnance against an unfashionable profession – she inveighs against the profession as it was only too often seen in her day – filled by worldly absentee incumbents with no sense of vocation who were in need of an unearned income. She speaks from hearsay or narrow experience, but her attitude again underlines her potentially proper sense of values, not the shocking lack of moral standards deplored by Fanny:

'Oh!' Mary says,

> 'no doubt he [the clergyman] is very sincere in preferring an income ready made, to the trouble of working for one; and has the best intentions of doing nothing all the rest of his days but eat, drink and grow fat. It is indolence, Mr Bertram, indeed. Indolence and love of ease – a want of all laudable ambition, of taste for good company, or of inclination to take the trouble of being agreeable, which makes men clergymen. A clergyman has nothing to do but to be slovenly and selfish – read the newspaper, watch the weather, and quarrel with his wife. His curate does all the work, and the business of his own life is to dine...'

This may seem perverse, but it is in fact a very accurate portrayal of her own brother-in-law, the Reverend Dr Grant.

In fact, Mary's virtues and charms carry conviction, it is only her fallings-away that smell of contrivance. Those small lapses of taste that outrage Edmund in the early days of their acquaintance, the mild mockery of her uncle, and the facetious pun, 'of Rears and Vices I saw enough' are not ground for moral disapproval in our eyes any more than they would be to the Jane Austen who could write in her letters of the Admiral whose legs were too short and his tail too long.

The famous letter in which Mary seeks news from Fanny of Tom Bertram's illness is somewhat unconvincing in several ways. In the first paragraph Mary shows a perfectly sincere and proper concern about Tom's illness, and for the distress of his family, and an equally proper implied criticism of his sisters, 'so unwilling to have their own amusements cut up, as to shut their eyes to the truth'. Then follows the heartless passage which arouses Fanny's disgust at Mary's 'cold-hearted ambition'.

> Fanny, Fanny, I see you smile, and look cunning, but upon my honour I never bribed a physician in my life. Poor young man! if he is to die, there will be *two* poor young men less in the world; and with a fearless face and a bold voice would I say to anyone, that wealth and consequence could fall into no hands more deserving of them. I put it to your conscience, whether 'Sir Edmund' would not do more good with all the Bertram property than any other possible 'Sir'.

Jane Austen is too skilled an artist not to write these passages in Mary's authentic tones; but even Mary would not be so naïve and imperceptive as to write in this way to Fanny. She would not be human had not some thoughts of the results of Tom's possible death crossed her mind, but frank and ingenuous though she is, she would have kept such reflections to herself. This is part of the necessary process of the destruction of Mary.

The final scene between Mary and Edmund, where we are expected to join with him and Fanny in shocked condemnation, is not so much contrived and unconvincing, as open to a more generous interpretation. Mary is a realist, and truly concerned about people in a way that Fanny and Edmund are not. She loves her brother and she loves Edmund, and struggles to find a way to restore a bad situation, even if it means pasting over cracks. Her reactions are not highly moral, but they are grounded in sympathetic tolerance and a practical, rational desire to make the best of things, which is far more humane and less self-absorbed than the Mansfield Park attitude. Fanny, Edmund, and Sir Thomas are only desirous, for their own reasons, to cast out the evil and preserve the citadel inviolate. There is a marked change of tone from the attitudes and actions over Lydia Bennet's elopement with Wickham in *Pride and Prejudice*. Of course, the betrayal of a husband by a bride is a more deeply disgraceful act, but the social circumstances are not dissimilar. Jane Austen was well aware of adulterous associations in real life, divorces in fashionable circles, and irregular relationships, all of which are mentioned in her letters; all such deviations are regarded as deplorable, but only in *Mansfield Park* do we find the hysterical overtones of an emotional condemnation. The news affects Fanny like a physical illness:

> The horror of a mind like Fanny's as it received the conviction of such guilt, can hardly be described... There was no possibility of rest. The evening passed without a pause of misery, the night was totally sleepless. She passed only from feelings of sickness to shudderings of horror; and from hot fits of fever to cold. The event was so shocking, that there were moments even when her heart revolted

from it as impossible, when she thought it could not be. A woman married only six months ago, a man professing himself devoted, even *engaged* to another and that her near relation – the whole family, both families connected as they were by tie upon tie, all friends, all intimate together! – it was too horrible a confusion of guilt, too gross a complication of evil, for human nature, not in a state of utter barbarism, to be capable of!

The culmination of Fanny's hysteria is reached in her conclusion that:

it appeared to her, that as far as this world alone was concerned, the greatest blessing to everyone of kindred with Mrs Rushworth would be instant annihilation.

Edmund's dismay is at Mary's failure to react to the situation in *his* way, to see it as an action so immoral and evil as to put the perpetrators beyond the bounds of forgiveness or reconciliation for ever:

To hear the woman whom no harsher name than folly given! So voluntarily, so freely, so coolly to canvass it! No reluctance, no horror, no modest loathings!

Mary is only hoping, after all, that Henry may be persuaded to marry Maria, a hope that Edmund repudiates with disgust not for the sound reason that such a marriage was not likely to make either of the partners happy, but because the two parties do not deserve such a socially acceptable solution. Maria must be cast out of the charmed circle,

Henry must pursue whatever vicious and dissipated courses his folly has driven him to. The element of charity is certainly more evident in Mary's attitude than in his, however much one may condemn the cynical disregard of moral principles that her attitude reveals.

Some people feel that Mary's tone in the face of these moral confrontations sounds out falsely, like a cracked bell; what seems false to me is the inconsistency of tone whereby she is forced by her creator out of the role of near-heroine, outshining Fanny in nearly every respect, in order to tally more nearly with Fanny's jaundiced view of her, and in order to reject her finally from the sacred precincts of Mansfield Park. In Fanny, Jane Austen attempted to create the heroine as a saint; but in Mansfield Park it is Jane Austen herself who is out of tune. By the time she came to write *Persuasion* the balance is restored, her vision cleared, and in Anne Elliot she created her perfect heroine.

Sense and Sensibility:
Men in a Minor Key

There is a great deal of passionate feeling in *Sense and Sensibility*, more passion, though not more feeling, than in any of the other books, but it is not to be found embodied in the male characters. The book has at its core the glowing and vital Dashwood women, and round them are grouped – they can scarcely be said to revolve – a rather drab collection of secondary characters. Admittedly, the Steele sisters and the John Dashwoods are worthy of a prominent place in the Jane Austen gallery of horrors, Lucy with her calculating charm, and Miss Steele with her mindless vulgarity, and the Dashwoods a portrait of a greedy, heartless and small-minded woman and her weak and mercenary husband; but the Palmers and the Middletons who attend the heroines almost constantly throughout their trials, are a very dull set – one can sympathise with Marianne's impatient boredom, if not with her manners. The attempts to make them more amiable as a result of Marianne's misfortunes only weakens them. We are *told* Mr Palmer becomes kinder and more attentive but we are not permitted to see him being so; and we find it difficult to imagine that Mrs Palmer's butterfly apology for a mind could settle on anything long enough to be attentive to the sisters' serious anxieties.

Mrs Jennings' heart is always warm, and her sympathies abundant; she is the sort of person who is more tolerable in the adversity of her friends than in their prosperity, even if her panacea for a broken heart tends to take the form of the 'finest old Constantia wine' which was so beneficial for her late husband's colicky gout. She is a character about whom Jane Austen seems to have had a change of mind; always good-humoured, her avid curiosity is apt to oust her crude brand of sympathy in the earlier part of the book. She is intolerably vulgar, inquisitive and insensitive at first, with a brash lack of perception about the feelings of other people. Later, her judgement and finer feelings all improve. If she could be so aware of the bruised feelings of Marianne after Willoughby had jilted her, it is strange that she could be so persistently impertinent to Colonel Brandon under the stress of mysterious bad news.

'No bad news, Colonel, I hope,' said Mrs Jennings, as soon as he entered the room.

'None at all, ma'am, I thank you.'

'Was it from Avignon? I hope it is not to say that your sister is worse.'

'No, ma'am. It came from town, and is merely a letter of business.'

'But how came the hand to discompose you so such, if it was only a letter of business? Come, come, this won't do, Colonel, so let us hear the truth of it.'

'My dear madam,' said Lady Middleton, 'recollect what you are saying.'

'Perhaps it is to tell you that your cousin Fanny is married?' said Mrs Jennings, without attending to her daughter's reproof,

'No, indeed it is not.'

'Well, then, I know who it is from, Colonel. And I hope she is well.'

And so on and on, pestering the unfortunate man until he simply ignores her in a way which reminds us very much of Mr Knightley in *Emma*. In comparison, her response on hearing of Marianne's misfortune is, 'Poor soul! I am sure if I had had a notion of it, I would not have joked her about it, for all my money...' There is much more of the vulgar Madame Duval from Fanny Burney's *Evelina* in the early Mrs Jennings than in the final version of her character. The nature of the composition of *Sense and Sensibility* accounts for the discrepancies – *Elinor and Marianne* was written sometime prior to 1797, which was the date when *Sense and Sensibility* as such, based on the earlier work, was begun; but it, in its turn, was not prepared for the press until 1811, and it is impossible that it did not receive some critical attention at the author's hands at this late date; but it would be difficult to smooth away all discrepancies of characterisation.

Sir John Middleton's universal benevolence is even more undiscriminating than Mr Weston's in *Emma;* like nature, he abhors a vacuum, and does not much mind who fills it.

As for her heroes in this work, Jane Austen so firmly underplays them, in their appearance, demeanour and personality, that it is as if she wishes to set off, by contrast, the brilliance of her heroine, Marianne, and her anti-hero, Willoughby. Edward Ferrars was 'not recommended to their good opinion by any peculiar graces of person or address. He was not handsome, and his manners required intimacy to make them pleasing.' He was diffident, and although intelligent and well-informed, without ambition to shine in public either as a man of affairs or a dashing young buck – 'all his wishes centred in domestic comfort and the quiet of private life.' He is as middle-aged in outlook as Colonel Brandon is in fact; though it might be borne in mind that Colonel Brandon is two years younger than Mr George Knightley in *Emma* who is never reckoned ineligible – on account of his age – to be the husband of Emma, or Jane Fairfax, or even Harriet Smith. The question of Colonel Brandon's advanced age is, it is true, raised always by Marianne or her younger sister Margaret; when they see in him 'an absolute old bachelor' it is at them that Jane Austen is laughing, not the Colonel.

> ...she was reasonable enough to allow that a man of five and thirty might well have outlived all acuteness of feeling and every exquisite power of enjoyment. She was perfectly disposed to make every allowance for the Colonel's advanced state of life which humanity required.

He, no more than Edward, is allowed to be handsome, but 'his countenance was sensible and his address was particularly gentlemanlike.'

In making her heroes no more than ordinarily good-looking or accomplished, Jane Austen is deriding the romantic novel of sensibility where heroes and heroines were paragons of beauty and virtue; and deriding too Marianne's aspirations for the ideal lover, young, beautiful, and throbbing with enthusiasm and sensibility. Willoughby is the answer to her prayer in every particular; their idyll is indeed a unique episode in Jane Austen's work, a brief lyrical episode which rises above the pervading irony, and which is untouched by Elinor's conventional anxieties, bathed in the glow of Marianne's ardent and single-minded idealism. Willoughby is introduced in the most romantic manner possible, rescuing a damsel in distress, and without, initially, a hint of danger or undesirability. Elinor is alarmed at Marianne's indiscretions and lack of decorum, but even to her, and certainly to their mother, Willoughby is almost beyond criticism. He is excessively handsome, graceful in manner, and – unlike Marianne – courteous, considerate and friendly to everyone – except perhaps, Colonel Brandon! The dialogue in which Marianne, Elinor and Willoughby discuss the Colonel is revelatory of all their characters, and gives one the first hint of a baser metal beneath Willoughby's jewelled exterior. Elinor esteems and appreciates Colonel Brandon, and pities him for his evident growing interest in Marianne, which can only be in vain, and because he is so conspicuously ignored and slighted by the other two; she even rises to a certain degree of wit in his defence; Marianne, eager and prejudiced, agrees with all that Willoughby says and expresses her opinion, that of a 'woman of feeling', without attempt at wit or irony – 'he has neither genius, taste nor spirit – his understanding has no brilliancy, his feelings no ardour, and his voice no expression.' Willoughby, however, is irrepressibly lively and witty at the Colonel's expense, full of rather facile jibes:

> 'Brandon is just the kind of man whom everyone speaks well of, and nobody cares about; whom all are delighted to see, and nobody remembers to talk to!'

When Elinor protests that he is held in high esteem by the 'park people', he exclaims:

> 'Who would submit to the indignity of being approved by such women as Lady Middleton and Mrs Jennings that could command the indifference of anybody else?'

His humour however makes him socially more adroit than Marianne, who has no humour at all. He laughs off Elinor's more serious protestations with:

> 'I have three unanswerable reasons for dislik-
> ing Colonel Brandon; he has threatened me
> with rain when I wanted it to be fine; he has
> found fault with the hanging of my curricle,
> and I cannot persuade him to buy my brown
> mare.'

He could have said with more truth and less frivolity that his reasons were that he had just seduced his ward, that the Colonel knew what a rogue he was, and that *he* knew that the Colonel was a better man than he.

He and Marianne share a lively, impulsive nature, and an almost irresistible charm of person and manner; but where Marianne is as she appears, without guile and incapable of falsehood or even the disguise of her feelings, he is, at bottom, calculating, self-indulgent and deceitful. When one later realises that Willoughby has seduced Colonel Brandon's ward and abandoned her to her fate, his sallies strike a tawdry note, and his wit seems a little cheap. He is not so much an immoral as an amoral person, whose habits of self-indulgence and extravagance lead him into individual actions which he cannot resist, whose conse-quences he fails to foresee, and which lead him into courses of behaviour which he dislikes or even knows to be bad or undesirable, but which he becomes resigned to as inevita-ble. His long and self-pitying confession to Elinor does not to any serious extent redeem him, it reveals only what was clear at the time, that his love for Marianne had become a serious emotion, and that he was prepared to take some risks and ask her to marry him; the fact that his intended proposal was prevented by his benefactor's discovery of his behaviour to poor Eliza, and her demand that he should marry her, does not redound much to his credit. Edward Ferrars' loyalty to his outworn obligation shines in com-parison. Willoughby neither obeyed his aunt by redeeming the young woman whom he had betrayed, nor did he throw his cap over the windmill and give up everything for love; he chose the shabbiest, the most caddish course, and made a cynical and loveless marriage to ensure the luxury and comfort that he could not deny himself. The Dashwood ladies were prepared, after his confession, to think of him with far less critical feelings, but they all three had been to a greater or less degree in love with him, Elinor never more so than at the end of the highly charged scene of his interview with her, with Marianne lying so near death's door above them:

> She felt that his influence over her mind was heightened by circumstances which ought not in reason to have weight; by that person of uncommon attraction, that open, affectionate and lively manner which it was no merit to possess; and by that still ardent love for Marianne, which it was not even innocent to indulge. But she felt that it was so, long, long before she could feel his influence less.

Although it is customary to say that Marianne is treated badly by Jane Austen (one critic goes so far as to say that she is 'betrayed and not by Willoughby') being married off to a middle-aged admirer in a flannel waistcoat there is no doubt that she gets the better man of the two. Colonel Brandon suffers throughout the book from the shadow of an impenetrable gravity, which is not allowed to assume the guise of a romantic mystery, which would endow him with some sort of glamour, although this is what it proves to be, in the best traditions of romantic fiction. Jane Austen may be giving another dig at the romantic school here, flattening the figure of mystery into a more prosaic shape. Colonel Brandon does not open his mouth until the end of the eleventh chapter, and is then only allowed a 'faint smile' as he engages in a brief conversation with Elinor; fraught though it is with meaning, and full of hints of 'tender recollections of past regard', it leads to no great expansion of interest in him, or excited speculation, for it is the prudent Elinor who hears him, and realises 'he has said more than he felt was wise, – Elinor attempted no more. Marianne, in her place, would not have done so little. The whole story would have been speedily formed under her active imagination; and everything established in the most melancholy order of disastrous love.'

Throughout most of the ensuing action, he appears similarly oppressed by secret anxieties and inner perplexities – he is grave, thoughtful, silent, distracted, at best engaged in mild and polite conversation, at worst 'in low spirits', that least romantic condition, until he brings himself to ask Elinor outright if Marianne and Willoughby are engaged. Elinor's answer is crucial; had she stated only what she knew, that is, that she knew of no positive engagement, in spite of appearances, Colonel Brandon would no doubt have revealed his personal knowledge of Willoughby's character as a libertine, and the worst of Marianne's anguish and public exposure night have been avoided; but, partly to prevent Colonel Brandon holding false hopes for himself, and partly making assumptions from Marianne's behaviour more hopefully than assuredly, she asserts more than she knows, and Colonel Brandon leaves dejectedly – with his story untold. It is after the crisis in Marianne's affairs that his character begins to assert itself more positively, when he can help the Dashwood ladies in practical ways. The offer of the living at Delaford to Edward Ferrars is swiftly made, as an act, as Elinor rightly assumes, of 'general benevolence and particular friendship', and his expedition in fetching Mrs Dashwood to Marianne's bedside from Barton to Cleveland makes us realise that it is as a man of action that he shines, as his reported activities on behalf of the all too many distressed ladies who figure in his past life bear witness. Once comfortably established in Mrs Dashwood's imagination as the suitor for the hand of Marianne, he assumes a suitability through her eyes that no one was aware of before:

> 'his manners, the Colonel's manners are not only more pleasing to me than Willoughby's ever were, but they are of a kind I well know to be more solidly attached to Marianne. Their gentleness, their genuine attention to other people, and their manly unstudied simplicity is much more accordant with her real disposition than the liveliness, often artificial, and often ill-timed, of the other. I am very sure myself, that had Willoughby turned out as really amiable, as he proved himself the contrary, Marianne would yet never have been so happy with *him* as she will be with Colonel Brandon.'

This is a piece of partial and prejudiced pleading, typical of the optimistic and elastic spirit of the lady, but there is more truth in her argument than Elinor will admit. Mrs Dashwood, though lightly drawn, is a particularly charming example of those married women whom Jane Austen delights to depict, of whom Mrs Weston, Mrs Gardiner and Mrs Grant are other specimens. Without being too specific, one recalls her devotion to her friend Madame Lefroy of Ashe, who evidently had similar qualities of charm and sympathy and intelligence. Mrs Dashwood has all Marianne's quick responsiveness and charm of manner, but without her selfish thoughtlessness, and with a real desire and ability – entirely lacking in Marianne – to set people at their ease and make them welcome in her home. Although her optimism and impulsiveness lead her astray in practical matters and even affect her judgement, she is basically governed by a greater conformity to the principles of her society, and a stronger hold on fundamental values than Marianne; that is, she is not so easily misled by the ignis fatuus of sensibility; one recalls Marianne's sublime personal logic of self-justification to Elinor, who has criticised her behaviour:

> 'I am afraid,' replied Elinor, 'that the pleasant-
> ness of an employment does not always evince
> its propriety.'
> 'On the contrary, nothing can be a stronger
> proof of it, Elinor; for if there had been any
> real impropriety in what I did, I should have
> been sensible of it at the time, for we always
> know when we are acting wrong, and with
> such a conviction I could have had no pleas-
> ure.'

Mrs Dashwood's enthusiasm is an innate trait of personal-ity, and not raised to the status of a cult, as with Marianne. She is as Marianne will become, when suffering and experience have made her less selfish but no less impulsive, as loving and fervent as ever, but directing her enthusiasm to real and tried objects instead of the will o' the wisp of romantic sensibility.

Jane Austen is a little cavalier in her dismissal of Marianne to Delaford Manor in the last pages of *Sense and Sensibility*, and her, 'with such a confederacy against her,... what could she do?' seems a sadly unromantic fate. But with the modification of her juvenile specifications for a lover, and no change in her capacity for devotion and loyalty and ardour, and with his renewal of spirits and liveliness, Marianne would surely devote herself to her new role with the single-minded enthusiasm which was her only way of facing any situation; and Jane Austen indicates as much – 'Marianne could never love by halves; and her whole heart became, in time, as much devoted to her husband, as it had once been to Willoughby.' One could hardly say more!

★

Edward Ferrars is crippled from the outset even more than Colonel Brandon, by the most inexplicable depression of spirits, an absolutely insuperable obstacle for any hero to overcome. His awkwardness and ill manners and moods of alternating cheerfulness and gloom make everyone thoroughly uncomfortable, and Elinor wretched. On his first visit to Barton, Marianne observes:

> the unaccountable coldness which she had often observed at Norland …there was a deficiency of all that a lover ought to look and say – He was confused, seemed scarcely sensible of pleasure in seeing them, looked neither rapturous nor gay, said little but what was forced from him by questions, and distinguished Elinor by no mark of affection. Marianne… began almost to feel a dislike of Edward.

Mrs Dashwood, with her unreserved welcome, and 'captivating manners', affects a revival of spirits, but not for long; soon, his 'gravity and thoughtfulness returned on him in their fullest extent, and he sat for some time silent and dull.'

The problem is not only the matter of an oppressive secret and a nagging conscience – and surely no other hero was ever burdened with such an inhibiting secret for almost the whole of the story! – but he himself confesses to a deficiency in personality:

> 'I never wish to offend, but I am so foolishly shy, that I often seem negligent, when I am only kept back by my natural awkwardness. I have frequently thought that I must have been intended by nature to be fond of low company, I am so little at my ease among strangers of gentility!'

This helps to account for his succumbing so readily as a youth to the charms of Lucy Steele, a girl who would certainly have helped him by making most of the running; this early attachment seems to stick in the throat of some critics: 'Edward's infatuation with someone as vulgar as Lucy Steele is out of key with everything we know about him' (R. Garis, *Learning, Experience and Change*). Perhaps 'infatuation' is the wrong word; we know nothing of the facts, but 'capture' may well suit the case better. Edward's boyhood, spent in a household with his mother, his sister and his younger brother, may have given him little experience of true elegance of mind, or much idea of the nature of affectionate relationships; Lucy would have been pretty and kind and attentive, treatment to which he would have been totally unaccustomed.

Edward is strong and honourable enough to stand by an engagement which has long ceased to have any emotional validity, but has not the strength or the integrity to keep away from Elinor when he realises they are falling in love with one another. His visits are a silent scream for help, and he does not cut a very heroic figure in the process. The contrivance by which he is disentangled and left free to marry Elinor, Lucy's elopement with Robert Ferrars, is one of the author's least convincing devices, not because it is not potentially plausible, but because it is pushed forward, hugger-mugger, off-stage and without any sort of hint or preparation, no doubt to maintain the element of complete surprise, and make Elinor's realisation more dramatic and moving.

Had Jane Austen given a little space for us to see Lucy's mind at work, weighing the favoured Robert against the disinherited Edward, ingratiating herself with Robert by playing on his vanity, we should have gained in entertainment and realism more than we should have lost in sheer surprise. Robert Ferrars is one of Jane Austen's splendid comic characters in embryo and it would have been a pleasure to have more of him. To balance Edward's weakness, Elinor is a strong character, firmly conformist even to the extent of making compromises for the sake of social demands or appearances, which range from the white lies of polite intercourse – she has so often to cover up for her sister's devastating frankness – to the dangerous duplicity of her fencing with Lucy, where she is in danger of appearing as hypocritical and false as her adversary. Both she and Edward are redeemed by intelligence and a great deal more humour than they are allowed the full use of in the course of the story – and even more sensibility than Marianne would admit them to possess. In short, the two couples are destined to enjoy a high degree of that rational sort of happiness which Jane Austen deems most suitable for marital bliss, and a more positive relationship than she promises – flattening superlatives and excess of emotion to the end – in her final words, 'though sisters, and living almost within sight of each other, they could live without disagreement between themselves, or producing coolness between their husbands.'

Men and Mores in the Novels of Jane Austen

Jane Austen never eavesdrops on the private conversations of men; the women are overheard in the privacy of the bedroom, the solitude of country rambles, over the family breakfast table, and in the intimacy of the boudoir, but the billiard room, the smoking room, the gunroom or the estate office are never trespassed upon. Men's voices are heard in the drawing room and the ballroom, or in the open air, in the company of females, even if not in direct conversation with them but with each other. Perhaps the nearest we get to overhearing men's conversation between themselves is in *Emma* when George Knightley and his brother John, a lawyer visiting Hartfield from London, talk together after dinner:

> The brothers talked of their own concerns and pursuits, but principally those of the elder, whose temper was much the most communicative, and who was always the greater talker. As a magistrate, he had generally some point of law to consult John about, or, at least, some curious anecdote to give; and as a farmer, as keeping in hand the home-farm at Donwell, he had to tell what every field had to bear next year, and to give all such local information as could not fail of being interesting to a brother whose home it had equally been the longest

part of his life, and whose attachments were strong. The plan of a drain, the change of a fence, the felling of a tree, and the destination of every acre for wheat, turnips or spring corn, was entered into with as much equality of interest by John, as his cooler manners rendered possible; and if his willing brother ever left him anything to enquire about, his inquiries even approached a tone of eagerness.

Men were seen visiting, dining out, dancing, but never pursuing any professional or money-making activity. In fact most of them are not gainfully employed, in the sense of receiving a salary or engaging in money-making activities, at all. At the period in which Jane Austen lived, and in the society of which she wrote, a young man with inherited money and property was not expected to take up or train for a profession.[1] In *Mansfield Park,* however, when Mary Crawford expresses surprise that Edmund intends taking orders, he replies, 'Why should it surprise you? You must suppose me designed for some profession, and might perceive that I am neither a lawyer, nor a soldier nor a sailor.' 'Very true; but... you know there is generally an uncle or a grandfather to leave a fortune to the second son...'

---

[1] The professions open to 'gentlemen' were extraordinarily limited, and this state of affairs persisted throughout the nineteenth century; Jane Austen's niece Elizabeth Knight had a family of fifteen children, ten of whom were boys, and of these three were in the Navy, five were in the Army, one was a scholar and a clergyman, and the youngest emigrated to Queensland where he became a grazier and property owner. An interesting footnote to a footnote is that a bill recently discovered amongst family papers reveals that perhaps for only a brief period, in 1803 or '05 (the writing is illegible) Henry Austen was engaged in the wine trade in London – a fact probably suppressed by the family as rather disreputable.

But for the young man who owned property, the care of his estates would occupy much or little of his time, according to whether he was a George Knightley or a Henry Crawford. In any case, there would usually be an estate manager or a steward or a bailiff to look after the practical day-to-day running of the estate. In Jane Austen's own family, her brother Edward Knight was the owner of extensive property in Hampshire and Kent. He himself, no doubt, was fairly fully occupied with the supervision of his estates, but his numerous lively and cheerful sons spent much of their time in amusing themselves hunting, shooting and visiting in other country houses. One finds the extreme of this in the character of the benevolent Sir John Middleton, in *Sense and Sensibility*, who hunted and shot, and spent the remainder of his time in a determined effort to fill his house with company, in order to compensate for 'that total want of talent and taste which confined their employments, unconnected with such as society produced, within a very narrow compass.' There are hints in her letters that Jane Austen met such men at Godmersham, her brother Edward's home in Kent, and the nephews came under her critical scrutiny too – 'Now these two boys who are out with the Foxhounds will come home and disgust me again by some habit of Luxury or some proof of sporting Mania…'

If expectations of a mercenary nature were not fulfilled, a young man of good family could find himself in some embarrassment, and precisely this predicament provides a powerful motive of action in many of Jane Austen's books. Frank Churchill dared not declare his engagement to a penniless girl (Jane Fairfax, in *Emma*) lest his expectations from his disagreeable aunt should be frustrated; Willoughby, in *Sense and Sensibility*, jilts his lovely Marianne rather than forego his inheritance and his taste for luxury; nowadays, of course, he would be trained for a profession or some business, and would be capable of earning his living, and the lady would be in a like position. If Jane Austen's novels are anything to go by, the custom had a very deleterious affect on the characters of young men, encouraging them in habits of idleness and extravagance in youth, and selfishness and self-interest when they had reached the time to settle down; and was an outlet – one of the few available to a woman – for tyranny and small-minded self-indulgence for a woman in a position to hold the purse strings.

The only young man who actually expresses his regret at not being qualified for a profession is Elinor Dashwood's courtier in *Sense and Sensibility*, Edward Ferrars, and a secret reason is that youthful idleness exposed him to the dangers of an ill-judged love affair. Mrs Dashwood added that the demands of a profession would at least provide him with a destination and a motive when he reluctantly left them, a wry commentary on the dire emptiness of the young man's existence.

Younger sons for whom there was no, or little inheritance very often entered the church, and a family living, or one in the gift of a relative or friend, would be found for them. Neither in the novels nor within her own family experience is there evidence that it was common for young men on the brink of ordination to experience profound heart-searchings or moral scruples; indeed, in the single case recorded in her letters, of Anna Austen's fiancé Benjamin Lefroy, who rejected an offer of a lucrative living on the grounds of conscience – he did not want to rush into a commitment to a religious vocation for mercenary reasons – the families, both clerical ones, joined in disapproval of his action. There is no doubt that many made very satisfactory parish priests, however worldly their original impetus might have been. In *Mansfield Park*, in which the theme of ordination plays an important role, the worldly Henry Crawford states, of Edmund Bertram's future living:

> 'Seven hundred a year is a fine thing for a younger brother; and as, of course, he will still live at home, it will be all for his 'menus plaisirs'; and a sermon at Christmas and Easter, I suppose, will be the sum total of sacrifice.'

Later, Sir Thomas and Edmund set him right as to *their* view of a clergyman's duties. Sir Thomas declares:

> 'I hope and believe that Edmund will occupy his own house at Thornton Lacey, ...I should have been deeply mortified, if any son of mine could reconcile himself to doing less... a parish has wants and claims which can be known only by a clergyman constantly resident, and which no proxy can be capable of satisfying to the same extent. Edmund might, in the common phrase, do the duty of Thornton, that is, he might read prayers and preach, without giving up Mansfield Park; he might ride over every Sunday, to a house nominally inhabited, and go through divine service; he might be the clergyman of Thornton Lacey every seventh day, for three or four hours, if that would content him. But it will not. He knows that human nature needs more lessons than a weekly sermon can convey, and that if he does not live among his parishioners and prove himself their well-wisher and friend, he does very little either for their good or his own.'

To which Edmund adds:

> 'Sir Thomas undoubtedly understands the
> duties of a parish priest – we must hope that
> his son may prove he knows it too.'

There are in the novels of course, many professional men; but with the exception of John Knightley in *Emma*, who is a prosperous lawyer in London, there are none thus regularly employed who belong to the class of country gentry into which Jane Austen's heroines hope to marry; and Mr John Knightley is from a family of irreproachable local standing and good breeding. There are soldiers, sailors and clergy-men in profusion from this class of society, but on the whole Jane Austen's small town attorneys and apothecaries occupy a rather ambiguous position above the tradesmen but inferior to the landed gentry. One recalls her advice to her niece Anna, writing her first novel:

> I have... scratched out the Introduction be-
> tween Lord P. and ...Mr Griffin. A Country
> Surgeon (don't tell Mr Lyford) would not be
> introduced to Men of their rank.

The nuances are subtle, and there is a good deal of over-lapping, in real life as well as in her fiction. Sir Thomas Bertram, the most dignified, respected and aristocratic of all the father figures in the novels, makes his money – and works very hard at it – as a merchant in Antigua. The point is entertainingly demonstrated in *Emma* by the heroine's dilemma over the expected dinner invitation from the Coles. The Coles were resident in Highbury, and were a 'very good sort of people', friendly, liberal and unpreten-tious; but on the other hand, they were of low origin, in trade, and 'only moderately genteel'. Affluence made them socially ambitious, and Emma considered their presumption in aspiring to attract 'the best families' worthy of a sharp refusal – 'nothing should tempt *her* to go; she only regretted her father's known habits would be giving her refusal less meaning than she could wish.' But much to her chagrin, when the invitations to dinner were issued, not only did none arrive for her or her father, but the rest of Highbury society – including Mr Weston's son, Frank Churchill, who was a new object of interest to her, accepted the invitations with enthusiasm. It was one thing to feel the insult of an ill-judged invitation, and quite another not to have the power of a refusal! However, the invitation, held over for the most thoughtful of reasons (the ordering of a screen from London to protect Mr Woodhouse from draughts), came at last, and after consultation with the Westons, was accepted.

Jane Austen delights in her revelations of her heroine's social snobbery, and that it is a personal foible and not characteristic of her – and Jane Austen's own society, is made clear. 'This lesson [i.e. the refusal of the invitation] she very much feared, they would receive only from herself; she had little hope of Mr Knightley, none of Mr Weston.' This social ambiguity is borne out too by her attitude to the worthy and attractively portrayed Robert Martin, who is as much a friend of Mr Knightley's as a tenant; but he is, in Emma's estimation, 'the very last person to raise my curiosity; [he] is in one sense as much above my notice as in every other he is below it.' Her attitude to him is deliberately pitched to diminish the regard of her protégée Harriet Smith for him, but it is one of the most disconcerting passages of many in the book to the modern admirer of this imperfect but fascinating heroine. That Jane Austen's own attitude was less rigid or hidebound by the niceties of social distinctions is further borne out by the evidence of the letters, as well as by examples elsewhere in the novels, as, for example, Anne Elliot's shame at her father and sister's anxious manoeuvrings to ingratiate themselves with their noble connections, the Dalrymples: 'had Lady Dalrymple and her daughter even been agreeable, she would still have been ashamed of the agitation they created, but they were nothing. There was no superiority of manner, accomplishment, or understanding.' And she holds up to derision Sir Walter's disparaging comments on Anne's impoverished friend Mrs Smith.

In her letters, her criticism, often outspoken, of lack of gentility, 'manner', or good sense, (particularly good sense) are applied without regard to social position. In real life, as in fiction, Jane Austen always laughed at pretensions to gentility or superiority, from whatever rank of society. What she valued was superiority of understanding and elegance of mind, to use her own language. When she was at Godmersham in 1813, the family of Finch-Hatton were neighbours, at Eastwell Park, but Jane Austen was rather consciously not particularly impressed. 'George Hatton[2] called yesterday,' she wrote in October 1813, 'and I saw him, saw him for ten minutes; sat in the same room with him, heard him talk, saw him bow, and was not in raptures. I discerned nothing extraordinary.' A week or so later, 'Lady Elizabeth Hatton and Anna-Maria called here this morning

---

[2]George Hatton – he succeeded his childless cousin in 1826 as 10th Earl of Winchilsea, and in 1850 he married, as his third wife, Fanny, the oldest daughter of his college friend Edward Royds Rice of Dane Court in Kent, whose wife was Elizabeth Knight, a niece of Jane Austen and sister of Fanny. The disparity in age – twenty-nine and fifty-nine – did not prevent the brief marriage being both happy and fruitful (three sons and one daughter). Jane Austen would in fact have relished George Hatton's character and eccentricities had she known him in later life – he combined fanatically conservative and anti-papist views (he fought a duel with the Duke of Wellington over the latter issue) with extreme good nature and cheerfulness in his domestic and private capacity.

[sisters of George Hatton]; Yes, they called, but I do not think I can say anything more about them. They came and they sat and they went.'

On the other hand, her response to the apothecary–surgeon who attended her brother Henry during his illness in 1815, Dr Charles Haden, was uncritically enthusiastic.[3] He was intelligent and charming and the best possible company; indeed, it is probable, reading her almost hysterically merry defence of him to her sister, that the latter had sounded a warning – 'who is this apothecary, and are you sure he is not getting altogether too fond of Fanny?'. '…you seen to be under a mistake as to Mr H.' she wrote. 'You call him an Apothecary; he is no Apothecary, he has never been an Apothecary, there is not an Apothecary in the neighbourhood. …he is a Haden, nothing but a Haden, a sort of wonderful nondescript Creature on two legs, something between a Man and an Angel, but without the least spice of an Apothecary.' She added with approval, 'He never does appear the least above his Profession, or out of Humour with it.' Apart from his interest in Fanny, he paid *her* a great deal of attention and read her work – 'Mr H. is reading *Mansfield Park* for the first time and prefers it to *P. and P.*' and engaged in delightful arguments about music or the theatre or her own books; she was in short a little in love with him herself, and it is delightful to think of this gay and stimulating interlude for Jane Austen, following a period of great stress and anxiety over Henry's illness, and not long before the onset of her own fatal sickness. In the company of her niece Fanny, who was almost as congenial to her as was her sister Cassandra, of an almost-recovered Henry, who 'could not help be amusing' and the incomparable Mr Haden, she could relax and enjoy herself almost as in the flirtatious days of her youth; as she said of the weather that

---

[3]See above, M.C.H., *Jane Austen and the Young*, p.50, and footnote.

autumn, 'nice, unwholesome, relaxing, close, muggy weather! – I enjoy it all over me, from top to toe, from right to left, longitudinally, Perpendicularly, Diagonally!' – a fine description of well-being!

★

The impression sometimes given of Jane Austen as a spinster living in a feminine society, who had little experience of men, interest in their ways or ability to depict them, is very far from the truth. One suspects she was one of those women who sparkle and shine in men's company more than in that of her own sex. She delighted in the visits from nephews, brothers and their friends as they passed by on the busy thoroughfare outside Chawton Cottage, enjoyed the gaieties of London life with Henry and his circle. She appreciated a good talk with a well-informed man of taste, as we have seen with Charles Haden, or with Mr Lushington, MP who stayed at Godmersham in October 1813:

> I like him *very* much. I am sure he is clever, and a Man of Taste. He got a volume of Milton last night, and spoke of it with Warmth. He is quite an MP – very smiling, with an exceedingly good address, and readiness of language. I am rather in love with him. I dare say he is ambitious and insincere.

From both the letters and the novels one learns how tedious formal visiting very often was, a way of passing the time for those without, in Mrs Elton's phrase, 'Resources', but a futile waste of time for those, like Jane Austen, with only too much to do. Though there was little that was not absorbed and put to good use, however trivial or boring. It was nothing unusual for a half-hour's morning call to be passed partly in silence, or largely filled with vapid nothings. The novels abound in such instances, as in *Sense and Sensibility* when Lady Middleton first calls upon the Dashwood ladies. 'On every formal visit a child ought to be of the party, by way of provision of discourse,' comments Jane Austen. 'In the present case it took up ten minutes to determine whether the boy were most like his father or mother, and in what particular he resembled either, for of course everybody differed, and everybody was astonished at the opinion of the others.' One recalls too, in the same novel, the call paid reluctantly on her sisters-in-law by the disagreeable Mrs John Dashwood, when, 'of the quarter-of-an-hour bestowed on Berkeley Street, she sat at least seven minutes and a half in silence', and her own dinner party which was so ostentatious, with 'no poverty of any kind, except of conversation.' In Jane Austen's own experience, the visit of the Finch-Hatton ladies has already been mentioned, and about the same time, Jane Austen, with her brother Charles and others from Godmersham found themselves obliged on a visit to Canterbury, to 'saunter about anywhere and go backwards and forwards as much as possible to make out the time', to avoid the dire fate of a full two-hour visit on old Mrs Milles and her daughter, who seem to have been just such a couple as Miss Bates and her mother:

> Miss Milles was queer as usual, and provided us with plenty to laugh at. She undertook in three words to give us the history of Mrs Scudamore's reconciliation, and then talked on about it for half-an-hour, using such odd expressions and so foolishly minute, that I could hardly keep my countenance.

Another visit which she and Fanny paid is entertainingly described and includes one of the irresistible non sequiturs in which she so delighted, but it must have been a tedious social occasion:

> The ladies were at home; I was in luck, and saw Lady Fagg and all her five daughters, with an old Mrs Hamilton from Canterbury and Mrs and Miss Chapman from Margate into the Bargain. – I never saw so plain a family, five sisters so very plain! They are as plain as the Foresters or the Franfraddops or the Seagraves or the Rivers excluding Sophy. – It was stupidish; Fanny did her part very well, but there was a lack of talk altogether, and the three friends in the house only sat by and looked at us. However, Miss Chapman's name is Laura, and she has a double flounce to her gown.

It must not be supposed that her expectations were very high, however; 'Mary found it dull,' she wrote on one occasion, 'but I thought it very pleasant. To sit in idleness over a good fire in a well-proportioned room is a luxurious sensation.'

Public affairs are conscientiously excluded from the novels, though it would be quite unrealistic to suppose therefore that they were not and had not always been matters of lively interest and concern in the Austen household; but they are not in Jane Austen's brief, and it is taken for granted that the topics suitable for discussion with young ladies are rather limited; in *Northanger Abbey* Henry Tilney in conversation with Catherine Morland (admittedly a naïve and ill-informed young lady), 'by an easy transition from a piece of rocky fragment, and the withered oak which he had placed near its summit, to oaks in general, to forests, the enclosure of them, waste lands, crown lands and government, shortly found himself arrived at politics; and from politics, it was a short step to silence.' On the other hand, the most cultivated of Jane Austen's heroines, Anne Elliot, has a very high expectation of good company:

> 'My idea of good company, Mr Elliot, is the company of clever, well-informed people, who have a great deal of conversation.'
>
> 'You are mistaken,' replies Mr Elliot, 'that is not good company. That is the best.'

From her earliest years, Jane Austen was in the company of older members of her family, her parents, her brothers, uncles and aunts and friends, who had contacts of all sorts with the outside world, and who were well-informed, articulate, and all with more than average literary interests and abilities. Her great-uncle was the Master of Balliol, her father and her brothers James and Henry were Oxford men (where the two latter had edited and largely written themselves a periodical based on the *Idler* of Dr Johnson, called *The Loiterer*); her brother Edward had made the Grand Tour, and her cousin Eliza – who was at Steventon Rectory frequently when Jane was a girl, both as a visitor and later as a refugee from revolutionary France – was god-daughter to Warren Hastings, in whose career and trial all the family took a keen interest; Eliza's husband the Conte de Feuillide, was guillotined in 1794, a tragedy which would certainly have brought the violent events in France very close to the Austen family, even had there been no other circumstances within the family likely to do so. But there were strong service links in the family; Henry had served for a period in the Oxfordshire militia, at a period when the threat of invasion was not an idle one, and two of her brothers, Francis and Charles, were in the Navy, and served, mostly at sea, throughout the long-drawn-out revolutionary and Napoleonic wars; her cousin Jane Cooper, with whom she and Cassandra had been at school, had married a naval officer, Thomas Williams, under whom Charles served as a midshipman in the frigate *Unicorn*. It was impossible that the family did not take the liveliest interest in public affairs of all sorts, and no doubt they were better informed than most country people, with so many sources of information.

But few of these matters are touched upon in the novels. Never did an author more rigorously and deliberately limit her field of detailed investigation; but intention rather than ignorance controlled her plan.

The deep and detailed examination of her female creations is Jane Austen's principal object in the novels; young women in the restricted society which she knew, and to which she consciously confined herself, young women particularly in relation to the grand subject of marriage, and thus in their relationship with their families, their friends, and the men who form the object of their interest, pursuit or desire. In Jane Austen's day, the economic and social position of the women of her class was such as to fill us with dismay, though it was not only accepted almost universally as normal, but resulted, without doubt, in a high proportion of successful marriages, and contented though stultified and often short-lived matrons. The role of women of the middle class of society at this time was largely decorative and procreative in the framework of marriage. Domestic labour was cheap and plentiful, so that organisational rather than practical domestic skill was all that was required in running a household.[4]

---

[4]Many women of course, exercised their talents in a variety of different ways to the great benefit of their community. Madame Lefroy of Ashe for example, learned how to inoculate against smallpox when that

In *Pride and Prejudice* Mrs Bennet was offended when Mr Collins implied that her daughters might be required to help in the kitchen; she 'assured him with some asperity that they were very well able to keep a good cook, and that her daughters had nothing to do in the kitchen.' In *Sense and Sensibility* Mrs Jennings, an ever-practical busybody, reckoned that on five hundred pounds a year Edward Ferrars and Lucy could contrive very happily with 'two maids and two men' (though on the income from two thousand pounds capital 'they must get a maid of all works'). At Chawton Cottage, a small house run by Mrs Austen and her two daughters on a very small income, Jane Austen talks of 'two maids and a man'; such a staff was considered almost the minimum consonant with domestic decency.

Young ladies were brought up with a haphazard education, which may have been excellent – far better, in some cases than our formalised schooling – or non-existent, depending upon the inclination or the ability to learn, the quality of the governess or masters employed – if any were – or the school – more rarely – selected. Elizabeth Bennet explained to Lady Catherine de Burgh the system of education employed for herself and her sisters – 'such of us as wished to learn, never wanted the means. We were always encouraged to read, and had all the masters that were necessary. Those who chose to be idle, certainly might.' Lady Catherine was rather shocked at this lack of system, and so to a certain extent are we. A governess was never employed, as far as we ever hear, for Jane and Cassandra Austen; they went to school, mainly to the

---

discovery was made, and inoculated literally hundreds of people in and around her husband's parish (Lefroy Papers, courtesy of Ms Helen Lefroy).

Abbey School in Reading,[5] until Jane was about nine or ten, but her father and mother, as well as her older brothers, especially the oldest, James, guided her subsequent education and helped to form her taste in literature. The Austen family was exceptionally cultivated, especially in literature – Jane's father, an ex-Oxford don, was a professional teacher – he tutored young boys who boarded at the Rectory with them – and James and Henry were both young Oxford graduates with a taste for literature.

Most of the training given to young ladies was in drawing, music and sewing, and very competent some of them became – Jane's work was particularly neat and fine, she played the piano with some competence and her sister sketched. Jane Fairfax, Marianne Dashwood and Anne Elliot were all very musical and accomplished performers, Emma Woodhouse had talent in both accomplishments which she was guilty of neglecting; surprisingly Fanny Price was denied both of the two latter skills by her creator, no doubt the result of a neglectful and impoverished early childhood. Even at best, these accomplishments were designed principally to create a marriage-marketable product, and also to help fill the long periods of idleness and boredom in the lives of country gentlewoman, particularly in those prolonged seasons when even mild out-of-door activities were denied them owing to the inadequacy of the roads and footpaths, and the impractical nature of their costume.

---

[5]Mrs Sherwood, author of *The Fairchild Family*, attended this school a little later (c. 1790) and it was evidently a pleasant place at that time. Mrs Goddard's school, in *Emma*, might have been modelled on it, 'a real, honest, old-fashioned boarding school, where a reasonable quantity of accomplishments were sold at a reasonable price, and where girls might be sent out of the way, and scramble themselves into a little education, without any danger of coming back prodigies.'

Although Jane Austen has been attacked for her mercenary attitudes, when one probes beneath the surface, one
finds that this is not so, surprisingly, if one considers the
nature of her society and her own circumstances. It is true
that every eligible person, particularly of the male sex, has a
price tag (Dr Chapman's lists of characters in his edition of
the novels, emphasise this, as each name is followed by a
figure representing their fortune or dowry, if it is known).
It is true too, that her language, her metaphors and images
are drawn to an amazing extent from the world of commerce, property and the counting house. But none of the
heroines, in spite of considerable pressure, is motivated by
monetary considerations in her choice of a husband;
admittedly, not too much strain is put upon them in their
final selections – they are not called upon to face the
extremes of poverty for the sake of love; Elinor Dashwood
and Edward Ferrars have rather a thin start, but they have
expectations, and Anne Elliot and Captain Wentworth will
face vicissitudes of a different sort, danger and separation in
time of war. But Fanny Price resists almost intolerable
pressure from those she most respects and wishes to please,
rather than accept the wealthy and charming Henry, whom
she does not love. Elizabeth Bennet enrages her mother by
rejecting Mr Collins with his comfortable income and his
expectations of inheriting her father's estate; and although
Charlotte Lucas makes out a very good case for herself
when she makes a loveless marriage for the sake of security,
we are made to understand that it is a very sorry and rather
despicable affair. Mrs Dashwood, with a minute income
and three almost dowerless daughters, replies with firmness
to Sir John Middleton when he asserts that Willoughby is
'very well worth catching.'

> 'I do not believe,' said Mrs Dashwood with a
> good-humoured smile, 'that Mr Willoughby

> will be incommoded by the attempts of either
> of *my* daughters towards what you call *catching
> him*. It is not an employment to which they
> have been brought up. Men are very safe with
> us, let them be ever so rich...'

It is only the ill-bred and unpleasant characters who talk in
these terms, Miss Steele, with her 'smart beaux', Miss
Bingley or Mrs John Dashwood. Mrs Dashwood's departure from her old home at Norwood is hastened by her
anger at Mrs John's insinuations about Elinor's attempts to
'draw in' her brother Edward Ferrars. The vulgar and kind-
hearted Mrs Jennings, urging the two Dashwood girls to
accompany her to London, makes no bones about her
intentions:

> 'I have had such good luck in getting my own
> children off my hands, that she [Mrs
> Dashwood] will think me a very fit person to
> have the charge of you; and if I don't get one
> at least of you well married before I have done
> with you, it shall not be my fault. I shall speak
> a good word for you to all the young men, you
> may depend upon it.'

Young men, particularly rich ones, may have felt themselves threatened by predatory maidens and their mothers,
but the ladies had few weapons at their disposal apart from
their personal charms or wiles; even their physical movements were circumscribed. The departure of a potential
swain after a prolonged visit without making a firm declaration is a familiar situation in the novels, leaving behind
perplexity, disappointment or grief. It is only the passionate
and single-minded Marianne who seizes the opportunity to
go in pursuit, and she only exposes herself to further

anguish and shame. Elinor remains puzzled and unhappy at Edward's moody and unaccountable departure, Maria sits wordless in the face of Henry Crawford's selfish defection. These are the humiliations to be borne in such a society; even the friendly Colonel Fitzwilliam finds it necessary to warn Elizabeth Bennet that he must marry a fortune; 'is this' thought Elizabeth, 'meant for me?' and coloured at the idea.

If a young woman were dowerless, her only alternative to the humiliating drudgery of 'governessing', or the equally humiliating role of dependent spinster, was the capture of a husband with a comfortable income. That governessing *was* drudgery, and a fate to be dreaded by a person of refinement, is made clear by Jane Fairfax, who has to face that fate. 'There are places in town, offices', she explains, '...Offices for the sale – not quite of human flesh – but of human intellect,' and later, hinting at the ambiguous social position that a governess was doomed to occupy, 'It would be no object to me to be with the rich; my mortifications, I think, would only be the greater; I should suffer more from comparison.' If a young woman were an heiress, she was in danger of falling prey to an unscrupulous fortune hunter, out only for her money, which would come under his control on their marriage; whatever the income, and in spite of the dangers, the only really satisfactory, really respectable role for a woman was marriage. Jane and her sister Cassandra, both resolutely rejecting the compromise of marriage in order to obtain an 'establishment',[6] were fortunate in belonging to a family

---

[6] Jane Austen accepted an offer of marriage from her friend's brother, Mr Harris Bigg-Wither in 1802, only to reject him the following morning; nothing is known of Cassandra's opportunities after the death of her fiancé Tom Fowle, in 1797; there are facetious references in the letters, but references to anything serious, had there been anything of the sort, would certainly have been suppressed by Cassandra.

rich in love and a need to be together as often as possible; fortunate that in addition to the very modest income they and their mother jointly possessed,[7] their brothers were ready and able (the two sailors with some difficulty!) to prevent the three ladies from want, by supplementing their income and providing them with a house, part of Edward Knight's Hampshire estate. But from first to last in her letters, Jane Austen is aware, humorously or ruefully, of the irksome, inhibiting shortage of money. Her instincts were generous: 'Money is dirt!' she wrote, refusing to quibble over a postage charge, and exclaimed, 'I am rich', in urging the acceptance of a dress length as a present. But there is a great deal of careful costing of ribbons and bonnets, gratification at the occasional gift of money, and thrifty planning of expenditure; disappointment is very hard to conceal when half-hoped-for legacies go elsewhere ('Legacies,' she says, 'are a wholesome diet'); and though one should not marry for money, it is folly to marry without it. 'Single women,' she points out to her niece Fanny, 'have a dreadful Propensity for being poor – which is one very strong argument in favour of Matrimony.'

The men, therefore, figure in the novels to be married or refused, to protect, inhibit, persecute or serve, according to their age, character, relationship or station. But not as pasteboard, two-dimensional figures; for an artist like Jane Austen, with her gift of vitalising a character with a single phrase, it was almost an impossibility. J.I.M. Stewart, in an essay called *Tradition and Miss Austen*, says:

> We know very well that we are not being in-
> troduced to her young men entirely in the

---

[7]Cassandra's fiancé left her £1,000; Mrs Austen had an income of £140 p.a. after her husband's death in 1805, augmented by her sons; until Jane Austen began to earn a little money from her books, she had no independent income at all.

round. But they are aware of what they are about, and they seldom evince that sort of failure in masculinity which afflicts, for example, some of the heroes of Henry James... in short, nothing in Miss Austen's manner of ignoring what she ignores falsifies what she exhibits.

This is to re-emphasise Jane Austen's intent in her characterisations – some of her male characters are more successful than others of course, but for the most part her limitations are self-imposed. If a character is a caricature, if it displays only one or two facets, this is by design. If Mr Collins, for example, were depicted not only in his complacency, obsequiousness and folly, but as possessing, say, a scholarly interest in New Testament history, or a passion for birds or botany, he would not only be less effective as a figure in high comedy, but as an agent in the portrayal of Elizabeth's development; the dismay and distress of his proposal, the incomprehension of Charlotte Lucas's acceptance of him would be so much less emphatic.

There is however, a paradoxical and puzzling element in Jane Austen's handling of her male characters. If one reviews the anti-heroes, or villains and near-villains in the novels, one finds that they are all endowed with an exceptional amount of charm of manner and beauty of person, as well as rather more than their fair share of intelligence. There is Willoughby in *Sense and Sensibility,* whose 'person which was uncommonly handsome, received additional charms from his voice and expression', and who was 'a young man of good abilities, quick imagination, lively spirits and open, affectionate manners'; Frank Churchill in *Emma*, (not quite a villain, except in the estimation of Mr Knightley and Mr Woodhouse) was a *very* good-looking young man, height, air, address, all were unexceptionable, and his countenance had a great deal of the spirit and

liveliness of his father's; he looked quick and sensible...
there was a well-bred ease of manner, and a readiness to
talk. In *Pride and Prejudice,* Elizabeth Bennet felt that she did
not judge the new officer in the militia, George Wickham:

> with the smallest degree of unreasonable ad-
> miration. The officers... were, in general, a
> very creditable, gentlemanlike set; but Mr
> Wickham was as far beyond them all in per-
> son, countenance, air and walk, as *they* were
> superior to the broad-faced, stuffy Uncle
> Philips, breathing port wine.

In the unfinished *Watsons*, Tom Musgrave is cast in the role
of the anti-hero, and he is one of the most entertaining and
fully realised characters in the fragment. His reputation is
established before his appearance on the scene; he was
'certainly a genteel, good-looking young man', but
Elizabeth Watson warns her sister of his character on the
first page of the work – 'A young man of very good fortune,
quite independent and remarkably agreeable, an universal
favourite wherever he goes,' but 'a great flirt, and never
means anything serious.' He was not intended to have the
weight of the others, a lightweight coxcomb, a toady in the
Osborne circle, without the social perceptions that come of
intelligence and good breeding.

    Northanger Abbey is unusual in dividing the function and
characteristics of the 'anti-hero' between two people, John
Thorpe and the brother of the hero, Captain Tilney.
(General Tilney is a sort of elderly ogre in the tradition of
the Gothic novel which is the object of Jane Austen's satire
in the book, a character unique in the Jane Austen oeuvre.)
John Thorpe is entirely without the beauty, manner, charm
or good sense we expect from the anti-hero, being a:

> stout young man of middling height, who,
> with a plain face and ungraceful form, seemed
> fearful of being too handsome unless he wore
> the dress of a groom, and too much like a
> gentleman unless he were easy when he ought
> to be civil, and impudent where he might be
> allowed to be easy.

He never distracts the heroine's feelings from her true object, but he precipitates the critical course of the action by his impertinent interference, and causes her repeated distress by his offensive behaviour. Captain Tilney, without having an important function in the mainstream of the plot (he resolves the dilemma of James Morland's engagement to a worthless girl in the sub-plot, by enticing her away with his superior glamour) has all the required attributes, 'a very fashionable-looking, handsome young man,' a confirmed flirt and with, apparently, very few principles of behaviour.

When we come to Mr Elliot in *Persuasion*, we find a man of much greater maturity, a widower, older than his earlier prototypes; his attractions are solider than theirs, and the more dangerous. Added to a fine appearance, Anne perceived that:

> everything united in him; good understanding,
> correct opinions, knowledge of the world, and
> a warm heart. He had strong feelings of fam-
> ily-attachment and family honour, without
> pride or weakness; he lived with the liberality
> of a man of fortune, without display; he
> judged for himself in everything essential,
> without defying public opinion in any point of
> worldly decorum. He was steady, observant,
> moderate, candid; never run away with by

> spirit or by selfishness, which fancied itself
> strong feeling; and yet, with a sensibility to
> what was amiable and lovely, and a value for
> all the felicities of domestic life, which charac-
> ters of fancied enthusiasm and violent
> agitation seldom really possess.[8]

Truly, Anne was in great danger at this point of succumbing to a man whom later her friend Mrs Smith described in
the most extreme terms as the most villainous of any in
Jane Austen's rogues' gallery!

> Mr Elliot is a man without heart or con-
> science; a designing, wary, cold-blooded
> being, who thinks only of himself; who, for
> his own interest or ease, would be guilty of
> any cruelty, or any treachery, that could be
> perpetrated without risk of his general charac-
> ter. He has no feelings for others. Those
> whom he has been the chief cause of leading
> into ruin, he can neglect and desert without
> the smallest compunction. He is totally be-
> yond the reach of any sentiment of justice or
> compassion. Oh! he is black at heart, hollow
> and black!

The character of Henry Crawford in *Mansfield Park* is not
encapsulated for us in a neat introductory descriptive
passage, but emerges in the course of the action, in his own
conversation and in the reactions of the other characters to
him. We are told that, while not regularly handsome, he has

[8]Every word of this encomium would apply to Colonel Brandon in *Sense and Sensibility*; to deserve all this and to possess an unquestioned integrity into the bargain, is something! Perhaps Marianne did better for herself than is generally supposed!

'air and countenance', and lively and pleasant manners; in a short dialogue between Mrs Grant (the Crawfords' half-sister) and the brother and sister, the broad lines of Henry's character are exposed – witty, frivolous and selfish, and with more charm than is good for him – with a hint from Mary of the evil influence of his uncle – 'I assure you, he is quite detestable – the Admiral's lessons have quite spoiled him.' Later, his attractions are summed up through the eyes of the Bertram sisters:

> Her brother was not handsome; no, when they first saw him, he was absolutely plain, black and plain; but still, he was the gentleman, with a pleasing address. The second meeting proved him not so very plain; he was plain, to be sure, but then he had so much countenance, and his teeth were so good, and he was so well made, that one soon forgot he was plain; and after a third interview, after dining in company with him at the parsonage, he was no longer allowed to be called so by anybody. He was, in fact, the most agreeable young man the sisters had ever known, and they were equally delighted with him.

All these young men, with the exception of John Thorpe, have a superabundance of charm, vitality, humour and poise, and most of them have intelligence and taste as well. But Jane Austen condemns them all, denying them that quality she valued above all others – integrity. Whether they are driven by worldly considerations or by self-indulgence, or both, and whether their crimes lie in the past or the present, they all have a central weakness in their moral fibre; the range of error varies from cruelties and failures of taste, to the blacker villainies of seduction and desertion in

Elliot, Crawford and Willoughby. In the light of revelation, their tone, sounded alongside the true and the good and the genuine, is off-key.

In comparison, the successful heroes are, on the whole, lacking in glamour. Henry Tilney in *Northanger Abbey*, is the most delightful; his ironic humour, his shrewd observations full of tenderness towards Catherine and satiric perception towards others, reflect the author's own point of view. Captain Wentworth is the nonpareil, brave, noble, courteous and intelligent, and Mr Knightley is an admirable character, with lively sympathies based on sensitive observation and mature judgements; but he is rather an avuncular figure, with a protective and corrective role towards Emma – he has energy, but not the vitality of youth which Emma herself shares with the anti-heroes. But Colonel Brandon, Edward Ferrars, Edmund Bertram, however great their merits, are dull, conventional characters, without joy or sparkle. Charles Bingley is intended to be a loveable man, but he is without much depth or great interest, and Darcy, for all his great potential, is only three-quarters alive.

Overtly, these young men, the anti-heroes, represent Jane Austen's satire on the conventional hero-figure of the romantic novels she was deriding in *Northanger Abbey*, and which were in the background of her thoughts throughout. Willoughby is, of course, the essence of this figure, from his first introduction, galloping up on his horse like a knight of old, to rescue the damsel in distress, with his glowing beauty and his lively sensibility, which links him too with the *Man of Feeling* type of character made popular by Sterne and Mackenzie. But they all fit in to the pattern to a greater or a lesser extent, particularly, for example, in the way they are introduced; Mr Elliot, the mysterious stranger who fixes his gaze so approvingly on the heroine (causing the straying hero to examine her with new eyes), Frank

Churchill, the long-expected, much-vaunted handsome son, and George Wickham, with his hidden relationship with the proud nobleman, and his story of past injuries.

Why did Jane Austen wilfully reject so often and so firmly these characteristics she admired and enjoyed, and which she herself possessed? Vitality and wit and lively charm combined with articulate intelligence and accompanied by a degree of physical beauty and grace, these things she responded to in her own life, and were what she found in most of the people she most admired – her sister and her brothers, especially Henry, Dr Haden, Tom Lefroy, who was her earliest sweetheart, and no doubt many of whom we never hear, and all these characteristics are conspicuously her own. What made her distrust them? There are no hints of any failure of integrity in her brothers; the two Admirals, Francis and Charles, seem to have been shining lights in that respect as in all other virtues among their naval colleagues; Henry was the most volatile and unsettled of the brothers, and his bank failed in 1816, but we do not hear there was any dishonour attached to Henry as a result of the bankruptcy. It is the same impulse which led to the pervading tone in *Mansfield Park*, so different from all the other novels, in its denial of life and energy and change, its horror of sophistication and the evil influence of the world outside, in favour of quiescence, moral conformity, and prudence. There is an element of perversity or self-criticism in it; Jane Austen had very little of Fanny Price about her; like Beatrice, or Mary Crawford, or Elizabeth Bennet, she was born under a dancing star. There seem to be no hints in the letters for the amateur psychiatrist, and it must remain a matter for critical speculation, an element in her work too original and too consistent to be a literary convention, and too complex for explanation in any simple personal terms.

With her conscious confinement to her limited canvas, her 'Little bit (two inches wide) of ivory', her repetition of similar themes and use of the same sort of social groups, Jane Austen used the same categories of types repeatedly, the idle young bachelors, the country parsons, the autocratic elderly widows who held the purse strings and bullied their dependants, the country squires, the anxious mothers with a houseful of daughters and a shortage of money, and so on. Each of these characters, however, is an individual, not a stereotype. Jane Austen was so economical with her material that she constantly made use of ideas from earlier, even juvenile works, both for plot and characters, but she did not repeat herself. Take, for example, some of her young clergymen; Mr Elton, Henry Tilney, Edward Ferrars, Edmund Bertram, and the egregious Mr Collins. They are all clergymen, all young, all from the same social class of country gentry; they are all reasonably conscientious and principled people, who will fulfil their duties in the church and parish well and wisely according to their lights, and the customs of the time (though Mr Collins, of course, will never act wisely) and they are all anxious to be married. Their spiritual eligibility for their role is never a matter for question, though one can make one's own assumptions. In every other respect they differ totally from each other, and are furthermore fully rounded, fully realised individuals. Mr Collins is the most nearly a caricature, a richly comic creation, sublimely self-satisfied, never aware of his own shortcomings; but, doing what he is told by his patroness Lady Catherine and subtly guided by his clever wife, he will avoid the worst effects of his folly and stupidity. Henry Tilney, full of charm and humour, seems in the course of the novel to take his parochial duties fairly lightly, a standard practice amongst young bachelor parsons at that time; marriage would doubtless fix him more steadily in his parish, and his good sense, good humour and sympathetic character would make him a good parish priest. As clergymen, Edward Ferrars and Edmund Bertram would be rather similar, conscientious, sensible and not very exciting; but as personalities, they differ; Edward Ferrars' low spirits and awkwardness had specific and embarrassing reasons, and once they were removed, he became relatively lively and humorous, though of a domestic and unambitious nature. Edmund is of a profounder nature, more intellectual and reflective, and, of all the characters, he will give most serious thought to his duties, practical, moral and spiritual. He is without humour, but with great tenderness of heart and a quality of romantic sympathy with nature, or rather a seeking of sympathy from nature, that breaks new ground in the Austen heroes. Mr Elton, like Mr Collins, is in a comic vein, not a clown, but a self-important prig, worldly and insensitive, who acquires the wife he deserves; for Emma's subsequent felicity, one hopes he may be translated to other spheres, maybe a parish in the neighbourhood of Bristol, not too far from Maple Grove!

All the fathers of families in the novels – with the exception of Mr Morland, who seems to be an admirable specimen of his kind – leave much to be desired; this might seen surprising, in view of the undoubted love and reverence felt by his family for the Rev. George Austen, a man of singular gifts, charm and simple goodness. But it would be a mistake to assume that Jane Austen needed models close at hand for her creations, an idea she herself denied. Her fathers are all gentlemen from the middle rank of society, though Sir Walter Elliot and Sir Thomas Bertram, as baronets, are rather above it. Captain Price, Fanny's father in *Mansfield Park*, is a little out of line, as a naval officer (the only naval officer described by Jane Austen who is less than admirable, if one excepts the Crawford uncle off-stage); the deplorable state of his household is due more to mismanagement than downright poverty, and the lack of gentility in his behaviour is due to his rough character and irascible temper rather than a really low origin; he is completely circumscribed in his interests and uncouth in his domestic habits, but he does know how to behave in the company of gentlemen, and shows up respectably in the company of Henry Crawford, despite Fanny's horrified anxiety – her situation is reminiscent of Elizabeth Bennet's in *Pride and Prejudice* when Mr Darcy is exposed to the blast of her mother's vulgarity. 'I believe,' commented Jane Austen, 'there is scarcely a young lady in the united kingdoms who would not rather put up with the misfortune of being sought by a clever, agreeable man, than have him driven away by the vulgarity of her nearest relations.'

The characteristic these elderly gentlemen share in common is their inadequacy as fathers; neglectful and inattentive like Mr Bennet, partial, worldly and vain like Sir Walter Elliot, tyrannical and materialistic like General Tilney, ineffectually foolish like Mr Woodhouse, or tragically ill-judging like Sir Thomas Bertram. The most well-intentioned and conscientious, he suffers the most grievously – Sir Thomas, who gave his daughters all the education and accomplishments that money could buy, but not the personal affectionate guidance which would have counteracted the lazy indulgence of their mother and the partial adulation of their aunt, and given them principles and self-control. Maria deserted her oafish husband, whom he should never have allowed her to marry, and was, in consequence, lost forever to her family, and Julia made a foolish and ill-considered marriage. Mr Bennet did better than he deserved, and acquired a trio of sons-in-law to amuse, stimulate or impress him; to laugh at, to shoot with or to talk to. His cynicism and indifference had become too deep-rooted to cause his conscience more than a momentary pang at the contemplation of the near-disaster his neglect of his paternal duties had caused his daughters. After his first fruitless efforts to find the eloped Lydia – for it was Mr Gardiner and Mr Darcy who in fact found the runaways and solved all the problems – he relapsed into his ironic inertia, the episode producing little more than some cruel teasing of his youngest daughter Kitty, and a great deal of wry amusement at the antics of his shameless daughter Lydia and her self-assured husband. He continued to be content to leave the other girls to find husbands unsupervised by him, clamorously helped or hindered by their mother. Mr Bennet is one of Jane Austen's unique creations, of complete consistency and depth. He has charm, intelligence and culture, but is selfish and lazy; seduced in youth by the physical attractions of a pretty face and animal spirits, and without the integrity and toughness to create a positive life from the ruins of his hopes of domestic happiness, as in similar circumstances Sir Thomas Bertram had done. He has withdrawn from active participation in the human comedy, and become an ironic observer, amused and amusing, but at bottom unhappy, irresponsible and callous. The young Mr Palmer in *Sense and Sensibility* is just such another character in embryo, saddled with a silly wife, but in him, misanthropy takes the place of humour.

The nature of the fathers in each novel is portrayed to highlight some essential element in the personality or the position of the daughter–heroine. Anne Elliot's position in her family is one of isolation, neglect and humiliation:

> Anne with an elegance of mind and sweetness of character, which must have placed her high with any people of real understanding, was nobody with either father or sister; her word had no weight; her convenience was always to give way; she was only Anne.

She is the least self-regarding, the most modest of all the heroines, far more so than Fanny Price, and only rivalled perhaps by Catherine Morland, whose modesty is as much a quality of her extreme youth, ignorance and immaturity as it is innate.

Sir Walter Elliot is vain and shallow, interested in nothing but personal appearance and rank; one of the only times he contemplates Anne with favour – or indeed looks at her at all – is to comment approvingly on her improvement in looks; he thought her 'less thin in her person, in her cheeks; her skin, her complexion, greatly improved. Had she been using anything in particular?' Her very virtues make her inconsiderable in his eyes – her lack of pretentiousness, her preference for the background rather than the limelight, her honest refusal to flatter his insatiable personal vanity, her interest in people whose social position or physical appearance her father deplores, like Admiral Croft or Mrs Smith.

'Who,' he exclaims petulantly,

> 'who is Miss Anne Elliot to be visiting in Westgate Buildings? – a Mrs Smith, a widow Mrs Smith – and who was her husband? One of the five thousand Mr Smiths whose names are to be met with everywhere. And what is her attraction? That she is old and sickly. Upon my word, Miss Anne Elliot, you have the most extraordinary taste! Everything that revolts other people, low company, paltry rooms, foul air, disgusting associations, are inviting to you.'

Similarly the valetudinarian Mr Woodhouse enhances the vigour and physical ebullience that emanates from his daughter. He represents a negation of life, while she plunges in, irresistibly involved. She of course, creates chaos and confusion with her errors of judgement and her misguided behaviour; if Mr Woodhouse had his way, nothing would happen at all, neither dinner parties, nor balls nor expeditions, nor, most of all, weddings, and all would be well, left in a state of suspended animation!

There are a number of other father figures or avuncular middle-aged men in the novels, mostly a more admirable collection than the fathers themselves, all sketched in with a firm hand and a lively eye. Admiral Croft, as a distinguished member of Jane Austen's favourite profession, is one of her most delightful men, a bluff, open-hearted sailor, not very subtle, but not imperceptive of the important things that go on around him; he may never be able to sort out the names of the two pretty Musgrave girls, but he sees quickly enough that Sir Walter Elliot will 'never set the Thames on fire, but there seems no harm in him.' He and his wife are a well-matched team, an example of connubial happiness and affection not very common in the novels. They are both good-humoured and sensible, tough, self-reliant and open-hearted, but not gullible; the Admiral, it is true, is not subtle enough to perceive half the small-mindedness and duplicity under his very nose, but Mrs Croft is more shrewd and discriminating – she quietly reserves her judgement as to the absolute suitability of either of the Musgrove girls for her brother Frederick, and knows full well how to value Anne. Anne's appreciation of the couple again emphasises the gulf between her and her father and sister Elizabeth, with their talk of the propriety of present-ing the Crofts to their noble relations. Elizabeth's conclusion is that it will not do:

> 'Oh! no, I think not. Situated as we are with
> Lady Dalrymple, cousins, we ought to be very
> careful not to embarrass her with acquaintance

> she might not approve. …We had better leave the Crofts to find their own level. There are several odd-looking men walking about here, who, I am told, are sailors. The Crofts will associate with them.'

Passages like this, and, for example, Sir Walter's strictures on the coarse appearance of naval men, must have been fine family jokes within the family, with the two naval officer brothers. It must have been a matter of regret that, with *Persuasion* posthumously published, Jane was no longer with them to share the fun. The Crofts certainly come more from Jane Austen's 'life experience' than her 'reading experiences' if one can make any such assertions about her characters, given her power of transmuting her materials, from whatever source, into her own creations.

Mr Weston, the genial bridegroom of Emma's ex-governess, 'poor Miss Taylor', Sir William Lucas and Sir Thomas Middleton are a trio of middle-aged gentlemen with much in common, three rather simple-minded men of strongly sociable disposition, good standing, and country tastes. Sir Thomas Middleton is the least complex; his interests are hunting and shooting, and when the season is over, his recourse against total vacuity is to fill his house as often as possible with as many friends and acquaintances as he can persuade to accept his invitations. He is unfailingly kind and hospitable, but entirely without discrimination – company is his object, and if conversation or common interests fail, this can be covered up by an improvised ball, a game of cards or a noisy round game. Mr Weston is indiscriminatingly sociable too, as Emma is disconcerted to find – *her* especially early attendance at the ball at the 'Crown' is most particularly requested, but so is that of half the other guests. Emma 'liked his open manners, but a little less of open-heartedness would have made him a higher character.' She felt that 'to be the favourite and intimate of a man who had so many intimates and confidantes was not the very first distinction in the scale of vanity.' Emma's motives for criticising 'the unmanageable goodwill of Mr Weston's temper' are not as entirely above reproach as is Mr Weston's universal benevolence. She is accustomed to take the lead in Highbury society, and when she discovers that Mr Weston has enlarged their expedition to include the Eltons and their party, she is outraged at 'an arrangement which would probably expose her even to the degradation of being said to be of Mrs Elton's party!'

> 'I am glad you approve of what I have done,' said he very comfortably, 'but I thought you would. Such schemes as these are nothing without numbers. One cannot have too large a party—'
> Emma denied none of it aloud, and agreed to none of it in private.

Mr Weston has 'a warm heart and a sweet temper'; possessors of these traits Jane Austen always treats with the gentlest of irony, the tenderest of humour, such people as Jane Bennet, Catherine Morland, William Price, even Harriet Smith, that pretty little ninny who is more sinned against than sinning. Mr Weston's lack of perception, like Miss Bates's, is part of a universal benevolence and is almost a reproach to the more irritable sensibilities of Emma. In the past, Mr Weston has been a soldier and a successful business man, and his robust activity, unlike Sir Thomas Middleton's, is and has been directed to more useful purposes than a rather frantic pursuit of pleasure and company. He has had objectives, and pursued them with vigour – 'he had made his fortune, bought his house, and obtained his wife.'

Sir William Lucas is a self-made man, a foolish man quite incapable of living up to his social pretensions, but he is treated without malice because he himself has none; underneath his rather childish pretensions, he is a kind-hearted simple man. Mr Darcy – in his early unchastened phase – may be disgusted by Sir William's ludicrous references to the court of St James, but his creator is not.

Mrs Bennet's brother, Mr Gardiner, is the only fully developed character in the novels who is in trade, and it is interesting that he is one of the most truly admirable of them all, with a charming and intelligent wife who is worthy of him. The only puzzle is how he came to have two such sisters as Mrs Bennet and Mrs Philips, but as Jane Austen said in one of her letters, it must be 'a proof of how unequally the gifts of Fortune are bestowed.' Mr Gardiner is described as a 'sensible, gentlemanlike man, greatly superior to his sister as well by nature as by education. The Netherfield ladies would have had difficulty in believing that a man who lived by trade, and within view of his own warehouses, could have been so well-bred and agreeable.' When Elizabeth and her aunt and uncle Gardiner meet with Darcy at Pemberley, Darcy's home, Mr Gardiner is seen as a dignified, self-respecting man, to whom the great land-owner is immediately drawn; in the ensuing crisis, brought on by Lydia's elopement, he is the man of action; in comparison with the descriptions of the reactions of some other male characters to shocking news – changes of complexion, staggering against a wall, and other manifesta-tions of romantic emotion – he behaves in an entirely practical manner, counsels moderate hope, and sets off in purposeful pursuit as soon as he has restored Elizabeth to her distressed family.

It is he and Mr Darcy between them who succeed in settling the sorry business. And it is clear that after the marriage of Darcy and Elizabeth, he and his wife will be among their most frequent and welcome guests. He is a new phenomenon, a cultured, gentlemanly tradesman who is not aspiring to break into the class of the landed gentry, an urban rather than a rural phenomenon, and one for whom Jane Austen had particular sympathy and liking.

It is a very lopsided business to contemplate or write about the men in Jane Austen's life and writing without reference to the distaff side; nor has it been entirely possible. The immensely subtle and constantly shifting relationships between the characters, conveyed by the seemingly casual, often trivial incidents and dialogue, with the overtones of authorial attitude indicated by the ironic tone, these are the main elements of Jane Austen's unique distinction. Her company of players is as varied and as acutely observed as her own social world; she chose to concentrate on young women in their domestic and matrimonial struggles, and the men, to that extent, are subordinate in their roles; they are relatively commonplace, such, as Macaulay says, 'as we meet every day. Yet,' he goes on, 'they are all as perfectly discriminated from each other as if they were the most eccentric of human beings.' Her method of differentiating these so diverse yet so circum-scribed characters is the essence of her genius – 'the touches so delicate, that they elude analysis, that they defy the powers of description, and that we know them to exist only by the general effect to which they have contributed.' We think of Fanny Price 'sighing alone at the window', giving way to her feelings of jealousy and self-pity, of Edmund Bertram looking grave at Mary Crawford's sallies, and being 'left to sit down and stir the fire in thoughtful vexation', of Mr Knightley, whose gravity is so much more Olympian than Edmund's, drawing in his horse beneath Miss Bates's window in Highbury, and revealing, in a brief dialogue, almost all we need to know about him – his vigour, his command, his courtesy and kindness, his humour, and – for even an Olympian has his weakness – his jealousy. We recall Mr Weston's cheerful self-approbation, with his, 'I thought you would approve...', and Admiral Croft, lost in contemplation of an ill-drawn boat in a print shop in Milson Street, and quick to acknowledge Anne with his 'usual frankness and good-humour'; of Mr Elton, as 'he sighed and smiled himself off'.

With these small and seemingly slight strokes Jane Austen builds up her portraits, no touch irrelevant and no phrase misplaced. With a marvellous economy of means and material she gets her characters to work for her, revealing themselves and each other in every incident and every word they utter, each episode relating to what has happened in the past, and providing clues for and illuminating what is to be revealed in the future. It is this that makes her, more than any other writer who was not a poet, worth reading over and over again.

The Miracle of *Emma*

Never can a writer have so precisely followed her own instructions as did Jane Austen in her novel *Emma*.

> Three or four Families in a Country Village is the very thing to work on ...exactly ...such a spot ...is the delight of my life; ...make full use of them while they are so favourably arranged...

she wrote to her niece Anna. The Aristotelian unity of place is pretty well adhered to in the novel, as no action occurs at a greater distance from the town of Highbury than Box Hill, seven miles away. One hundred and fifty pages elapse before the almost somnolent tranquillity of Highbury, Hatfield, and their neighbourhood is broken by the intrusion of any newcomers from the outside world; for the arrival of Isabella and John Knightley from London for their regular Christmas visit can hardly be included in that category. Old Mr Woodhouse would regard their arrival as a return to sanctuary.

It is a triumph of Jane Austen's unobtrusive art that she yet makes that first volume of *Emma* as entrancingly interesting as the two following, more action-packed volumes. After the initial exposition of setting the scene, describing the actors and establishing their relationships, the events that are described are no more than the exchange of visits between old friends, two dinner parties, some walks and a great many long and revealing conversations.

The major event that has just taken place before the novel begins is the marriage of Emma's ex-governess and beloved friend to their neighbour Mr Weston, an event which furnishes material for much discussion, and the opportunity for the author to expose some of the characteristics of her actors; Mr Woodhouse's fussy and irrational anxiety and depression at an event which represents change, which in any form is anathema to him; Emma's cheerful capacity to see the best in everything, as well as her incorrigible tendency to see herself as the prime mover and influence in every local activity; and George Knightley (*always* known as Mr Knightley, as the older son) with his rational outlook and his affectionate awareness of Emma's capacity for seeing things, not as they really are but as her fancy dictates.

The development of Emma's acquaintance with Harriet Smith occupies the following chapters. Harriet is a 'parlour-boarder' at Mrs Goddard's school in Highbury, the 'natural daughter of somebody'. Seventeen years old, very pretty and naïve, and suggestible to the point of feeble-mindedness, she is an ideal tabula rasa on which Emma can exercise her passion for guiding and manipulating other people; an enterprise of whose dangers her mentor Mr Knightley very soon becomes aware. Emma is under the impression that one of her main benefits to Harriet is educational; but in truth she teaches her nothing in particular except to stop her giggling and to have a better idea of polite society and of her own claim to a part in it.

Emma is never so much out of favour both with us and with George Knightley as in her behaviour over the farmer Robert Martin, of whom she declares that he is a member of an 'order of people with whom I can have nothing to do.' Inexorably she quenches Harriet's interest in him and while protesting that she herself must not interfere and that Harriet must make her own mind up, she almost literally dictates Harriet's letter of refusal to his proposal of marriage. Mr Knightley has the highest regard for Robert Martin, whose farm adjoins his own property, and he is horrified to hear of Emma's interference: 'You have been no friend to Harriet Smith, Emma,' he exclaims, and emphatically denies Emma's assertions that her protégé should aim higher than a yeoman–farmer – 'he is as much her superior in sense as in situation …she is pretty, and she is good-tempered, and that is all…'

The role of Harriet as a *protégé* is the give-away, for Emma is extremely class-conscious, what we would regard as snobbish. 'What! think a *farmer* …a good match for *my* intimate friend! …marrying a man whom I could never admit as an acquaintance of my own!…'

Whether contemporary readers perceived Emma as a snob, whether Jane Austen herself meant us to see her as at fault in this respect, we are certainly repelled at this moment by such a blatant example of social exclusiveness and blind prejudice. Mr Knightley, less blinded by social niceties – after all, he and Robert Martin are both of them farmers – is angered by the lack of judgement which can rate Harriet's featherweight attributes higher than Martin's solid merit.

What is at the core of Emma's impulsive and irresponsible activities is boredom, unrecognised by herself, but only too apparent. She has health, wealth, leisure, an intelligence and energy unmatched by any of her circle, and nothing whatsoever to do. The image of Emma spending her days calling on the Bates's or walking with Mrs Weston, and her evenings playing backgammon with her almost imbecilic father is almost too dreadful to contemplate! We are told that her attempts to improve her own education and skills are abortive, and that she is ashamed at her neglect of her parish duties – that sort of application and the carrying out of routine duties is not for her. She is a creature of impulse and imagination. Without the company of Mr Knightley, her life would be arid indeed, and even he does not provide her with the particular stimulus her nature needs at this stage in her development. He is quite self-sufficient, one might say that she can do as little for him as she feels she can for Robert Martin! That is, of course, until they both – she and Mr Knightley – wake up to the fact that they need each other.

It is not surprising that Emma's pent-up energy should be happily expended upon shaping and 'educating' this malleable innocent, and her imagination exercised in creating a lofty and romantic future for her. The egregious Mr Elton now appears on the scene to fulfil this romantic role, yet another character regarding whom Emma's judgement goes badly astray. Mr Elton is the new young vicar of Highbury, anxious to please and full of animation and agreeable manners, ripe for matrimony. He is summed up by the rather reserved John Knightley admirably:

> 'I never in my life saw a man more intent on
> being agreeable than Mr Elton. It is downright
> labour to him where ladies are concerned.
> With men he can be rational and unaffected,
> but when he has ladies to please every feature
> works.'

Having selected Mr Elton for this part in her romance, Emma wilfully and enthusiastically ignores every clue to his real intentions; determined that he is in love with Harriet, she interprets his every action in that light, and what is more deplorable, she convinces Harriet herself that that is the case. The revelation of the real state of his feelings, when, under the influence of Mr Weston's good wine, he

declares his love for *her* in the privacy of her carriage is one
of the supreme scenes in all comic literature. It is the first
of a series of revelations to Emma that her judgement has
been at fault, causing humiliation to herself and distress to
her victim/protégée.

Thus, keeping a gallery of lively and interesting characters in the wings to appear in Volume II, Jane Austen
achieves her first miracle in this remarkable novel by
holding the reader's interest with the minimum of resources. With the introduction in Volume II of Frank
Churchill and Jane Fairfax and the appearance of Miss
Bates and her mother, the canvas is widened; the opportunities for high comedy are increased, and the advent of
the two newcomers gives occasion for Emma to plunge
ever deeper into romantic speculation.

The character of Emma must rank as one of the chief
miracles achieved by Jane Austen in this novel. 'A heroine,'
she declared, 'whom no one but myself will much like.'
Emma has so many characteristics which we cannot admire,
and behaves so often in a way which we find unacceptable,
it is almost miraculous that we do not, in fact, lose all
patience with her, but continue to be involved in her future
happiness. She reveals herself as arrogant, self-willed, ill-
judging and dangerously manipulative; as Mr Knightley
points out, when scolding her for 'abusing the reason you
have,' – 'Better be without sense than misapply it as you
do.' Yet every time she horrifies us with some outrageous
assumption or some piece of bad behaviour, she redeems
herself by the revelation of opposing qualities. There is a
fundamental honesty and candour ('candour' in the
Johnsonian sense of freedom from malice and total honesty, rather than the modern meaning of truthfulness
without regard for the consequences) and even modesty in
her which makes us forgive her her fall from grace. Her
good nature is invariable, and her kindness and patience is

exemplified by her treatment of her father, whose welfare and peace of mind are always a priority with her. Although she is accustomed to be the Queen of the Highbury world, and accepts that role as of right (the challenge from vulgar Mrs Elton is one of the joys of the book) there are occasions when she is prepared almost to allow herself to be humiliated if she feels the situation justifies it; she cannot understand entirely the reasons for Jane Fairfax's adamant refusal to accept her kindly overtures after the Box Hill incident, but she accepts the repeated rebuffs without any sense of wounded pride because she pities Jane's plight, and in addition, is in a state of penitence for her own bad behaviour during the excursion.

Emma suffers severely from the revelations of the ill-effects of her errors of judgement, and is full of good resolutions, which, alas, are sometimes as short-lived as her programmes for self-improvement in music, art or literature. But her pain at least is more for the victims of her delusions than for her own *amour propre*.

> It was a wretched business, indeed! Such an overthrow of everything she had been wishing for! – Such a development of everything most unwelcome! – such a blow for Harriet! – that was the worst of all! Every part of it brought pain and humiliation, of some sort or other; but, compared to the evil to Harriet, all was light; and she would gladly have submitted to feel yet more mistaken – more in error – more disgraced by mis-judgement, than she actually was, could the effects of her blunders have been confined to herself.

The Box Hill affair has another dimension however, for on that occasion Emma was really acting out of character, and the prime mover was not herself. The party, owing to Mr Weston's incorrigible *bonhomie*, was larger than she had hoped for, and its members less congenial – she was in danger of 'the degradation of being said to be of Mrs Elton's party'! Frank Churchill was in a wayward and unaccountable mood (having quarrelled with Jane Fairfax the previous day) and amused himself by flirting publicly with Emma. The brittle attempts to get the party going were not successful; the Eltons bridled and were affronted by activities not of their choosing; Jane was driven away by an exchange with Frank of whose significance only they themselves were aware; Emma, overexcited and unhappier than she knew, was driven to insult Miss Bates in a manner that even that euphoric lady could not misunderstand, and the party finally dispersed with Frank in a state of affected high spirits, which the company found 'almost unpleasant. Such another scheme, composed of so many ill-assorted people, she hoped never to be betrayed into again.'

Mr Knightley's reproof, well-merited as she knows it to be, completes the wretchedness of the day. The true cause of the failure of the excursion and the creator of the unpleasant atmosphere and underlying tension is of course Frank Churchill, who here behaves as caddishly as any of the author's heroes are ever permitted to do. His frenetic public display is entirely directed at Jane Fairfax, without regard for Emma's feelings, or Jane's, or anyone else's. Jane is miserable, Mr Knightley jealous and disapproving, Emma is driven to bad behaviour, poor Miss Bates wounded, and everyone is uncomfortable. Emma's feelings of shame are profound, but we can feel a certain sympathy for her on this occasion, she is so outrageously manipulated by Frank.

When eventually the situation between Frank Churchill and Jane Fairfax is revealed, Emma's reaction is quite uncompromising:

'What right had he to come among us with affection and faith engaged, and with manners so *very* disengaged? ...How could he tell what mischief he might be doing? How indeed! How near she had been to falling in love with him herself and to revealing that she believed him to be in love with her. And as for Jane Fairfax how could *she* bear such behaviour? ...to look on, while repeated attentions were offered to another woman, before her face, and not resent it. There is a degree of placidity, which I can neither comprehend nor respect.'

Emma was wrong with respect to Jane, as she soon became aware; there was no placidity there, only guilt, resentment and anger, and also jealousy, which accounted for a great deal of the reserve and unresponsiveness which had irked and puzzled Emma. Emma's conclusion on Frank is an echo of Mr Knightley's views:

'Much, much beyond impropriety! ...So unlike what a man should be! None of that upright integrity, that strict adherence to truth and principle, that disdain of trick and littleness, which a man should display in every transaction of his life.'

The effect of this episode is of almost exaggerated importance in the social life of Highbury. It makes it clear that in such a very small community there is no room for secrecy, deceptions and masquerading. The repercussions of such deceptions are too destructive, and may affect the innocent bystanders as well as those more closely involved. To

Emma, whose nature is open and frank, the duplicity appears abominable:

> 'what has it been but a system of hypocrisy and deceit – espionage and treachery? – To come among us with professions of openness and simplicity; and such a league in secret to judge us all! Here have we been, the whole winter and spring, completely duped, fancying ourselves all on an equal footing of truth and honour, with two people in the midst of us who may have been carrying round, comparing and sitting in judgement on sentiments and words that were never meant for both to hear'

(Perhaps a little bit of double-think here on Emma's part, as she herself had certainly been guilty of harbouring unfounded and fantastic suspicions about poor Jane Fairfax, and must have had no very comfortable feelings about what Frank may have reported.)

Emma's heart is unaffected by the disclosure of Frank Churchill's secret, but her conscience is again tormented by her part in what she sees as yet another disappointment for poor Harriet; here of course, she is delightfully hoist with her own petard, when Harriet discloses that it is Mr Knightley she has set her sights on, and not Frank Churchill! But meanwhile, she is 'extremely angry with herself.' She adds, 'If she could not have been angry with Frank Churchill too, it would have been dreadful,' – a touch which cannot but endear us to this flawed heroine. She echoes Mr Knightley's strictures – 'Emma, you have been no friend to Harriet Smith.' She was afraid she had done her nothing but disservice, …common-sense would have directed her to tell Harriet that she must not allow herself to think of him. 'But with common-sense... I am afraid I have had little to do.'

It is this honesty and self-knowledge, however easily clouded the latter characteristic can become, which makes Emma irresistible. There is an ebullience and robustness in her character (whence derived? – certainly not from her father!) which, together with her frankness and her true goodness of heart gives her the dimensions of a genuine heroine. It is improbable that even Mr Knightley's firm guidance will prevent future ill-judged escapades from time to time, but under his watchful eye no doubt nothing worse than embarrassment, self-reproach and repentance will be the result.

A third miraculous feature in the novel is that for special reasons it is a book which gives greater delight on second or any subsequent readings. Everything in the plot structure depends on secrecy and subterfuge, ambiguities and misunderstandings. So carefully is the series of events worked out that from even the first chapter there are clues which can be picked up to indicate the true state of affairs almost impossible at the first reading, but giving the greatest delight on subsequent readings.[1] Almost every move of Frank Churchill and Jane Fairfax can be accounted for, not as on the surface, but rising from and related to their secret liaison – the postponement of Frank's visit to his father until after the arrival in Highbury of Jane, the frequent calls on the Bates with Frank's attention to the repair of Mrs Bates's spectacles, the trip to London for a haircut, Jane's determination to walk out for exercise in the direction of the post office regardless of the rain, and so on. Dialogue also bears double meanings, which become apparent at later readings. The brief farewell meeting between Frank and

[1] Lady James (P.D. James), has recently made a study of *Emma* as a detective story; I claim in my defence that this essay was written many years earlier!

Emma after the projected ball has been cancelled is a particular triumph of *double entendre* and misapprehensions. These ambiguities are not confined exclusively to the secret lovers; George Knightley becomes affected as his relationship with Emma seems to be threatened, and he has jealousy to conceal; and certain plans he has for his favourite Robert Martin, misinterpreted, give rise to some disquiet in Emma's breast, and hope in Harriet's! – before they reach a happy conclusion.

All this gives *Emma* a tautness and compactness singular even in Jane Austen's novels. There are no sub-plots, because every strand is so intricately interwoven with every other. Fundamentally it is a novel more 'light and bright and sparkling' than *Pride and Prejudice*, more secure in its environment than *Mansfield Park*. *Pride and Prejudice* raises issues of class and of the hapless position of women in society, and the themes of *Mansfield Park* are just as significant, the question of a cloistered society and of serious moral issues. Apart from some interesting ambiguities in an apparently ordered social structure, the important issues in *Emma* are moral ones – the consequences of deception and self-deception and injudicious interference; but in this case nobody is cast forth into outer darkness, and, as in a true fairy tale, they all live happily ever after. Ignoring the substrata of issues raised and social structures questioned, the novel is truly well entitled; it is about Emma, a flawed and many-faceted heroine, and her comedy of errors; a consistent, well-balanced and totally satisfying novel.

A Portrait of Jane Austen

In the summer of 1788 the Rev. George Austen and his wife Cassandra took their two daughters, Jane and Cassandra, to Kent to visit their great-uncle Francis Austen, a prosperous solicitor of Sevenoaks. He was by then over ninety years old, and his second wife had died some years earlier. She (born Jane Chadwick, late Lennard) had been Jane's godmother, Francis himself was godfather to Cassandra. This perhaps reflected the close and affectionate nature of the relationship between Francis Austen and the girls' father George Austen; George had lost his own parents in his childhood, and his uncle Francis had paid for his education at Tonbridge School and then at Oxford; upon George's marriage he had bought the livings of Deane and Ashe in Hampshire, intending to offer him whichever first fell vacant. His benevolence persisted, in spite of an increasing number of grandchildren, for on his death at the age of ninety-three, George received a bequest of £500.

It is not improbable, in the writer's view indeed most likely, that it was in the course of this visit that the portrait of Jane Austen now known as the Rice portrait was painted. It was in the possession of the family of Francis Austen in Kent until it was presented to a family friend in about 1817. It was at that time known as the 'Zoffany Portrait' but there are no grounds for the attribution, and it is now not considered possible that he was the artist.

A more plausible candidate is an artist called Ozias Humphry, who was originally a miniaturist until his eyesight deteriorated and he turned to larger canvasses. With Francis Austen he enjoyed the patronage of the Duke of Dorset whose estates at Knole adjoined the town of Sevenoaks. He painted a number of miniatures for the Duke, and a portrait of Francis Austen, also a commission from the Duke. His brother was the Rector of two parishes in the neighbourhood, first of Kemsing and Seal and subsequently of Birling, both in the gift of the Sackville family. He married a Miss Elizabeth Woodgate, a member of a local family of some standing in Kent.

Interesting though this attribution may be, the question of the identity of the artist is irrelevant to the problem of the identity of the subject. The portrait depicts a young girl in her early teens in a high-waisted muslin dress, carrying a green parasol; the hair is mid-brown and cropped short; the features have a marked similarity, not only to those of other members of the Austen family whose likenesses exist, but to the few extant sketches which claim to be of Jane Austen.

Sometime about 1817, Colonel Thomas Austen, a grandson of Francis Austen (born, like his cousin Jane, in 1775) who had inherited his grandfather's property, presented the portrait to a lady called Elizabeth Hall (1789–1831), who was about to marry or had just married Thomas Harding Newman (1779–1856) as his second wife. The Newman family were acquaintances of the Austens – indeed a family tradition reported that Thomas had proposed to and been rejected by Jane in his youth. The Halls too knew at least some branches of the family; they came from Hollybush, Staffordshire, and Jane's cousin Edward Cooper was the Rector of the neighbouring parish of Hamstall Ridware. Visits were exchanged between the Austens of Hampshire and his family. Colonel Thomas presented the portrait to Elizabeth Hall because she 'was a great admirer of the novelist'. Possibly he was aware that his friend Dr Harding Newman would be no less delighted to have the picture. Elizabeth died rather young in 1831, in her early forties, and the picture remained in the possession of her husband; on his decease it passed with the rest of the estate into the hands of his son (Elizabeth's stepson) also called Dr Harding Newman. As his father had been a friend of Thomas Austen, so the son was a friend and Oxford colleague – they were dons together at the same college, Magdalen – of a great-nephew of the novelist, John Morland Rice, the fourth son of Elizabeth née Knight, the younger sister of the more celebrated Fanny. In 1880 Dr Newman was reaching the end of his life (he died in 1882) and was giving thought to the disposition of his worldly goods. He sent a picture to his colleague and friend John Rouse Bloxam, and added in his letter:

> I should like to give another painting of Jane Austen the novelist by Zoffany to her relative, your neighbour Morland Rice. It is of a girl about fifteen, and came into my family, the gift of Colonel Austen of Kippington to my mother-in-law, or rather my stepmother, my father's second wife, who was a great admirer of the novelist. I can remember Colonel Austen visiting this place.

After Harding Newman's death in 1883, Bloxam wrote, in the course of a letter to another friend:

> …talking of paintings Harding Newman, nephew of Dr Newman, has just sent me a full-length portrait by Zoffany of Miss Austen, the novelist, to give to Rice, who is a connection of the lady. Rice is much pleased with it – I know that Newman intended to leave it to

Rice, but did not – but his nephew to his great
credit has given it…

From this period there was a general and continued
acceptance of the portrait as representing the juvenile Jane
Austen. No one hitherto had questioned it. Lord
Brabourne, Fanny Knight's oldest son, and a close friend of
his cousin Morland Rice, used the picture as a frontispiece
to his volume of Jane Austen's letters in 1884; Constance
Hill included it in her book *Jane Austen, Her Homes and Her
Friends* in 1901; Richard Brinley Johnson's work on Jane
Austen in 1920 used a rather flat sepia copy of the picture,
much reduced in size. No members of the family – and in
1884 there were many surviving who knew a great deal
about her and her immediate family – protested or suggested that this was indeed not of Jane Austen.

Perhaps the most conclusive piece of confirmatory testimony came from the daughter of Anna Lefroy, née
Austen; Anna was the oldest child of Jane's older brother
James. She and her cousin Fanny Knight were born in the
same year (1793) and were the oldest of Jane Austen's
nieces; Anna was closest geographically to her aunts, indeed
had been cared for by them as a child when her mother
died in 1795. Anna's third daughter Fanny Caroline was
born in 1820, after Jane's death, but she became the family
historian, collecting and recording. After the receipt of his
portrait in 1884 Morland Rice wrote to a cousin Henry
Morland Austen asking for information about the picture;
the latter reported that he had seen 'Miss Lefroy yesterday'
and that 'she knows more than anybody about the Family
History.' He continued, '…she would have no doubts
about its genuineness.' She thought the date of the picture
was 1788 or 9, which fits with the visit of the Austens to
Kent. She seemed to assume that the portrait was painted in
Bath, a not unnatural assumption and quite plausible. The

one fact that seems incontrovertible is that the picture started its history in the possession of Francis Austen of Sevenoaks and his descendants, and must have been commissioned and paid for by him.

It was left to one of the most distinguished and influential Jane Austen scholars of his day not so much to question the portrait's authenticity but to reject it from the canon altogether, in a single statement; a statement concerning material the nature of which he himself claimed total ignorance, i.e., the costume!

The scholar was Dr Chapman, and in his book *Jane Austen, Facts and Problems* (OUP, 1948) he wrote:

> It had a pedigree that any layman might think watertight, but it cannot be Jane Austen. It is a portrait of a young girl which can be dated by the costume to about 1805 (when Jane Austen was thirty) or later.

For this judgement he relied – without question – on the opinion of two current experts, Mrs Doris Langley-Moore of the Bath Museum of Costume, and Miss Anne Buck, Keeper of the City of Manchester Gallery of English Costume. Their judgements seem to have been based on an inexplicably small selection of comparable portraits, perversely chosen from the early nineteenth century. They ignored the very large number of examples from the last quarter of the eighteenth century which have since been brought forward, by, amongst others, Richard Wheeler in his *The Rice Portrait of Jane Austen* (Codex Publications, 1996). One is led to the conclusion that the expertise of these scholars lay more in the collections of extant costumes than in the more complex problems of social history. Unfortunately the opinion of a scholar of Chapman's standing, however fragilely founded, was accepted without question by the Jane Austen Society, and also by the National Portrait Gallery who had recently, on the advice of Chapman, acquired the unfinished sketch of Jane Austen by her sister Cassandra, a sketch universally and probably correctly accepted as of Jane Austen by her sister, but whose provenance, in fact, is rather more tentative than that of the Rice portrait. Family tradition, so decried by the experts, is here the only evidence.

Much ink and paper has since been expended on the subject, but gradually a very large body of evidence has been accumulated to show that the costume worn by Jane Austen in the portrait is consistent with the date previously accepted, evidence both literary and historical, and that derived from dated miniatures and portraits.

In conclusion, this is a portrait that fits all the known descriptions of Jane Austen's appearance and personality; even, or perhaps especially, the rather sour one of her cousin Philadelphia Walter who met them all on their visit to Kent in 1788. She initially preferred Cassandra, and called Jane whimsical, prim and affected. (Later, she described them both as beautiful girls.) Jane had already embarked on her precocious literary activities, designed for home consumption, full of the wildest exaggerations of current literary trends and of human foibles. She was already a 'chiel amang us takin' notes', and it is not difficult to see in the Rice portrait the emerging of an exuberant, observant and lively personality.

BOOK TWO

The Life of Elizabeth Rice of Dane Court: Born Austen/Knight, a Niece of Jane Austen

Austen Family Pedigree (partial)

Francis
1698–1791

William = Rebecca Walter
1701–1737   (née Hampson)

Rev. George = Cassandra Leigh
1731–1805   1739–1827

Francis Motley
1747–1815

Rev. James = Anne Mathew   George   Edward   Henry   Cassandra   Francis
1765–1819   1766–1838 (Knight) 1771–1850 1773–1845   1774–1865
                                     1767–1852

Col. Thomas   Jane = W.J. Campion
1775–1859   1776–1854

Anna = Ben Lefroy
1793–1872

Elizabeth = E.R. Rice
1800–1884   1789–1878

Fanny Caroline
1820–1885

John Morland Rice
(Fellow of Magdalen Coll., Oxford)
1823–1897

Jane   Charles
1775–1817   1779–1852

Introduction[1]

In the preface to their book *Jane Austen, Her Life and Letters* William and R.A. Austen-Leigh wrote of 'the uneventful nature of the author's life, which, as we think, has been a good deal exaggerated. Quiet it certainly was; but the quiet life of the member of a large family, in the England of that date, was compatible with a good deal of stirring incident, happening, if not to herself, at all events to those who were nearest to her, and who commanded her nearest sympathies!'[2] This applies exactly to the life of Jane Austen's niece Elizabeth Knight (née Austen), the sixth child of Edward, Jane Austen's brother (who assumed the name of Knight in 1812) and the younger sister of the more famous Fanny.

The whole of Elizabeth's married life – she married Edward Royds Rice in October 1818 – was spent at Dane Court just outside the village of Tilmanstone in East Kent. There she brought up her fifteen children, tended her garden and her birds, visited her neighbours and died in the sixth year of her widowhood at the age of eighty-four. Nothing could appear more tranquil and uneventful; but apart from the vicissitudes, some of them dramatic or tragic, which inevitably occur in any large household, her ten sons brought many of the stirring events of the latter

---

1 The bulk of the material in this book is drawn from the letters and other material of the Rice family, owned by Henry Rice Esq. who is a great-great-great-grand-nephew of Jane Austen and to whom I am indebted for permission to draw upon them.

[2]W. and R.A. Austen-Leigh, *Jane Austen, Her Life and Letters*; London, 1913.

half of the nineteenth century right within the doors of the peaceful manor house, tucked into its green hollow in a quiet corner of Kent. Of the ten brothers, five were in the Army, three in the Navy. Between them, they served in every quarter of the globe, and fought in Burma, India, China, Africa and the Crimea. Her husband's political career (he was Liberal Member of Parliament for Dover for more than twenty years) took her to London a great deal, and of course made them all aware and informed concerning the main political issues of the day. And her daughter Fanny's marriage to the Earl of Winchilsea, as well as her oldest son's marriage into the family of the Vernon Harcourts, widened her social and political horizons still further.

The letters of Elizabeth Rice that survive – all to members of her family and most to her daughter Louisa – are almost entirely domestic in subject matter and unpretentious in tone. There is a great deal about health and weather – universal preoccupations in those days of inadequately heated houses and difficult travelling conditions – a great deal about family plans and movements, and the exchange of family news. Even at this level of the retailing of comparative trivia, there is in her letters a pre-Victorian tone, quite bracing and often ironic.

Under the stress of bereavement – she lost three sons in their youth – her letters avoid the sickly sentimentality which creeps sometimes into those of her daughters; and there are many incisive judgements on the character or the appearance of acquaintances which put one in mind of her illustrious aunt.

'The Deedes go tomorrow,' she wrote in May 1858.

> Mrs D. is nice and quiet and indolent and essentially selfish but she is very comfortable to listen to prosing on about all her own con-

cerns and not taking even the slightest interest in anything else, but I like her for not being able even to pretend to care. Lou Deedes is rather ugly I think and soon will be very – she is the sort of girl with rough arms and red cheeks that I never want to look at, but Caroline likes her and I believe she is nice and with good in her…

Her account of a visit to her sister Fanny Knatchbull's house at Provender might even warrant some of the strictures for callousness levelled at Jane Austen for some of her more robust remarks:

> …the Church is damp and the house cold. I do not the least wonder at Matilda [one of Fanny's daughters] dying there, I only wonder she lived so long.

Her appraisal of members of her own family was no less clear-sighted and shrewd. Her firstborn, Admiral Edward Rice, was a man of great sweetness of disposition, but was evidently full of naval briskness and efficiency:

> I was sorry I only saw you a minute before you went [she wrote to her daughter] I was going to, but when left with Edward I happened to get into a sort of talk with him that one never can in his busy or man-of-war moods which are one or the other generally prevailing.

Tilmanstone is still a remote and tiny village, and Dane Court still stands, transformed into luxury flats. But the Rice family, members of which once occupied nearly every house of any size in the immediate neighbourhood, in a group known as the 'Colony', which owned the land for miles around, built the school, employed the villagers and tended them in sickness, formed the cricket team, supported the Church and filled the churchyard, are all scattered and gone.

What follows is an attempt to describe the life and personality of an individual known, if known at all, as one of the nieces of Jane Austen; a niece whom one might put in the second rank of the Austen nieces. Fanny Knight, her older sister, and Anna Austen were the most intimate with their aunt, and were both adult by the time of Jane Austen's death in 1817, the latter indeed already married and a mother. Elizabeth was seventeen, and Caroline Austen, the half-sister of Anna was twelve, though living as she did at Steventon, close to Chawton, she saw her aunts more frequently than did Elizabeth at Godmersham.

But that Elizabeth knew her aunt quite well is without doubt; such contacts as are known will be mentioned later; but it is very much to be regretted that Elizabeth never – as far as we know – wrote down her recollections and impressions of her aunt. She read the novels aloud to the family, wonderfully well, according to her daughter, and commented when asked for an opinion, that the engraving made from Cassandra's sketch of Jane was very like, though the eyes were a little too large.

What does emerge from a study of all four nieces is the impression that the cast of Elizabeth's mind was the most akin to her Aunt Jane's, particularly in her ironic brand of humour and her unsentimental attitudes, as revealed in her surviving letters.

A Wedding

On an autumn morning in the year 1818, a wedding took place in the little church of Godmersham in Kent. The bride was Elizabeth, second daughter of Edward Knight, (né Austen) of Godmersham Park and Chawton House in Hampshire, brother to Jane Austen; the groom was Edward Royds Rice of Dover. Onlookers observed that a handsomer couple had never entered the church; later, in Dover, where the groom was well-known, it was reported that people followed them in the streets in admiration of their fine appearance. He was tall, six feet two inches, and well-built, a keen sportsman and a vigorous and splendid horseman, she was dark-haired, fresh-complexioned and bright-eyed. Elizabeth was eighteen years old, her husband ten years older.

Although the families were neighbours in Kent, it was in Paris that the couple had first met. After the final defeat of Napoleon in 1815, France and particularly Paris was flooded with people from Britain, either officially involved with peacemaking and the re-establishment of business and other contacts, or simply for pleasure and social reasons.

The great Duke of Wellington, in Paris as Commander-in-Chief of the victorious allied armies, formed the focal point for both categories. Madame Sarah Rice, widowed mother of the bridegroom, was of Huguenot origin, hence the French title which it seems it was customary to bestow on such ladies, as in the case of the Austens' friend and neighbour, Madame Lefroy; she came to Paris with her younger son Edward for a prolonged sojourn of more than two years, where they enjoyed all the gaieties of the new French court and the entourage of the Duke. As an excellent rider, Edward was frequently a member of the Duc de Berri's hunting parties in the forest of Fontainebleu, and as a handsome young Englishman was in demand at the Duke's balls and assemblies. Madame Rice's visiting list still exists for this time and runs to several pages of interesting and impressive names. Without doubt she exercised her considerable gifts as a financier while she was in Paris; she was a banker in her own right, partner in the Dover bank of Rice, Latham and Co., and Paris must have been a fruitful and interesting place for speculation at that time.

To Paris also came Edward Knight, with his two older daughters, Fanny and Elizabeth, and two of his sons, Edward and George, and their aunts Louisa and Charlotte Bridges.[1] Except for a brief armistice after the Peace of Amiens in 1801/1802, the Continent had been closed to Britain for a whole generation, and Edward was one of many anxious to give his family the experience they had so long been deprived of. The party arrived in Paris in the middle of May, and stayed in France only about three weeks, returning home on 7th June, only a few weeks before the death of their beloved Aunt Jane.

George Knight was already a friend of Edward Rice, and one morning he brought his friend to the Knights' lodgings to meet his family. Elizabeth was suffering from toothache and had her face wrapped up in a handkerchief; her state can hardly have been conducive to romantic feelings. Nevertheless, Edward was immediately impressed, and said to George on their departure, 'What a remarkably pretty girl your sister is!' George concluded that it was a case of love at first sight.

---

[1] Charlotte Hawley m.1810 Rev. Brook John Bridges (d.1812). Louisa was her unmarried sister-in-law.

Back in Kent, Edward pursued his courtship assidu-
ously, shocking 'Kackie' (Sackree, the Godmersham
children's nurse) by taking Elizabeth off for long solitary
walks. At first, Elizabeth's deep attachment to her home at
Godmersham and the carefree, happy life she lived there
with her brothers and sisters, surrounded by innumerable
relations and friends, caused her to hesitate, and even to
refuse Edward's first proposals; but finally, finding herself
very much in love, she consented to the engagement. That
period, of several months' duration, was marred by an
enforced separation caused by an illness to which Edward
succumbed, the nature of which is not clear,[2] but which
condemned him to exile in Cheltenham, where he was sent
to take the waters. From there he despatched frequent
letters to his beloved, of an increasingly despondent nature;
she passed the time chiefly by visits to a number of friends
and relations, all of whose names will be familiar to readers
of Jane Austen's letters – the Rev. George Moore, at
Wrotham, Sevenoaks, who had married Harriot Bridges,
Elizabeth's maternal aunt, and concerning whose disposition and temper Jane Austen had declared herself very
dubious ('I do not mean ever to like him!');[3] Colonel
Thomas Austen of Kippington, Edward Knight's second
cousin – he was the grandson of that fine old attorney,
Francis Austen, who was second father and benefactor to
his nephew George, father of the novelist – and the Rev.
Brook Henry Bridges, at Danbury, Chelmsford, one of
Elizabeth's maternal uncles. Visits to London for shopping
– everything from the purchase of turbans to supervising
the fittings for her new carriage, helped to pass the period

---

[2] It is possible that it might have been connected with a fall from his horse
in this year, 1818, to which Edward referred in a cheerful letter to
Lizzie's father, in which he requested the loan of a copy of *Sense and
Sensibility*.

[3] Jane Austen, *Letters;* (no.49, p.177), ed. Chapman, OUP.

of enforced separation. It is a pity that none of *her* letters to Edward at this time survive; she had a great deal more humour in her composition than he had, a more original and quirky perception of people and things, and no doubt in these circumstances a conscientious desire to amuse and cheer the disconsolate exile. That consolation was needed, Edward's letters reveal all too clearly. He stayed at first at the Pulteney Hotel, where his mother always stayed when in London, for a few days in order to consult his physician, who despatched him to Cheltenham. He was very dismal:

> If I must be away from you, I am indifferent what it is – I have no wish to stay in Town having now no inclination to enter into the gaiety of it even were I well enough...

He arrived at Cheltenham feeling very unwell and dispirited, and continued to bombard Elizabeth with accounts of his poor health, poorer spirits, and boredom. He seemed to be unable to find consolation or entertainment in reading or congenial company, and had little awareness of the distress his outpourings were causing Elizabeth:

> you desire me to tell you what I do – nothing that can give me pleasure to relate or you to hear – indeed, time passes sadly slow ...my own thoughts ...seldom quit you, and only make me upset.

In a later letter he aroused himself from this slough of self-pity to write apologetically:

> it is painfull to be able to write such letters only as my last which you acknowledge made you wretched... and your account of yourself

> is far from satisfactory, indeed, my dearest
> Lizzie, your heart and head must not ache at
> once.

At last, a combination of rest and the Cheltenham waters and no doubt the spur of happiness ahead affected a cure for the afflicted Edward, and the wedding took place as arranged, on 6th October, 1818. At that period weddings were rarely the big ceremonial affairs they later became; one recalls the wedding of Emma Woodhouse in *Emma* – 'very much like other weddings, where the parties have no taste for finery or parade – very little white satin, very few lace veils; a most pitiful business!'[4] And the wedding of Jane Austen's other niece, Anna Austen, who married Ben Lefroy in November 1814, described by Anna's half-sister Caroline was certainly 'in the extreme of quietness'. She explained, 'Weddings were then usually very quiet. The old fashion of festivity and publicity had quite gone by, and was universally condemned as showing... great bad taste...'[5] None of the three ladies at Chawton Cottage – Jane Austen, her sister Cassandra and their mother – attended the ceremony, nor, one imagines, did they expect to do so. After the simple ceremony in the dark and extremely chilly church, and after partaking of the modest wedding break-fast which had been enlivened only by the addition of the wedding cake and the luxury of hot chocolate, the bride and groom departed for their new home in Hendon. The Lefroy family returned to their Rectory at Ashe, and Caroline and her mother Mary repaired to the 'Great House' at Chawton for a day or two; it was occupied at that time by the youngest Austen brother Charles and his family, where without doubt the three ladies from the

---

[4] Jane Austen, *Emma,* p.484, Chapman ed., OUP.
[5] Caroline Mary Craven Austen, *Reminiscences*, J.A.S., 1986.

cottage would be found. James Edward, Anna's half-brother, returned immediately to school at Winchester, and her father stayed at home alone with only the servants to keep him company, and his neighbour Mr Digweed from Steventon House.

Elizabeth's wedding took place in Godmersham Church, and one of the Bridges uncles who was in Holy Orders carried out the ceremony. Fanny reported in a letter to her old Governess Miss Chapman that Elizabeth:

> had four Bridesmaids, Fanny and Sophia Cage, Marianne and myself – all dressed in white gros de Naples Bonnets and Spencers. The bride wore a sprigged muslin gown trimmed very much with lace over a White Sattin slip – a dear Indian muslin Pelisse lined with white Sattin open in front part and trimmed also with lace and a white Gros de Naples Bonnet and feather. I know a bride's dress is always interesting so I do not apologise for these particulars.[6]

The immediate aftermath of the wedding was informal. The bridegroom went out shooting with some of his new brothers-in-law (at this time of the year, even a family wedding must not too much disrupt the serious business of the season), and Elizabeth scrambled out of her delicate sprigged muslin and made a tour of the grounds with her younger sister Marianne, all round the stables and chicken houses and over the roofs of the cow-houses, in a visit of farewell. Fanny continued:

---

[6]Knatchbull Papers, Kent Archives Office, Maidstone, Kent.

They went to Wingham House for a few days
at first as the E. Bridges were then all at
Ramsgate, and from there to spend some time
with Mrs Rice at Tunbridge Wells. They then
returned to Godmersham and when Papa paid
his usual visit to Chawton in November I accompanied Mr and Mrs Edward Rice to
Goodnestone, Sandling, Eastwell[7] etc., and
they returned with me to spend their Xmas at
Godmersham, and settled in their house at
Dane Court Jany. 1st.

This was to be Elizabeth's home for the next sixty-two
years, and here her fifteen children were reared. On their
arrival the lodge gates were opened by Wyborn, who was to
be for the rest of his working life the Rice farm bailiff, a
vital presence and influence to the Rice children as they
grew up. Fanny's letter to Miss Chapman was written from
Dane Court on 25th March, 1819; Elizabeth was already
pregnant with her first child, and Fanny gave a description
of the new home. Like her sister, she had reservations about
its situation in comparison with their earthly paradise at
Godmersham:

I have been here since the 16th of February,
and they will take me home and I hope stay
some time at Godmersham the 1st April. I
cannot call this a pretty place though it has
several advantages and Mr Rice is doing so
much to improve it, that I have no doubt a few
months will make a great difference. The
house stands low, and is surrounded with
wood, but the country immediately beyond

---

[7]The homes of Sir William Bridges, William Deedes (m.1791 Sophia
Bridges), and of the Finch-Hattons, respectively.

the place is not pretty, and the roads are infamous. There is an Avenue issuing from the front of the house and some nice paths in the woods adjoining. The house is being whitened at present and a flower garden is mentioned and there is to be a greenhouse built another year.

...The Vicinity of Dane Court to Goodnestone (home of the Bridges family) about 4 miles, is a great comfort and it is also a pleasant distance from Godmersham – only 20 miles. Cacky came here with me for a few days and as you may suppose enjoyed her visit very much. She has been remarkably well this winter. Marianne left the schoolroom when Lizzie married, and went to one or two winter balls. She is now keeping house at home and I believe she will accompany Papa and me into Hampshire about the end of April for 3 or 4 months after which Miss Clewes (governess) is going home for 2 months and I shall of course be stationary...

Fanny wrote a long letter to her sister two days after the wedding in reply to a 'comfortable' letter from her; it had reassured her after Lizzie's tearful departure from Godmersham for Wingham, and she could once more think of her 'as I delight to do, happy and like yourself.' Fanny reported the many congratulatory messages and calls, the distribution of wedding cake, and the rearrangement of bedrooms arising from Lizzie's departure. Evidently Aunt Cassandra Austen was at Godmersham – 'good Aunt Cass! she quite cried with pleasure at hearing your letter...' Fanny concluded by protesting she had no time nor inclination for anything but Lizzie – 'you divide my heart with Pork Steaks, roast Beef, Jellies, creams and Wedding cake.'

Elizabeth, born in 1800, was the second daughter and the sixth child of Edward and Elizabeth Austen, (Edward took the name of Knight in 1812, after his wife's death); so there was a difference of seven years between her and her sister Fanny who was the oldest of the family of eleven children. They were left motherless when Elizabeth Austen died after the birth of John Brook Austen in 1808. Fanny was then fifteen years old, and was faced with the considerable burden of assuming the overall direction of the very large household at Godmersham, comforting the widower as best she could, cheering the other children, and in general helping to restore the shattered household. That she was successful the later happy history of the family bears witness; Edward never remarried, but the house at Godmersham seems always to have been the centre of a lively and cheerful group of relatives and visitors, opening its doors to uncles and aunts and cousins, neighbours and friends, and yet never giving the impression of disorder or chaos. It will be remembered that Jane Austen wholeheartedly enjoyed the comfort and order and spaciousness of the house, where all was 'Elegance and Ease and Luxury' and one could 'eat Ice and drink French wine and be above Vulgar Economy.'[8]

One of the few references to her younger niece by Jane Austen in her letters occurred at this time of bereavement, when she wrote to Cassandra at Godmersham:

> Your account of Lizzy is very interesting. Poor child! One must hope that the impression *will*

---

[8]J.A., *Letters* (no.54, p.209), ed. Chapman, OUP.

be strong, and yet one's heart aches for a dejected mind of eight years old.[9]

Some time later, in September 1813, Elizabeth and her younger sister Marianne accompanied Fanny and their father to London, where her Aunt Jane was already visiting her brother Henry at Henrietta Street. Shopping and visits to the theatre were amongst their activities, the plays chosen to suit juvenile tastes; less agreeably, visits to the dentist were part of the programme, which Jane Austen described, in all the details of fillings and extractions, with sympathy for their sufferings: 'I would not have had him look at mine for a shilling a tooth, and double it!'[10]

What must be Elizabeth's earliest recorded letter forms the first part of a letter Jane Austen wrote to Cassandra from Godmersham Park in October of 1813 – remarkable more, as the work of a thirteen year old, for the fluency and ease of its style than for any special interest of content, and for the air of humour which is already apparent.

> I must now tell you something about our poor people. I believe you know old Mary Croucher, she gets 'maderer and maderer' every day. Aunt Jane has been to see her, but it was on one of her rational days. Poor Will Amos ...has left his house in the poor row, and lives in a barn at Builting. We asked him why he went away, and he said the fleas were so starved when he came back from Chawton that they all flew upon him and 'eenermost' eat him up. How unlucky it is that the weather is so wet! Poor Uncle Charles has come home

---

[9]Ibid., (no.58, p.221).
[10]Ibid., (no.83, p.328).

half-drowned every day. I don't think little
Fanny (Charles' daughter) is quite so pretty as
she was; one reason is because she wears short
petticoats, I believe. – Papa has given me half-
a-dozen new pencils, which are very good
ones indeed; I draw every other day. I hope
you go and whip Lucy Chalcroft every night.[11]

The Rice letters record a number of contacts between the
Austens of Hampshire and the Knights; in September 1807,
Edward Austen (he was not yet 'Knight') and his wife
Elizabeth were at Chawton House with the two eldest boys
Edward and William, and Fanny; Elizabeth Austen wrote to
little Lizzie, then aged seven, home at Godmersham with
her other brothers and sisters, in the care of the invaluable
Sackree. She told Lizzie that they were expecting a visit
from Grandmamma Austen and Aunts Cassandra and Jane
from Southampton, and that 'Uncle and Aunt James
Austen' were also expected from Steventon. Little James
Edward Austen, their son, who was nine, was to ride over
on a donkey, a distance of fourteen miles, quite a feat for a
small boy. The baby Caroline was too young to join the
party, which 'I regret very much, for she would be a nice
little plaything,' commented the baby-loving Elizabeth.

Elizabeth was seventeen years old when Jane Austen
died, and must certainly have known her aunt well;
although Jane's last visit to Godmersham was several years
before she died (in September/October 1813) the Knight
family visited their other property at Chawton regularly.[12]
Contact between that house and Chawton Cottage where

---

[11]Ibid., (no.86, p.341).
[12]Although Marcia Rice, granddaughter of Lizzie, thought that perhaps
Lizzie had not visited Chawton House during Jane Austen's lifetime, she
was wrong; the Knights *en famille* were there for two months April – May
1814 and for four months in the spring of 1813.

the three Austen ladies lived was almost a daily affair, whichever brother was in residence; for Edward was generous in allowing his less prosperous naval brothers the use of this second home. So it is a matter of great regret that there is no record of any reminiscences left by Elizabeth concerning either of her aunts, with the single exception, recounted by one of Elizabeth's daughters, that her mother told her of both her aunts coming into her room once and dancing for her! Pride in her achievement there certainly was; her novels were read aloud in the family, most memorably by Elizabeth herself – 'Grandmamma read Aunt Jane aloud as no one else could.' It was only later, after Elizabeth herself was dead, that the surviving family expressed regret that they had failed to persuade her to talk of what she remembered of her aunt. By that time, Jane Austen's reputation was beginning to grow, and any information would have been of more significance. In the mass of family papers and correspondence spanning the greater part of the nineteenth century, her name is not mentioned more than three or four times, and never except in a trivial context.

Henry Austen's home in London was a popular and useful meeting point for the various families. In August 1815 young William Knight wrote to his sister Lizzie at Godmersham from his Uncle Henry's house at 23, Hans Place. Fanny had been staying, maybe other members of the family too, but William, aged about sixteen, was passing a solitary evening – 'you cannot think how dull the drawing-room seems... I every now and then expect to see some of you coming downstairs...' Henry Austen, now a widower, was dining at Hanwell, where the Moore family included two daughters, one of whom Jane Austen suspected might be a possible second wife for him. Solitude added a spur to William's appetite, and he described in detail his consumption of fried whiting, beef 'stakes', 'assparraguss', Cheshire cheese and oranges. Henry's next visitor, early in October, was to be Jane Austen, who came to London to see her novel *Emma* through the press, but in fact had to extend her visit to nurse Henry through a serious illness.

The two families linked together by this marriage at Godmersham were already known to each other. Edward Rice had an older brother, Henry, born in 1776 (and thus almost the same age as Jane Austen). He figures in several of her letters as a member of the local social group, as a friend and a dancing partner. By 1800 he was engaged to be married to Lucy Lefroy, the daughter of a neighbour and particular friend of Jane's, Madame Anne Lefroy, wife of the Rev. George Lefroy of Ashe. They married in July 1801 – Jane, with high-spirited facetiousness, wrote to Cassandra, 'Mr Rice and Lucy are to be married, one on the 9th and the other on the 10th of July.'[13] There was a question of Henry Rice receiving the curacy of Deane, a living adjoining Steventon held by Mr Austen. It had been until recently occupied by the oldest Austen son James, but he would shortly be moving into his father's rectory at Steventon. But according to Jane, the spanner in the works was likely to be Henry Rice's mother, Madame Sarah.

> It has never been Mrs Rice's wish [she wrote] to have her son settled near herself – and there is now a hope entertained of her relenting in favour of Deane. Mrs Lefroy and her son-in-law were here yesterday. *She* tries not to be sanguine, but *he* was in excellent spirits, I rather wish they may have the curacy. It will be an amusement to Mary to superintend their household management, and abuse them for

---

[13] In fact, the wedding took place on 20th July, according to letters of Mrs Anne Lefroy.

expense, especially as Mrs L. means to advise
them to put out their washing.[14]

Mrs Sarah Rice lived in Dover, and Deane would be a fair
distance from her home. Why did she not want Henry on
her doorstep? Years later, she was happy to have Edward
and his wife as very near neighbours. Had her patience,
which later, as we shall see, became quite worn out, already
begun to wear thin? Mrs Lefroy is clearly a woman of good
sense, while her future son-in-law shows signs of the
ebullient optimism which so often accompanies an extravagant or improvident nature. Jane Austen, incidentally,
cannot resist a dig at her sister-in-law Mary, wife of James,
who was parsimonious and inclined to be bossy.

   A few days later, Jane Austen reported:

> I would not give much for Mr Rice's chance
> of living at Deane; he builds his hope, I find,
> not upon anything his mother has written, but
> upon the effect of what he has written himself.
> He must write a great deal better than those
> eyes indicate if he can persuade a perverse and
> narrow-minded woman to oblige those whom
> she does not love.

On the grounds of this passage, Madame Rice has been
assumed to have contributed something to Jane Austen's
gallery of ill-natured, selfish elderly women such as Mrs
Churchill, Mrs Ferrars, Mrs Norris and Lady Catherine de
Burgh. Madame Rice was certainly known in the Rice
family as a formidable woman, autocratic and overbearing,
and as the mother of Edward Rice and Lizzie's mother-in-

---

[14]J.A., Letters (nos. 31 and 33, pp.111–112 and 117–8), ed. Chapman,
OUP. Lucy and Henry Rice did indeed start their married life at Deane,
very close to the Lefroys at Ashe.

law she played an important role in the family for many years.

Lizzie's Mother-in-Law

Sarah Samson was born in 1755 at Whitechapel in London. Her family was of Huguenot origin from St Lô in Normandy, and had settled in East Kent in the seventeenth century. The family was well-known in Normandy for the manufacture of copies of imported Chinese porcelain, still known as Samson ware. The family had another claim to fame in their link with the Elizabethan poet Christopher Marlowe; Marlowe's sister Anne married a shoemaker of Canterbury called John Cranford, and their great-grand-daughter married a Captain Samson and became the mother of Sarah. Her father, the Captain, made his fortune in the East India trade, as Commander of a vessel called the *Hardwicke*. As the Company at that time had a monopoly on shipping to British India, this was a very profitable business, and the ships, armed like sloops of war, usually only made about three voyages, on which they expected to clear £10,000 each time. At the same period Henry Rice, whose family came from Llyn-y-bran in Glamorgan, and who was known in London as 'the handsome Welshman', joined his uncle who owned the East Indiaman *Dutton*. Eventually Henry succeeded to the ownership of the *Dutton*. After a prosperous voyage, he gave a ball on board in Dover harbour with the express intention of wooing and winning his older colleague's handsome daughter. In this he was successful. His bride brought with her a fortune of £30,000 together with a strength of character and business acumen rare for a woman of that time.

Rice retired from the sea as an elder brother of Trinity House, and settled near Dover at Bramling House; he established a banking and trading firm in Dover (Latham, Rice and Co.) with Samuel Latham, also of Huguenot origins, who remained a lifelong friend of the family. Apparently the firm acted as agents for the Rothschilds – Sarah had many dealings with them – and they used their fleet of small fast ships not only to trade but to transmit and make profitable financial use of news from the Continent. It is said that at the time of the French Directoire and the Consulat, Sarah made a considerable fortune by her adroit use of early information.

Henry Rice died in 1797, at the age of fifty-four, leaving Sarah with three children; a girl had died in infancy, Henry, born in 1776, went to Christ's College, Cambridge and took Holy Orders; John, the oldest, was reputedly the most gifted, and died at the age of twenty-six in India in 1799, cutting short a career already full of achievement. He had become an aide, interpreter and translator to Tipoo Sahib, the Sultan of Seringapatan, and there is amongst the Rice papers an interesting account of the capture of that place in May 1799 by Major-General Baird, and of the death of Tipoo Sahib in the course of the action. Edward was the youngest son, born in 1789 and was destined to be his mother's favourite.

Sarah was said by Samuel Latham to have been, not exactly pretty, but 'a smart-looking girl'. She liked to dress in white, as in a portrait of her as a young woman, and her grandchildren recalled her even in later years wearing a white bonnet, dress and white satin shoes at all times. The bonnet was never removed, indoors or out. Her visits were dreaded by the young, to whom she was evidently severe; one grandson went so far as to call her 'a terrible old woman'. Another earned her displeasure, probably permanently; he was called John Morland, and Sarah always called him John, in memory of her own lost son, which he hated, as he was always called Morny in the family. One day she said, 'John, John, do you love Grandma? John, do you love Grandma?' To which he replied emphatically, 'No, no, oh no!'

'Humph!' replied his grandmother, not unnaturally affronted, 'that settles it!' What 'it' was was not disclosed, but he thereby probably forfeited a tip or even a legacy.

At this time, after her husband's death, Sarah Rice moved to a house in Dover, no great distance from Dane Court. She was very fond of card-playing, and a grand-daughter reported ruefully that although her parents 'detested cards', Mama had to spend all her evenings at this occupation with her mother-in-law. The house in Dover, later the site of an hotel, was a fine one, with attractive grounds, but on one occasion when the Duke of Wellington was in residence at Walmer Castle (he was then Lord Warden of the Cinque Ports), a battery of artillery was placed between the house and the sea, impeding Mrs Rice's view and creating a great deal of noise and disturbance. She had all the windows in the house closed and the shutters put up, and then sent a message to the Duke, inviting him to visit her. He was naturally surprised at the state of things within doors. 'As long as your Battery remains where it is' she explained, 'this is how I must live.' The Battery, needless to say, was immediately removed.

Another anecdote reminds one of Jane Austen's Lady Catherine de Burgh, sallying forth into the village and bullying the country folk into good behaviour. Sarah was asked by a Dover clergyman to support his Sunday school; after consideration she declared that school on Sunday was work, and therefore she would support it only if it took place on a Monday!

The impression from all these accounts is certainly of an imperious, capable, self-willed woman, and one is inclined to sympathise with her children and grandchildren, dependent on her for support, and dancing to the tune of her money boxes. But that is not the whole story, as is shown by the large collection of letters in the Rice archive concerned with Madame Rice's financial affairs. Amongst the material there is not only a very large number of bills incurred by the Rev. Henry Rice, for everything from butcher's meat to building materials, all eventually paid by his mother, but also a series running from the beginning of the century to 1833 (when Sarah was an old lady of seventy-six), all concerning her son's complicated financial affairs, which became increasingly desperate and confused; the letters reveal much about the character of the writers, as well as the inexorable deterioration of their relationship.

Henry's debts began to accumulate as early as the period of his student days at Christ's College, Cambridge, in the final years of the eighteenth century. His mother settled his debts in response to a letter from a Fellow of the College in 1804, pleading on behalf of the 'little Tradesmen' who 'by being so long kept out of their money, you must be perfectly aware, [are reduced] to extreme inconveniences as well in reputation as pecuniarily.'

Getting into debt as a student was common enough in those days, but another letter from a Fellow of the college, J. Hopkins, reinforces the impression of Henry Rice as a man with too little care for correct and considerate procedures. The writer urged that some small college debts should be settled, in order that Henry Rice should be enabled to proceed – belatedly – to his degree (a graduate could not take his degree as long as college bills remained unpaid). In addition, Mr Hopkins had more or less guaranteed that he would proceed to his degree to the Bishop who had ordained Rice. 'I hope,' Hopkins concluded, 'Mr Rice means to return to college to take his degree, for his own credit, for the credit of the college, and, I may add, to satisfy my feelings on the subject.'

In the early years of the nineteenth century, Henry and his young family lived first at Deane near the home of the Lefroys at Ashe, and then at Cholderton, a parish in Wiltshire. Already by 1804 he was writing to his mother acknowledging the receipt of sums of money and the settling of bills by her, protesting that this would be 'the last application of the kind I will ever make', and begging her not to 'accompany your discharge of my debts with your displeasure.'

This early letter is ironic in view of what was to follow over the course of the next thirty years. In fact, the letter, with its anxiety to justify expenditure, its apologetic tone and its fear of maternal displeasure, implies clearly that financial problems with his mother were no new thing.

In about 1807 Madame Rice bought for her son the living of Great Holland, a country living in a parish near Frinton on the Essex coast. By the standards of the time, it was a comparatively rich one, and should, one would have supposed, together with the allowance of £420 a year his mother made him, as well as continual 'hand-outs', have established him in relative prosperity. The value of the living, Glebe and Tithes, he reckoned as £661.16 or more, the price for the purchase of the advowson he insisted was 'extremely reasonable', and 'although I confess the County of Essex is not the situation I should prefer as a residence, and the house wants much done to it before it could be made a comfortable residence,' yet he hoped his mother would agree to the purchase, for 'my dear Mother, I am at a time of life to be settled, indeed with my family it is absolutely necessary...'

From this time forward the tone of the surviving letters between them changes – protestations, demands, excuses from him, anger, frustration and finally despair from his mother. By January 1811 he was writing from Cholderton:

> My dear Mother,
> I had hoped, after the conversation we had in town, you would have afforded the assistance I need, without any further application on my part, but as usual my expectations have failed, I will not now dwell on a subject which constantly gives me pain, but will only state that my inconveniences are very great – my request is – that whatever you think proper to allow me, you will name, that in future I may know what I have to depend on without any application to, or expectation from you – and that we may in future meet, free from that constant altercation which money has occasioned. Happy shall I be if this can be arranged between ourselves, without even Edward's knowledge and that it may be settled with that delicacy, which is necessary to secure the affection between mother and son – I can say with the utmost sincerity of heart that my first wish has been to see my mother happy – which being accomplished – I flattered myself she would have endeavoured to render her sons comfortable...

Was the above a touching plea to a tyrannical parent who delighted in keeping a rigid control over her son by her refusal to unloose the purse strings, which, after all, contained money left by her husband for eventual distribution to his surviving sons? The young Jane Austen would probably have taken that view. But later events reveal a different picture; Henry was always badgering his mother to allow him whatever he was to be entitled to from his father, and 'let him get on with it'. But had Sarah agreed to this, even if it were possible under the terms of the will, without doubt the money would soon have been squandered, and she would have been put under intolerable pressure to give him further financial assistance, to the detriment of her own income and even of the expectations of her other son. It would also have destroyed the bonds of affection between them even more speedily than the current unsatisfactory situation.

The increasingly desperate methods Henry Rice employed in order to raise money included raising annuities, borrowing at exorbitant rates of interest, and getting involved in litigation, either voluntary (to claim a small legacy), or involuntary (when he was sued by his own brother-in-law for the redemption of a bond), but either way unprofitable. His letters take on a bullying tone of emotional blackmail, the ill health of himself, his wife or his children being invoked, and self-pity is always more evident than self-reproach.

In 1819 Henry and his family, now living at Maxton just outside Dover, were driven by financial necessity to remove to Dunkirk, where they lived for several years, too impoverished to return home. Our source is a handful of letters from Henry's wife Lucy to her brother the Rev. George Lefroy of Ashe in Hampshire (like James Austen, he succeeded to his late father's parish) in which she reported her melancholy tale of their chronic financial straits, ill luck, ill health, and finally the sad death of their only son Henry, aged seventeen or eighteen. He had been sent, perhaps as an assistant teacher, or maybe to finish his education to Heidelberg, under a Professor Schwarz, and there he fell ill and died. Lucy's letters are stoical – living in Dunkirk is less uncomfortable than she expected, and there is an agreeable if limited society. Her style lacks sparkle, but her letters confirm the conviction that Henry's financial affairs were as troublesome to his in-laws as to his mother. Lucy had been a friend of Jane Austen's, her sister-in-law was Jane's niece Anna, and the family still kept up friendly relations with the Austens in the neighbourhood.

Lucy's approaches to her brother for financial help were tentative and apologetic; her husband kept her in the dark to some extent about his financial affairs, but their plight was only too apparent to her:

> I have no doubt Rice's bankers have received what you sent them but you will be surprised to hear he has never mentioned the subject to me since he wrote to you from here before he went to town, this is to me very odd after all the anxiety and vexation I went through.

Her own applications were for small loans, no doubt to cover minor domestic expenses, and reveal a pathetic degree of personal poverty:

> My dear Brother [she wrote] I hardly know how to make the request... and am perhaps unreasonable for doing so and therefore beg if it is inconvenient to you you will not grant it, but if not and you would have the kindness to send me £10 or £15 it would be of the greatest use to me and would make me leave this much more comfortable [this was on the eve of their departure for Dunkirk], believe me my dear Brother it is not to squander away or I would not ask for it and as I am convinced we shall live there much cheaper I promise you I shall put by something every week and hope by that means I shall be able to return it to you

when we come back again, I assure you this is
for myself I am asking, Rice knows nothing
about it nor do I wish him to know it therefore whatever fault there is is mine I know you
will let me know when you receive this
whether you can or cannot grant my request
and also I hope you are not angry with me for
having made it.

When the family returned to England we do not know, but
by early February of 1824 their address was Norton Court,
and Henry was writing to his mother in a now familiar
vein. A demand for £250 in 1824 was satisfied, but was
evidently no more than a palliative, as Henry could never
bring himself to disclose the full extent of his debts and
entanglements. Now and then the unfortunate Lucy was
driven to write to Madame Rice; in spite of her protestations of economy, it needs no subtlety to see what sort of
frightful entanglements her husband got himself into and to
speculate why he should have felt himself compelled to take
such actions.

I have taken the opportunity of Mr Rice's absence [she wrote] to write to you. I am unable
to enter minutely into a statement of the present embarrassment but I shall proceed to tell
you it arises from no extravagance of the present time but solely from having been obliged
to borrow a large sum of money before we left
Cholderton for which he was to pay interest –
unfortunately for his present comfort this interest was suffered to accumulate and some
time back he was compelled to borrow a further sum in order to pay it off in addition to
the Annuity he has insured his life for, the

whole sum, which, as you may suppose, has decreased his income very considerably... rather than have applied to you himself I know he would have resigned his Living and have ended his days abroad but for the sake of our children I am most anxious to avoid this alternative... I shall be miserable till I hear from you and I can assure you that the fear of your displeasure is no small addition to our present unhappiness...

Madame Rice wrote to Lucy kindly but firmly explaining that Henry had exhausted not only her patience but also the whole of his share of his late Father's property and Shares.

I could wish to spare your feelings by not expressing my displeasure and what I do feel at being troubled again on money concerns respecting your husband after telling him... that now all money concerns were entirely at an end between him and me and I lamented to say from his hitherto incessant line of conduct must all social intercourse which as a mother I might have hoped to enjoy, but which nothing can restore to me but being permitted to witness his future integrity by living within his income and not incurring any expence that he cannot afford, as on that depends his future comfort, as the Ill Effect of not doing so must now fall entirely on himself...

She concluded by referring to a letter she had received from him which had deeply offended her – it was 'unpardonable to him as a Christian. I may forgive him but as a Mother I cannot efface [it] from my memory...'

Henry and his family had by this time moved to Great
Holland, and he had embarked upon a course of rebuilding,
furnishing and planting in a style which seemed, at least
according to his mother, to be far beyond his means. She
paid most of the bills she considered reasonable, but many
were not, and relations had become strained to breaking
point. Henry's letters now stressed what he regarded as his
deprivation of filial rights, couched in a tone of high-
minded self-righteousness:

> I trust I shall never be wanting in duty or af-
> fection to my Mother [he wrote] but from the
> abject situation in which you placed me, on
> my stating to you a short time since the dis-
> tress I experienced, when you would not
> condescend to communicate with me, but in
> defiance of all delicacy to what I might feel,
> placed my letters in the hands of an Agent,
> through whose kind interference in my behalf,
> I find I was solely indebted for the small assis-
> tance you afforded me. From this, and from
> the total neglect you have since shewn towards
> me and my family, with the addition of twice
> stopping at Norton and refusing to enter my
> doors in the presence of my servants, I feel
> myself precluded from a line of conduct (I la-
> ment to say) which, as your son, I should have
> been happy in pursuing, fearful that, where I
> should have hoped to find affection, I should
> be subjecting myself to a repetition of the
> treatment which I have so lately suffered.

This egotistical letter, repulsively hypocritical and offensive
in tone, yet met with the desired result, though only after a
good scolding for his remarks about his Mother's 'agent'

who in fact was her old friend and colleague Mr Samuel Latham. But Henry can never have brought himself to disclose the full extent of his debts and entanglements, as invariably within a month or two he found himself again in desperate difficulties. Soon after this, Henry wrote a really despairing letter to his Mother, his sense of injury and persecuted innocence much to the fore:

> What is to become of me? what can cause this desire in you to persecute me to the utmost? ...nothing can prevent the immediate seques-tration of my living if these accounts are not settled – why is this cruel act of injustice re-sorted to? Have I not suffered enough? my cup believe me, is nearly full. Whatever is the result in mercy answer this by return of post as I must now quit this place of Sunday night. Your affect. H.R.
>
> You know too well my inability to command a sixpence.

His Mother's response to this angry scream for help was written on the same day to Mr Parker, her solicitor:

> March 22nd 1833
>
> My dear Sir,
> I have enclosed a copy of both letters received this morning, the indignation I felt at my son I can scarcely describe and is such as cannot be answered by me. I see that he is determined never to cease being a scourge to me notwith-standing all I have sacrificed for him ...I told my son all money concerns was ended be-tween us, as the Bills were all paid that I agreed should be paid ...I fear you will hardly

be able to read this I am so tired – perhaps – you may as well write him to Great Holland on receipt of this and say that I have desired you to see Mr Harrison, – I am so tired – I can only say I remain yours truly S. Rice

If anything should be done – be careful that everything is properly done.

One can only be sorry for this old lady of seventy-eight with her meticulous care for accuracy and fairness in her financial dealings with her family and indeed everybody else, distraught by a lifelong struggle with her improvident, extravagant and not always truthful son. There does seem to be a puzzle underlying this situation – why was this respectable country clergyman with a good living and a small private income from his mother so constantly in dire financial straits? Why did not Mrs Rice yield up to him whatever sums he might be entitled to from his late father's estate, and leave him to manage as best he could, saving herself thereby many years of distress on his account? Her son Edward at Dane Court never seemed to trouble her in the same way, and there are no records of his bills being paid by his mother, as was the case with Henry. A combination of family tradition and letters to Mrs Rice from her attorneys help to provide the answer. The Rev. Henry Rice was incorrigibly extravagant, a compulsive gambler and an aficionado of prizefighting; thus goes the tradition in the family. Not a scrap of specific evidence can be gleaned from the surviving correspondence to support this, except for a remark in a letter from Mrs Rice's attorney that the Rev. Henry would not be likely to leave London as long as any of the recent advance of £500 she had made still remained in his pockets. And a letter from him to Mrs Rice as early as August 1818 leaves one in no doubt as to his opinion about Henry's character and integrity.

Her attorney, Mr Robinson, wrote to her enclosing the account of some 'purchase money', and added:

> I confess that I was not surprised Mr R. [Henry] should ask for part of the money as he wd. not have been so anxious to have sold it unless he thought he should get some of the produce. What I have before sayd I now repeat – that you must make up your mind to have frequent applications and you must also determine to the extent you will go. It appears to me quite useless to write for accounts of expenditure and to think of giving advice, for you may rely upon it all your Letters are laughed at and the advice contained in them treated with contempt. Indeed, if a person who has arrived at the age of 38 cannot know how to conduct himself so as to keep within his income, I think it will be a very difficult task to convince him of his error, but you have had such repeated instances of such being the case that remonstrance is useless. You must determine and act accordingly. I know it vexes you and with good reason – I really think you should have an acknowledgement of the several sums he has had from his Father's property. I do not apprehend that Mr R. can sell his Life Interest in the Living but he may grant Annuities upon it, which will be done on very bad terms, such property not being an eligible property… I am Madam, your obedt. servant, Edmund Robinson.

Strong words indeed to a mother about her son! But what Mr Robinson anticipated came to pass a few years later when it was discovered that Henry Rice had indeed raised money by granting several Annuities, not only disastrously reducing his income thereby, but then allowing himself to get into appalling arrears over the extortionate rates of interest. The attorney pointed out that he had fallen into very bad hands and 'really, considering the ruinous rate of Interest he is liable to pay the question naturally arises whether it would not be prudent to repurchase the annuities at once.' This Mrs Rice accordingly did, to the extent of several thousand pounds, but not in time to prevent a sheriff's officer coming to Great Holland and temporarily taking possession.

> This last act of Mr Rice's friends [wrote the attorney] is if possible more nefarious than their previous conduct, but it is not more than might have been expected from such a quarter …with regard to your son's present embarrassing position, he had better be relieved immediately and presuming that you will send me an order upon Barnett's I have told him he may draw for the amount upon me.

He concluded:

> I am afraid your son may consider that he will be entitled to a much larger sum from his Father's estate than actually exists, and his expenditure may be proportionably conducted.

These expectations seem to have been the stimulus at all times to Henry Rice to live beyond his means, and must have been the reason for his frequently resentful tone to his mother – he was only claiming what be considered was rightfully his! He reminds one of many a young man in novels of the time, including those of Jane Austen – young men with a taste for luxury whose expectations are a disincentive to hard work or economy, and a trap to tempt them into extravagance and financial disaster. Certainly the letters reveal more, much more, to the discredit of the son than the mother, and must to some extent give the lie to Jane Austen's opinion in this case.

Sarah Rice lived all her widowhood in Dover, and relations between her son Edward and his family must have been close and cordial, in spite of the unenthusiastic attitude of some of the grandchildren, and the tedium of endless games of cards! Edward accompanied his mother on journeys to France – he was also involved with his mother's banking business, although he resigned his interest after his mother's death, and on visits to his brother, notably in 1824, when Henry was stricken with an unidentified malaise, attacks which 'are now in a great degree nervous, but from whatever cause they arise the effects of them seem very serious...'

Sarah Rice died in Dover in 1841 aged eighty-six, a well-known and much respected citizen of the town. Her death was reported in the *Dover Chronicle* of 4th December, 1841 – 'the much respected mother of our excellent representative', and her funeral a week later in the unctuous style of the time, describing the five mourning coaches moving slowly through the streets of the town, thronged with spectators, to the family vault in St Mary's Church.

> It afforded us true gratification [the report continued] to witness the universal testimony of regret and respect manifested on this occasion. Throughout the long line of procession the shops were closed, and the large mass of

spectators bore witness to the warm interest felt by all… in the body of the Church we observed many of the most respectable of our townspeople, anxious to pay their last tribute of respect to one so deservedly esteemed by the town in general…

On 10th January of the following year, Samuel Latham wrote in a letter to Edward Royds Rice, '…I do not know when I have been more annoyed and surprised than on perusing on Saturday the Article in the *Dover Chronicle* to which you allude, and really thought Fenton must have lost his senses.'

The article that gave rise to this indignant response had appeared in the *Dover Chronicle* on 8th January, under 'Local Intelligence'; it was by a Mr Sherwill, a local antiquary, and was entitled 'Forgetfulness'. It described how an old lady, in 'enjoyment of every earthly good', had come across an indigent old man on the South Pier at Dover, in the depths of winter, shivering for want of an overcoat. She had promised to raise a subscription amongst her friends, 'during the card-parties of [the] winter', to buy him one. Many persons contributed their half-crowns and shillings, the old lady died, the man did not get his coat, and the subscribers did not have the satisfaction of seeing their 'mites' protecting him from the cold. Apparently the identification with Madame Rice was clear to everyone, hence the indignation of Edward and her old friend Samuel Latham, who attributed the libel to 'some Marine Parade Tory…' to damage the paper and to annoy you and your friends.' It was a highly improbable story, that a wealthy old lady who could well afford to buy twenty greatcoats out of her own pocket, would allow the object of her benevolence to languish through two cold winters while she collected florins from her friends and acquaintances. To us it is a storm in a teacup, but how the old lady must have turned in her grave to have the financial integrity of herself or her heirs and executors thus impugned!

Dane Court and its Owner

The house to which Edward Rice brought his bride in the November of 1818 was a modest Georgian manor house just outside the village of Tilmanstone, in Kent, about seven miles from Dover. Its situation is picturesque, the house sits in a hollow surrounded by low tree-clad hills; until the devastation caused by the gales of 1987 the grounds boasted a great deal of fine timber, especially an avenue of lime trees, and even now, in an area mainly agricultural, copses and woods of deciduous trees diversify the landscape. Caroline Cassandra, one of the Rices' five daughters, has left scraps of reminiscences and biographical material, and she points out that many of the houses of east Kent were built in low-lying and sheltered spots, partly to gain protection from the prevailing south-west gales, and also 'with a view to concealment', that area being more susceptible than most to invasion.

In the early nineteenth century the house, rectangular in outline and deeper than its modest frontage would indicate, was stuccoed and whitewashed and liberally festooned with creepers. Later, under the brisk naval regime of the oldest son and heir, Admiral Sir Edward Bridges Rice, (who enjoyed a certain degree of *folie de grandeur*) the house was stripped and refaced with red brick, and extensively enlarged, although the number of regular occupants had sunk to himself, his wife and his only son. Records reveal that he mortgaged his son's property as well as his own to carry out these alterations, no doubt considered desirable and even necessary at the time, though deplored by later generations.

Pevsner suggests that the main core of the house dates from about 1742. The facades of the front entrance and the garden front are classically Georgian, with two storeys of generous sash windows and a steep tiled roof bearing a row of dormer windows, and an imposing pillared doorway with niches occupied by classical statues.

Extensive outbuildings and kitchen premises of an earlier date in a mellow red brick confirm the belief that the main building stands on the site of an earlier house. Caroline Cassandra reported that during repairs to some older part of the building at the beginning of the nineteenth century, a book dated 1530 was found. In the time of the Civil War, Dane Court was owned by Richard Fogge, whose family memorials can be seen in Tilmanstone Church; he was a supporter of the Royalist cause, and in common with many of his contemporaries, such as the Verneys of Claydon, lost and suffered much during that terrible time.

Other subsequent owners of the house included Hattons, who no doubt were connected with the Finch-Hattons of Eastwell Park, near Godmersham, a family which later formed a closer attachment to the Rice family when George Hatton, the 10th Earl of Winchilsea, married Fanny, Edward and Lizzie's oldest daughter.

The main preoccupation, and indeed the profession of the new owner of Dane Court was the care of his farms and his property which he was continually extending by the purchase of neighbouring land. There is evidence that the family in this way was making a determined effort to reject the elements of trade and commercialism in its background.[1] Sarah, Edward's mother, was born in Whitechapel,

---

[1] Elizabeth Rice at a later date deplored her family's connection with the Portal family, whom she considered vulgar and ostentatious, though

not, even then, the most genteel of neighbourhoods, and Edward Rice's Aunt Bridget Rice married a fishmonger in St Clement Dane's called Richard George. Perhaps the dislike, even abhorrence expressed by some of her grand-children of Madame Sarah Rice arose from her unabashed involvement in business and financial affairs, which perhaps embarrassed them as their connections grew ever more aristocratic; that involvement, incidentally, which had made possible in the first place the lifestyle of Dane Court – the lifestyle of country gentlefolk with their stake exclusively in the land. To complete the dissociation Edward Rice dissolved the banking partnership with Samuel Latham in 1836.

---

perhaps not so excessively as her sister Fanny, just as her grandmother Cassandra Austen (Jane Austen's mother) had done in 1825. When Elizabeth's brother, William Knight married Caroline Portal in that year, old Mrs Austen commented, '...well, my dear, only think of old Joe Portal's daughter marrying my grandson!' Joe Portal was the grandson of a French emigré but he had married a Miss Hasker, whose parents kept a marine store and clothing shop in Portsmouth, a connection which made him and his family socially suspect. In 1875, Elizabeth's son Charles Augustus married his cousin Adela Mary Margaretta Knight, whose mother the second wife of Edward Knight II, was another, younger daughter of 'old Joe Portal'. Elizabeth did not attend the wedding (though she did not disapprove of it) but wrote in comment, '...I have no respect for *nouveaux riches* and take no interest in crimson velvet gowns or ruby lockets consequent on them... and I have always been sorry that the family is so involved with them – any set of people where Portals are the finest must be at a lowish ebb...'

There is in the Rice archive a bill for a large quantity of French wine due from the Rev. Henry Rice to the firm of Austen, Maunde, wine merchants! (6th June 1805 or 3, the handwritten account is obscure.) This can be none other than the partnership of Henry Austen, Jane's brother, and his friends Maunde and Tilson, whose bank foundered in 1816. The fact that no other hint or record of this probably brief excursion into commerce has ever been found, emphasises the impression that such ventures were frowned upon by the family. If their other customers were as slow as the Rev. Henry Rice to settle their accounts, the firm may well have been short-lived.

Thus Edward's life was spent farming his land and supervising his tenanted farms, hunting and shooting on every possible occasion, and from 1836, active as Liberal Member of Parliament for Dover. He held the seat for twenty years, in spite of his firm refusal to resort to bribery to win votes, as his wife bears witness in more than one account of their electioneering together. In July 1852 she reported to her daughter Louisa:

> I had such a nice drive in the Phaeton yesterday with Papa and Ba [Lionel, the youngest of the fifteen children, then ten years old] we went to Ringwould through Sutton to look up 4 or 5 Dover voters – 2 gave their votes directly, 2 would not promise wh. of course means that whoever pays for them will have them and the other boldly said he must have remuneration for his, so we only got 2.

Since the Reform Act of 1832, with the increase in the numbers of independent but not very prosperous voters, bribery continued to be very common; one admits to a certain degree of sympathy for the sturdy voters in the confrontation with Edward reported by his grandson – he wrote:

> Mr Rice had one or two amusing experiences when he was a Member of Parliament for Dover. On one occasion a deputation of voters came to see him and said that they would very much like him to be their member. He thanked them for their good wishes and hoped that they would vote for him. But this did not seem to satisfy them. They said that they were anxious to vote for him, but wanted a little en-

couragement. He asked them what sort of encouragement they meant, and they said, 'Well, Sir, the other side are giving £5 encouragement but we would very much like to vote for you, and so we will do it for £4.' I never heard who they voted for. The Dover views on the ethics of bribery were not perhaps legal, but I think quite logical. Another man on whom my grandfather called to ask for his vote said 'Yes, Sir, I am quite ready to vote for you, but what will you give me for it?' My grandfather replied that he was afraid he could not give him anything. To which the man said, 'Well, now Sir, look here, you are a rich man, you have a country house, you come to Dover driving a pair of horses, you have got all you can want. I have nothing in the world but this vote. You come and ask me to give it to you for nothing, and then I suppose you will go away and call yourself a gentleman.'

Edward Rice never allowed personal interest to influence his actions as a Member of Parliament. With his close knowledge of local trade and the packet service in Dover, he became their leading advocate in the House, and was able to help them in many ways, as when he persuaded the Administration to support one of the Harbours of Refuge built for naval and commercial shipping in the late '40s. These activities ensured solid support from the voters, but in other areas he was his own man, as in his support for a Government grant to Maynooth Catholic Seminary in Ireland, which evoked an angry round robin from a large number of his supporters. The reaction of his friend and future son-in-law Lord Winchilsea, a rabid anti-Papist, must have been explosive. Edward's energy and integrity were further endorsed when a proposal was put forward that he should be appointed Speaker of the House of Commons. Fortunately, this never came to anything, as, in spite of his physical vigour, he was the victim of considerable nervous tension when serious decisions had to be made, as letters of his children and of Elizabeth testify, which made the periods of electioneering times of great domestic strain. He was High Sheriff of the County in 1839, a high honour and indicative of the general respect with which he was regarded.

In 1846 his conscience dictated that he should vote for the repeal of the Corn Laws – 'This will be the ruin of you, my boy,' he declared to his oldest son, 'but I cannot in conscience do otherwise.' His son considered that the cost of freight would keep the price of imported grain sufficiently high to render home-grown produce competitive, and in this he was right, at least for some years.

Edward Rice was the youngest of Sarah's three sons, being born in 1789, sixteen years after the birth of the eldest, John, an isolating factor which no doubt contributed to the energetic independence of action which characterised his life. His brothers had been at school at Westminster, but he was sent to a private tutor, who was reported to have been the tutor to Princess Charlotte. At the age of eighty-eight, 'with memory much impaired', he said, 'I must record as my opinion that the disadvantages of a small private school are very great – as boys are often sent there as being unfit for any other school to the great injury of their companions.' That such evil influences had little effect upon him is emphasised when we learn that later when entered as a commoner of St John's College, Oxford, he found the habits of hard drinking amongst the undergraduates there so little to his taste, that he asked for, and obtained permission to transfer to Worcester College; his friends, mostly from Christchurch, would mockingly take a post-chaise to visit him in his isolation.

Edward was a very respectable scholar, worked hard, and was disappointed not to obtain a first-class degree. His great delight, however, was physical exercise, running and walking huge distances in his youth, and riding all his active life. An incident he recounted with pride took place in about 1816 when Louis XVIII left his exile in London to return to Paris, accompanied by about 'five hundred gentlemen'. The route all the way to Dover was *en fete*, but the gentlemen dropped off one by one as their horses or they themselves tired, until only Edward Rice and one other remained. This latter said, 'Well, Sir, I think my horse is as fresh as yours.' To which Rice replied, 'True, but I have a fresh horse awaiting me at Rochester.' So he was the only gentleman left to witness the sight of the vastly corpulent monarch being swung aboard the waiting ship seated on a chair at the end of a crane. He must sometimes have thought ruefully of that sight in later years; in 1862 at the age of seventy-two he fell downstairs and injured his spine. His legs remained paralysed and his arms partially so, but he contrived to fend off total inactivity by having himself, seated in a special chair, swung into a small pony carriage by means of a hoist kept by the front door. His grandson reported that 'he had a particular objection to be seen swinging in the air by his grandchildren, but we occasionally managed to hide behind a corner of the house, and get a glimpse of the performance.' At over nineteen stone, he must have been an impressive spectacle. In this trap, driven by himself, he travelled all over the neighbourhood, and to Dover, often at breakneck speed, and survived many a tumble, bellowing loudly until help came to pick him up, whereupon he would resume his journey. He survived this catastrophic accident sixteen years, his friend and physician claiming that he did not die sooner because he refused to do so 'until the last possible moment.'

Along with his physical energy went great physical courage and a hot temper, slow to flare up and quick to subside. The former is exemplified by his handling of a large mob of nearly 2,000 men during machine-breaking riots, who had assembled on Barham Downs, probably in 1839, a year he was High Sheriff. Accompanied only by a groom, he set off as night was falling, and rode slowly into the midst of them, talked to them and warned them of a troop of (fictitious) cavalry he had summoned, and persuaded them to disperse quietly to their several villages.

His temper, being kept firmly under control, was the more effective when it was given free rein. When some of his sons had been shooting over land occupied by a tenant farmer, one of them had the ill luck or bad marksmanship to pepper the farmer's son with shot, though without very serious consequences. Although Mr Rice was extremely apologetic and conciliatory to the farmer, he refused to be mollified and kept repeating, 'If it had been anyone else's son, he would have been in gaol by this time.' The Squire's control finally gave way, and he propelled his wheelchair at full speed straight at the farmer, bellowing, 'Get out of the room, Sir!' The farmer, alarmed at this juggernaut bearing down upon him, leapt back, and fell into a large mahogany wine cooler, out of which he hastily scrambled and fled from the house.

The Duke of Wellington, in spite of being a staunch Tory, was an admirer and supporter of Edward Rice. When Edward stood as a Liberal candidate for Dover the Duke would not countenance sponsoring a Tory candidate to oppose him. 'No, no,' he said, 'can't do better...' Their acquaintance went back further than the Duke's tenure of the Wardenship of the Cinque Portes, with his seat at Walmer Castle. After Waterloo, when the Duke was in

Paris as Commander-in-Chief, it will be remembered that Edward and his mother graced his court. Edward's daughter, Caroline Cassandra, who of all his daughters was most devoted to him, proudly described how he was selected with three more of the handsomest men in Paris, to open one of the Duke's balls with four of the handsomest ladies in a dazzling quadrille. But he had received no invitation, owing to the jealous dislike of one of the Duke's aides. It was only because of a chance meeting with the Duke out hunting that the omission was rectified, and he was able to open the ball, resplendent in fancy dress, with his mother's Indian diamonds in his hat.

Edward Rice was evidently a man who, though intelligent and well-educated, found action and the straightforward routines of running an estate and his farms a lot easier than decision-making about personal and political issues. His anxieties about whether to stand again at each successive election threw him into such a state of nervous indecision as to reduce his whole family to a condition of unsettled wretchedness. Part of a letter which Louisa wrote to her brother Edward when the latter was serving in Burma as Flag-Captain in his Uncle Charles Austen's ship HMS *Hastings* gives a picture of the general turmoil which prevailed during an election campaign.

> Dearest Mama has made a little progress perhaps since I wrote, but not much, she has had no proper chance yet so many people have unfortunately pushed in at different times. John Deedes rode over to breakfast and spent the day Tuesday – and Brook [Bridges] called – and Cptn. Fay and Louisa – and stayed that evening until this morning – Sir Edward Dering has been here, canvassing though all day – he is so ridiculous and cheerful and

amusing – he has been of some use in advising Papa – though after all I am afraid his principle [sic] advice won't be followed. Lord Chelsea began canvassing Tuesday, and Papa after wretched indecisions and settlings which made him feel quite ill went down there yesterday at Bass's (his agent) request, to canvass, or, as he meant to do, if he could, get out of it – and issue an address saying so which Sir E.D. said he could perfectly honourably do and no one would say a word, not even the Dover Liberals, though they would, of course, hate it. He says, and so do all, that they use Papa very ill, and ungrateful in not bringing him in for nothing – so they do, very, if they want him to stand. When he got there yesterday he found about 60 of his committee assembled which he did not expect, but Bass said he had been obliged to do, and of course they must take measures to fight now. Papa has sent early in the morning to Goodnestone for Morland [his son, a Fellow of Magdalen College, Oxford] to meet him at Dover, which he did, and he (Papa says) and all the Committee managed to persuade him not to give up, so he set forth with a long tail, he says, to canvass, hating it – he didn't get back till about half-past eight and kept Sir E.D. …who bothered over at 2, starving – poor Papa was very tired and very low – but Sir E.D. chimed in very well and was so cheerful and cheering I was very glad he was there – G.C.O. [Oxenden] was in fits at him all dinner time… at his election anecdotes and advice – he is so grave all the time…

This morning at half-past 8 Papa drove off to go on canvassing or make one final effort to give it up – which we feel sure he will not do – so you may feel sure he is going on – he will have at least ten days canvassing he says – Mama thinks he will be beaten – I don't – but as the election won't take place for some time I hardly know what it is worthwhile to say – don't say in a letter to Augustus or anybody that might repeat it to their friends, that he might be beaten, it seems nonsense saying anything – but you know how wonderfully particular he is and how he cares for what everybody and anybody says – he really does want to give it up now, I am sure…

An important factor in Edward's decisions about continuing to serve in Parliament was the influence he could, or thought he could exert on the careers of his sons in the services. Promotion was still very much a question of wealth or of patronage and influence, and every ounce of pressure he could apply in appropriate quarters to ensure the advancement of his sons he felt it his duty to do. When a Liberal government was in power, his influence was the more effective, but even in opposition he would have useful access to the 'corridors of power'. The situation was no doubt exacerbated by the comparative shortage of money to help advance the family in their careers; they all had their own way to make and the girls had to be provided for. It was a catch twenty-two situation, as an election campaign night cost as much as £1,000 (a fact bewailed by the boys writing to each other from their different ships and stations round the world) and membership of the Commons, unsalaried as it of course was, was an expensive privilege, including the cost of a London house, travelling and many other items of expense.

The family, exchanging letters in the mid-fifties, dreaded the possibility that Dane Court might have to be sold, or at least let, as their father's expenses mounted and his income dwindled. It never quite came to that, and in 1878, by great good fortune, every surviving member of his family was at Dane Court to stand around the graveside and bid their father farewell. Their father they all respected, admired and loved, their mother evoked even deeper feelings of devotion, but 'the Court of the Danes', as they facetiously called their home, claimed roots of the being of each individual which age and change seemed powerless to eradicate and resulted in a really remarkable 'colonisation' of the neighbourhood by a large number of the members of the family until death claimed the survivors well after the end of the First World War.

Elizabeth Rice: the Early Years

The early months of the married life of the young couple must have been very busy with wedding visits – the relations and friends of both families, particularly the Knights, were extremely numerous in Kent and Hampshire – and with settling in to their new home, and arranging everything to their satisfaction. Elizabeth sometimes found it lonely by herself after the bustle and company of Godmersham; her daughter Caroline Cassandra left a notebook with extracts from Edward's diary which showed he hunted nearly every day in the season, and of course he would be out on his property much of the time. Elizabeth was anxious to have the company of one or other of her sisters, but her grandmother Lady Bridges sternly put a stop to that; young married people, she declared, must depend upon each other for company, and not be reliant on visits from outsiders. (We do know, however, that Fanny was at Dane Court in March 1819, accompanied by the nurse, Sackree.) And of course, very soon a baby was on the way. In the years between 1819 and 1844 Elizabeth produced fifteen healthy children and seems to have had some miscarriages as well. The mortality rate amongst women as a result of childbearing was still at this time lamentably high, as an inspection of the records of any family will show. Amongst Jane Austen's generation, Elizabeth, mother of the eleven Knight children, died in 1808 after the birth of her eleventh child, and the first wives of both Frank and Charles Austen died in childbirth. Mary, wife of Frank, died after her eleventh confinement in 1823, Fanny, wife of Charles, as the result of her fourth in 1814. It is not clear how Anne, the wife of James Austen, the oldest of Jane Austen's brothers, died, at the age of thirty-six in 1795; she was six years older than her husband, so already rather old for childbearing when she gave birth to Anna in 1793. An account quoted by Professor Honan describes how she was suddenly taken ill when quietly at home with her husband, and he, after giving her an emetic, summoned the doctor who arrived only to find she had already died; he diagnosed a sudden rupture of the liver (for which one would think an emetic was not the ideal treatment).[1] There was no report of illness prior to her death, and she could of course have been in the early stages of pregnancy. In the next generation, amongst the Knight family, young Edward Knight's first wife, Mary Dorothea, died in 1838 at the birth of her seventh child, and Caroline, first wife of William Knight, at the birth of her eighth. One Knight daughter, Cassandra, who married Lord George Hill, died in childbirth in 1842, leaving four children, at the age of thirty-six. All these women, with the exception of Anne Austen, who probably died of other causes, were well under the age of forty, Fanny Austen only twenty-five. One is inevitably reminded of some of Jane Austen's remarks, especially on the efficacy of 'the simple regimen of separate rooms', and her sad comment on her niece Anna Lefroy – 'poor animal, she will be worn out before she is thirty. I am very sorry for her.'[2] One remembers too her advice to the other niece she loved, Elizabeth's sister Fanny – 'Do not be in a hurry... by not beginning the business of mothering quite so early in life, you will be young in Constitution, spirits, figure and

[1] Park Honan, *Jane Austen, Her Life*, (p.103).
[2] J.A. *Letters*, (no.141, p.483), ed. Chapman, OUP.

countenance, while Mrs William Hammond is growing old by confinements and nursing…'[3]

Elizabeth Rice must be considered fortunate indeed to have survived such a long period of continuous childbearing with her health apparently unimpaired. But it is not surprising that she felt apprehensive as the time for her first confinement approached. Edward was visiting his brothers-in-law at Chawton for the shooting, leaving Lizzie at Godmersham; he wrote her an encouraging letter, which at the same time reveals something of the current ignorance of what were the greatest hazards of childbearing, that is, the lack of any sort of antisepsis and elementary medical hygiene. It is not likely that Elizabeth's mother died, as he suggested, of a cold, almost certainly she succumbed to puerperal fever or from some other infection related to her confinement.

> Chawton, Friday morning. September 4th
> 1819
>
> My dearest Lizzy,
> I have this moment received your letter and will not go out till I have answered it not to scold you I assure you but to endeavour to make your mind easier if I can by convincing you that you can have nothing more to fear than any other woman in a similar situation and much less than many who have not the good health you have and from various causes of deformity etc. have reason to dread danger in their confinements – you have very good sense and if you would exert yourself I think it

---

[3]Ibid., (no.142, p.488).

would prevent your suffering from anything approaching to Superstition.

Do not be angry with me, my dear Lizzy, for making use of the word, but what you say about your Mother's death is very like it – hers I understand was caused by catching cold after her confinement,[4] otherwise she could have had little to fear after having had eleven children – you have been so well as yet that there has been some difficulty in making you take sufficient care of yourself. I have every hope that you will be equally well in your confinement – above all things, my dear Liz, recollect that nothing will tend so much to assist you through yr suffering (I fear there must be) as keeping up your spirits. If it will be of any comfort to you to have me back sooner than Saturday I will come *at a moment's notice*.

We have had no rain till last night, I have shot very badly and there is no scent, my new gun misses fire about every other shot – I must give it up – I like Chawton very much indeed, we have everything both here and at the Cottage as comfortable as possible. I am afraid we disarrange your Grandmother's dinner hour by dining at ½ past five and 6 o'clock, but she is good enough to say she does not mind it.

He concluded:

---

[4]Diana Dick, *Yesterday's Babies*; Bodley Head, 1987. '...childbirth fever was a very real threat for several more weeks... the fever was always heralded by violent shivering attacks, and it was assumed in such cases the mother must have caught cold.'

you are wrong my dearest Love if you suppose
'as a man' that I do not fear your suffering but
at the same time I am satisfied I have every
reason to have the best hopes of your doing
well – pray be of good cheer – yr. ever affect.
E.Rice

The next day Edward wrote again, and referred to several
members of the Chawton community; Elizabeth was still at
Godmersham, where the baby was to be born.

Chawton September 5th 1819

My dearest Lizzy,

I was very glad to receive your letter this
morning written in better spirits than your
last. I wish you could get rid of the pain in
your face. We are this moment come from
Church and as soon as I have finished this
epistle are going to call on Mrs Digweed, Mr
Papillon etc. – we have not had such good
sport shooting as George and William appear
to have had – Edward has shot very well, I
have always shot badly but never I think so
badly as this year – we have fagged uncommonly hard and are not at all sorry to have a
Day's rest today. You ask me how I like Miss
Lloyd[5] I am sorry I cannot return her the
compliment of admiring her in any way...
Your Aunt Cassandra begs you will tell Mrs F.
Austen that the parcel arrived safe yesterday –
that the children, baby and all are well and that

---

[5]Martha Lloyd, who had lived with the Austen ladies ever since the death
of the Rev. George Austen in 1805. In 1828 she married Francis Austen
as his second wife.

she will write herself in a Day or two. Adieu my dearest Lizzy, yr. ever affect. E.Rice,

(Crossing) – since I wrote the other three sides Edward and myself have been to Mr Papillon's, Mr Digweed and the Cottage – at Mr Papillon's we saw a niece of his with a very good pair of eyes[6] and Miss Parker, we have also been to see the Great Oak at the end of the Gravel Walk I really think Chawton very pretty, your Father must convert the House, tell him I will contract to do it very cheap. My love to Fanny, Maryanne etc. Mr Wharton's little dog is barking – adieu, I shall expect a letter from you on Tuesday morning and will write two lines to you on that day to tell you what will be our plan of returning – I hope not through Town for we spent so much on eating that I cannot afford it again. Respecting the name of the lady or gentleman who is expected we will talk of that before she arrives. I am very glad your Father stands Godfather I asked my Mother some time since to stand Godmother and she said she would.

We hear finally of the successful outcome of the confinement (the birth of Edward Bridges Rice, later Admiral Sir Edward, on 30th October) in a long letter Fanny Knight wrote to her cousin Fanny Cage. Fanny Cage and her sister Sophia were the daughters of Elizabeth Austen's older sister, another Fanny, and her husband Lewis Cage, both of whom had died; the orphaned sisters lived at Goodnestone Farm with their grandmother, Lady Bridges. This letter also discusses two of Fanny Knight's suitors familiar to readers

[6]No doubt this was Eleanor Jackson, whom Henry Austen was to marry in April 1820 as his second wife.

of Jane Austen's letters – John Plumptre, long rejected but still evidently a little bit hankered after, and the more lively James Wildman (my savage Consort) of Chilham Castle, who, as Aunt Jane diagnosed in 1817, continued to blow hot and cold. It also rather charmingly exemplifies the twenty-six year old Fanny's tendency to rather wordy philosophising! After apologising to her cousin for failing to respond with sufficient feeling to the news of the death of a mutual acquaintance at Goodnestone, she continued:

> what a difference a few miles makes in the current of one's ideas and the subjects that interest us most! proximity has more to do with everybody's feelings than anybody imagines and it is mortifying to reflect that one's dearest friend from whom one has been separated long would probably be less affected by one's loss than by the death of a common acquaintance or event or servant in the same house! Well, be it so, all is ordained for the best that regards the fascination of the human mind and if we were suffered to feel equally for misfortunes absent and present, past or future, where would be the end or who could calculate the sum of human misery?

She then recounted an anecdote about James Wildman of Chilham Court, who had been her 'savage Consort' at a party on Twelfth Night, when she was Queen of the Revels. She assured her cousin that he would never be her consort 'in reality', although 'he began sighing at me most manfully the other day – the hot fit is on just now, but I know by experience it will not last long, and I have no intention of fanning the flame.'[7]

> But my dearest Fanny [she continued] the agitation of all agitations you may easily imagine was occasioned by my darling Lizzy! never shall I forget what she went through, and never shall I forgive you if you tell people so. I was in the next room during the worst, and heard everything and the impression it made upon me will never be effaced I think. Poor sweet darling, I hope she thinks she now has ample amends, but I own, Fanny, I who always doated upon everything belonging to babies must acknowledge I would rather forgo the happiness of becoming a mother than have to endure what must be endured to accomplish it. I could not for the world have anybody but yourself know how miserable it made me because it is the sort of thing people always think it witty to laugh at or take lightly – but I literally have not been myself in body or in mind since, and instead of the joy one is supposed to feel on such occasions the irritability of my mind has been such that I have almost hated all the congratulatory letters

[7] J.A. *Letters* (no.140, p.179) 'Mr J.W. frightens me – he will have you. I see you at the Altar. I have some faith in Mrs C. Cage's observations, and still more in Lizzie's; and besides I know it must be so. He must be wishing to attach you. It would be too stupid and too shameful in him, to be otherwise; and all the family are seeking your acquaintance. Do not imagine that I have any real objection, and I like Chilham Castle for you; only I do not like that you should marry anybody.' Also letter no.141, 'I have pretty well done with Mr Wildman. By your description he cannot be in love with you, however he may try at it, and I could not wish the match unless there were a great deal of love on his side...'

which have arrived, and have been more disposed to despair than to rejoice. This you will perceive to be a great weakness and to have been in itself an excuse for deferring as long as possible writing confidentially – commonplace letters I could scribble off out of my head but my heart would not open till its acuteness had a little subsided and now I shall be all the better for having written this to you... She is going on very well and has indeed a lovely baby – the upper part of its face is rather Rice-ish, but the nose, mouth and chin will be like Lizzy's and it is altogether such a nice clean-looking child, so good and amiable and strong and healthy, that one quite doats upon it, and of course she thinks it perfect. She has sat up twice for more than an hour on the Sopha of an evening, but she is very weak though in the fairest possible way of amendment and makes an excellent nurse.

Fanny then reverted to her own personal affairs:

Many thanks for your Plumptre details – I had been longing for them, and they were most interesting but very surprising to me... My greatest comfort was always as you know the idea of his happiness, and to hear from you on whom I can depend not only for the truth, but for the truth unexaggerated, unadulterated, that he is so far otherwise – and also that he seemed to avoid speaking of me, and alluding to past events, produced such a revolution in my mind and caused such extraordinary sensations that I can hardly yet think of it with composure![8]

How amused would her Aunt Jane have been at this further example of Fanny's 'delicious play of mind', and her 'provoking and interesting' character. John Plumptre's reported unhappiness was not, one surmises, a source of unmitigated grief to her.

Fanny, who had been restless and changeable for so many years, was not to remain single for much longer; but surprisingly, she did not choose any of the eligible young suitors who had been in pursuit of her over the years. In October 1820 she married a widower, Sir Edward Knatchbull, 9th Baronet of Mersham-le-Hatch and Provender, Kent. He was born in 1781, which made him twelve years older than Fanny. His first wife had been Annabella Honeywood of Elvington, a village very near Tilmanstone, and she had died, leaving him with six children. At the age of sixteen, Fanny had written to her Governess Miss Chapman, that she was 'an inveterate enemy of second marriages, particularly if there is any family.' Now she wrote to her,

> If you have heard that I am engaged to be married to Sir Edward Knatchbull I am now writing to confirm that intelligence and I need not add that it gives my family the greatest satisfaction and that with a man of his excellence of character my prospect of as much

[8] John Plumptre had married in 1818 Catherine Mathilda Methuen of Corsham in Wiltshire, and settled at Fredville, near Dane Court, where the Rice family and his were very intimate; the Plumptres and the Knights were connected by marriage through the Bridges; at a later date William Plumptre became Lord Fitzwalter, resuming a lapsed title.

238

> comfort as this world can bestow is well-
> founded and I trust not unreasonable.[9]

So the vacillating Fanny, whom her Aunt Jane had called 'Silly and Sensible, commonplace and eccentric, Sad and Lively, Provoking and Interesting,' voluntarily accepted a renewal of a role which had been forced upon her a dozen years earlier when her mother died. There is no reason to suppose that it was not a love match, in spite of Fanny's unecstatic report to Miss Chapman, and the very restrained style in which Sir Edward couched his letter of proposal to her – '…It is not from any professions which I can make that I shall venture to found any claim to your esteem. Allow me to say that you are the only person in whose Society I can find Happiness and to whose example and care I could entrust the welfare of my children.'[10]

In 1826 Fanny's brother Edward was to marry – by elopement – her oldest stepdaughter, Mary Dorothea Knatchbull, which made Edward his sister's stepson-in-law! Some of the family found the situation shocking, including Fanny, though her disapproval was of shorter duration than that of her husband, who never forgave his daughter, and for eleven years did not speak to her.

Fanny produced no children for several years, and then, from 1825, when her first daughter Fanny Elizabeth was born, added nine more to the first family of six. Her husband died in 1849, leaving her to a lengthy widowhood of thirty-three years; of her nine children, six died before her, three in their twenties, so her life had more than its fair share of sorrow. But on 24th October 1820, Godmersham saw another happy wedding day, two years almost to the

[9]Knatchbull Papers, Kent Archives Office, Maidstone.
[10]Ibid. For more particulars regarding Fanny's engagement and progression towards a true affection for her betrothed, see Margaret Wilson, *Almost Another Sister*; Kent C.C., Arts and Libraries.

day after Elizabeth's. Elizabeth wrote an account of it to her brother Henry, a letter one would much like to read, but only Henry's reply survives. Henry was twenty-three, a junior officer in the 8th Light Dragoons, and was stationed at King's Lynn. He thanked his 'delicious Lizzy' for her 'exquisite account of the memorable 24th... I should like to have been there amazingly, ...how excellent of Fanny not to howl throughout the business – see what it is to be good!' His cheerful letter is full of descriptions of guns, shooting and horses, dinners in Lynn, 'middling – better than dining alone' – and a ball, where, after staying nearly half an hour he 'retreated without shaking a leg – at which the *mères de familles* were pleased to do me the honour to express their indignation to Mrs Richardson, remarking that 'he does not come to the ball then to secure pretty partners, but only to show off his own figure' – I dined with this lady the next day (whose daughters are the prettiest girls in the town, and reckoned great beauties here, I think them very moderate indeed) and as there was music in the evening and a he voice sadly wanted I lent my aid, and fortunately as well as singularly, with some success – at least, so they were good enough to signify to me – and thereby, I completely established myself in the good graces of the above dame...'

A month after Fanny's marriage, Elizabeth gave birth to a daughter, Fanny Margaretta, and almost exactly a year later, a second son, Henry, was welcomed in a letter to his son-in-law by Edward Knight senior from Chawton House:

> Your most welcome letter received this morning [he wrote] occasioned universal joy at our breakfast table, and I now send you our most hearty united congratulations on the safety of our dearest Lizzy and the birth of

your second son with the sincerest wishes that the future reports we are to expect may be as satisfactory as these we have received today. Marianne is already as anxious to nurse her little Nephew as if it were the first she had ever had, and I have received more kind messages for Lizzy, than in her present state it is prudent for her to hear. – Six o'clock. William is just arrived as happy and as merry as a Grik, he passed his examinations yesterday, came by the coach to Winchester, and from there post, he looks very well, rather less thin than usual, we have just dined and celebrated the grand events of the day in some excellent Claret.

William was soon to take Orders, and became Rector of Steventon, where his father built for him a new rectory in place of that which had housed Jane Austen's family and that of her brother James.

The breakneck speed of child-producing in the Rice family now slowed down a little, the next child, a son, not being born until June of 1823. The interval enabled Elizabeth to pay a few visits, including one to London, in the hot June of 1822; it was intensely hot, and they soon moved to Kippington, near Sevenoaks, the home of Colonel Thomas Austen. Colonel Thomas was the grandson of Francis Austen, the solicitor of Sevenoaks, the uncle of Jane Austen's father George, who had befriended, educated and supported him after the death of his father. Mrs Thomas Austen was an old school friend of Lizzie's, née Marianne Morland. Lizzie wrote from here to her sister Marianne:

...I left very little regret for the pleasures of London behind me for really the heat was beyond anything I ever felt. I certainly enjoyed myself extremely whilst I was there though we made the most of our time. I hope your bonnet and Sophia's frightful hat will have arrived this morning. I hope you will like yours, I meant to have put your feathers into the Box, but it was nailed down before I knew anything about it, so I am afraid you must wait for them till we come ourselves.

The recipient of this letter was Elizabeth's younger sister by only a year; she never married, and survived all her siblings to die in 1896 at the age of ninety-five. She spent quite a lot of time at Dane Court, but made her home, after her father died, with successive brothers – Charles, and then John, and latterly chiefly in Ireland, where her two younger sisters, Cassandra and Louisa, became successively wives of Lord George Hill. Incidentally, the latter, when he wished to marry Louisa Knight after her sister Cassandra, his first wife, died, had to do so on the Continent, in order to circumvent the iniquitous Deceased Wife's Sister Act, which had come into force in 1835 – too late, fortunately, to deprive Charles Austen (the younger brother of Jane Austen) of the solace of marrying his sister-in-law Harriet Palmer, who had taken over his infant family after her sister's early death.

Marianne had the reputation of being 'very witty', invariably cheerful and good-humoured, and physically energetic, enjoying walks in pursuit of wild flowers and birds' nests, the seeking-out of which was a passion at Dane Court. 'Gadge, my love,' was her favourite exclamation. A photograph of her in late life shows a bright-eyed old lady in an old-fashioned bonnet secured under her chin by an enormous bow, revealing sausage-like ringlets clustered on each side of her face.

Henry Knight received a letter too from Kippington, although only his reply survives, '…I have resolved to take up my pen before I go, just to tell you that I have nothing at all to say,' which is indeed the case as the letter is filled with trivial family particulars, remarkable only for a prime piece of facetiousness relating to Uncle Henry Austen, brother to Jane, and his second wife.

> …of course, you have heard of Uncle Henry [Henry Austen] having attempted to poison his wife and so far succeeded that she was given over!! but she has of late made a sudden and unlooked-for recovery – he was in custody for two days, but stole 90 guineas of Mrs Heathcote who came to bring him something to eat with which he bailed himself and is now at large – I have George's authority for the circumstances down to 'recovery' and my own reasons for knowing the latter part to be equally true…

One is reminded, reading these letters, of some of the comments their Aunt Jane passed upon them in her letters, with their passion for horses and field sports, their affectionate and facetious gaiety, and the occasional indication of something more serious.

As the decade proceeded, the Rice babies continued to arrive at regular intervals, the incessant pregnancies enlivened by family visits. After probably a short period of nursing Elizabeth would be able to leave her baby in the charge of the nurse with the older children and the nursery staff, and enjoy a change of air and company, at Godmersham or at Mersham-le-Hatch, with her as yet childless sister Fanny. That Elizabeth did nurse her babies is indicated in Fanny's letter already quoted – 'she makes an excellent nurse'; breastfeeding was the only known deterrent to conception, apart from abstinence, and not, of course, a very reliable one. We learn from letters of Mrs George Austen (mother of Jane Austen) that it was the custom at least in the late eighteenth century when she was writing, to breastfeed a baby for a few months, and then put it out to a foster mother, having first weaned the baby onto 'pap', some soft and easily digested milky substance. All her children were thus disposed of in the village until they were about eighteen months old – and seemed none the worse for it. In 1773, five months after the birth of Cassandra, Mrs Austen wrote to her sister-in-law Mrs Hancock:

> I suckled my little girl through the first quarter, she has been weaned and settled at a good woman's at Deane, just eight weeks; she is very healthy and lively, and puts on her short petticoats today.

As Maggie Lane comments (*Jane Austen's Family*, Hale, p.58):

> In view of the high level of child mortality, and the inevitably inferior hygiene and living conditions of the labouring classes, it seems the Austens ran a terrible risk; but it was a risk that paid off, for their children came back remarkably hardy, and not one was lost at an early age.

The Austens, with a small Rectory, a growing family, and a houseful of the Rev. George's young pupils, were very pressed for space. In the case of the wealthier Rice family, however, with a large establishment and plenty of room, the babies remained at home.

Elizabeth was at Mersham with Fanny in August 1822 when Edward wrote to her from Calais, travelling doubtless on business connected with the family banking and cross-Channel packet service interests – his mother, very much the head of the family business affairs, was with him.

> My dearest Lizzy,
> I dined at Dane Court yesterday and found Fanny (not quite two) quite well – drove down to Dover late last night and had rather a rough passage over this morning, it would have been a fine day for sailing but there was nothing coming but old Smoky – who clawed over in about 3 hours and a half to my surprise. I found my Brother[11] here on his way to England but he is going to return with me as soon as we have devoured some Soules and cotelettes which are very invitingly on the Table by the bye. I will order some Soules to be sent to Hatch tomorrow morning…

By April 1823 Elizabeth was expecting her fourth child, who was to be born in June, a third son, named John Morland, after Edward Rice's lamented brother and after Elizabeth's friend Mrs Thomas Austen, née Morland. Her father Edward Knight wrote her a pleasant letter from Steventon, where he was supervising the building of the new Steventon Rectory, for his son William. Edward Knight I was, judging from his few letters and from general report, a man of great gentleness and singular sweetness of disposition, happy in his family and his estates. While he must have been efficient in the management of his prop-

---

[11]Edward Royds Rice's brother the Rev. Henry Rice. In 1819 he and his family had been compelled to leave England and live for a period in Dunkirk for financial reasons. (See Chapter Two, p.214.)

erty, and competent in handling business affairs – he survived a dangerous lawsuit, and heavy losses incurred when his brother Henry's bank failed – he probably lacked the intellectual ability of his brother James Austen, and the wit and sparkling humour of his brother Henry and his sister Jane. One surmises he was most like his brother Charles, the sailor; they were to die within a month of one another, each universally beloved.

Edward wrote:

> Trusting, my dearest Lizzie that you will prefer having a few lines from me to not hearing at all, I have taken my pen to chat with you a short time before I begin my morning's ride. I drove William here yesterday, and I propose taking him home again to a late dinner today, after finishing the various business I have planned for the morning. I had time yesterday after service partly to inspect his new mansion, which makes a splendid appearance, the Walls both inside and out will be finished this week, and the Roof, which is already framed in the Meadow, put on in the course of the next. I am very well satisfied with such of the work as has been now done, as well as with the spot we have fixed on, but I feel quite …[illeg]… when I think how much it will cost and long for William to find a good rich wife to help furnish as well as fill his mansion. I have seen very little of Chawton yet, arriving there on Saturday near 5 o'clock, and leaving it yesterday before ten. I had a very cold journey from London, on the outside of the Alton coach and glad enough I was to get inside at Faversham, during a storm of snow. It has done me no

harm. I had a cold before, I don't think it is worse. William appears to be glad to have a Companion, and we shall have plenty of employment till the others arrive, in unpacking and putting to rights. My account of Louisa yesterday was so good that I felt very sanguine in my hopes of their being able to begin their journey on Thursday, as proposed, tho' I am aware that a further delay may be necessary, but I always like to hope for the best. I believe George liked my visit very much, and I was very glad to see his Chambers and mode of going on. I can now fancy all he is about, and I rejoice to see he is so much in earnest. I don't think very frequent visits from friends do him much good. I found your grandmother and Aunt Cassandra very much as I had left them in December, the cold winter does not appear to have injured either of them. We dined with them on Saturday, and repeat our visit tomorrow. I am sorry to hear from Aunt Louisa [his sister-in-law, Louisa Bridges] that Rice has got the Influenza, I trust it will be a slight attack and that you and the children will escape it, which is perhaps more than can be expected, but you have all my kindest and best wishes, and I shall be glad to hear from you whenever you feel disposed to write to me…

God bless you my dearest Liz, don't let Edward forget me [i.e., little Edward] ever yours most affectly. Edwd. Knight.

William did oblige his father by marrying, the first of the Knight brothers to do so, in 1825; his bride was Caroline Portal, a daughter of John Portal of Freefolk Priory in

Hampshire, (the 'old Jo Portal' of old Mrs Austen's wry exclamations) whose wealth was derived from trade. Many years later, William's older brother Edward was to marry her sister as his second wife. Elizabeth Rice shared her grandmother's reservations about the Portal *nouveau riche* style, but Jane Austen admired their fine eyes.

Elizabeth's daughter Elizabeth Louisa (Lou), destined to be her mother's lifelong support and companion, was born in the following month and a bare sixteen months later was followed by a third daughter, Marianne Sophia. Before the latter's birth Edward and Elizabeth managed a trip to Scotland with his mother and their old friend George Oxenden of Broome, Barham, one of the executors of old Henry Rice's will. They stayed at Braehaven, the home of the Duke of Montrose, and with other friends in Scotland. Elizabeth had a passion for beautiful scenery, particularly mountainous scenery, and revelled in the fine bracing air of the north, compared with the damps and mists she complained of in her corner of Kent.

But in spite of her complaints, her letters are full of enthusiastic descriptions of her garden, the sweet songs of the birds, the entrancing perfumes of the syringa and honeysuckles, and the enchantment of the woodland wild flowers. The forest and hedgerow birds that abounded in the garden and the park were a source of interest to all the family, and 'nesting' was a popular pursuit. Elizabeth also kept and bred cage birds and became something of an expert.

> I have just been nesting with Norah[12] [she wrote to her daughter Caroline in May 1850 from Godmersham Park] ...we only went

[12]Norah Hill, daughter of Lord George Hill and Cassandra Knight, who died in childbirth in 1842; Charlotte (b.1837) was the only daughter of Henry Knight and his wife Charlotte Worthey.

about the Piece and the Lime Walk and we carried the little ladder out of the Orange House with us... we found a good many and she found the most beautiful Golden Cresteds I ever saw, hanging at the end of a branch of a yew tree, down by the Piece – she is longing to come to Dane Court and I hope she will soon after you get home – she is taller than Charlotte and just like what she used to be – she likes nesting and reading better than anything – her hair is immensely thick and long – she wears it plaited in front like Louisa's and then joined to the back hair – I am so glad you like your music lessons and that you are going to have another fortnight of them – you and Marianne must practice singing together when you come home – she goes back with us on Monday and Morland comes home the next day – I am sorry you will miss so much of Cecil and so is he but it cannot be helped... The Park and Woods are more perfectly lovely than I can describe, the Cuckoo is cuckooing over the thatched seat and yesterday I heard it by the Tower when I was walking in the Park with Uncle George Hill...

Back home at Dane Court, with Caroline away visiting her Aunt Fanny Knatchbull, she reported on the state of the gardens:

I watered your garden before we walked last night and have been to see it this morning, the things in the new bed grow almost too strong, the mould is so rich, you can see nothing now but leaves and flowers all over it, the convolvuluses are beautiful, there were eight or ten flowers in full bloom on them just now, and plenty of Sweet pease blown and blue salvias, the rose geranium is immensely spread and the night-blowing stock and the carnations are blowing, one is nearly out, they are cloves – the jessamine has got one bunch of bloom out and three others are coming – the Venus looking-glass is beautiful, it looked so pretty this morning in the Rock work mixed with that little pink Deal flower – the Ranunculuses are not quite good ones I think and mine are just as bad – your Maria Leonida rose was quite covered with blights, till the day before yesterday when I syringed it all over, and cut off the brown buds – it looks better now a good deal, but not so healthy as it was – the East winds have blighted everything dreadfully – my Woolwich carnations in the fruit garden are blowing beautifully – there are two yellow with red edges, and some white with scarlet, and lake edges, I mean to raise as many young ones as I can from them and perhaps I may give you the ugliest some day if it seems likely to die – your little ass of a canary hen has laid 2 more eggs in the seed drawer, I have put them into the nest and hung it up again and given her a good box on the ear and now she is sitting on them… now I must leave off so Goodbye my dearest little Carry we all send our best love to self and Hatch.

At this time Elizabeth was a lively and active gardener, with her spraying and dead-heading and propagating, and her disciplining of contrary canaries. Later, chronic 'rheumatiz' and ill health kept her more confined and curtailed her active gardening, but she never lost her interest and involvement. The slightly caustic wit and teasing tone often comes through the expressions of anxiety about the health of members of the family; she is not fussy or carping, but her concern is often tempered with a humour which seems to distance her from her object – she is the reverse of sentimental. In the spring a few years later, her daughter Louisa was staying at Haverholme Priory in Lincolnshire with her sister Fanny Winchilsea, and Elizabeth wrote with a budget of family news, including the state of the garden:

> My dearest Lou, This is the first day I have felt really better and able to write so I am very thankful to tell you so and to discourse a bit – Leggatt's steel is doing me good and the S.W. wind still blows tho' it rains it pours and has all night. I went out yesterday but the wind was N.E. tho' the respirator kept it out of my chest it attacked my arms and hands and shoulders and I went to bed very painful and riz up much cured – Papa's cold is worse to-day and he mourns indoors and coughs more than he can and sips Barley water – he caught it in the Railway House having all his hair cut off and sitting without his hat in spite of my warnings – yesterday being a cold N.W. he shot cart to Ashley and sat there three hours looking at the burnt premises and measuring about with… and Sutton for new ones. Ernest and Flo are as happy as possible together, he goes about with his arm in a sling nesting and jumping over everything and helping in her garden – they read French together from 11 to

12. Walter draws a good deal, takes sketches of favourite places and colours them – his knees are better but he walks lame, Flo is most careful of me and devotes herself to darting about after open windows and doors and helps me in every possible way – I do not know about …(new maid) yet, she seems civil and zealous but I have learnt to distrust everybody – one is so taken in – I guess that she does everything pretty well and nothing very – the birds are singing so beautifully through the gently falling showers, if I was well I could find lots of nightingales' nests over close to the Iron gates in the garden. Eggledon has nearly finished 'bedding out' but he is as usual very idle about it – I do not know whether things smell sweeter here than anywhere else but the May which is profuse and the Persian lilacs and the Syringas which are just coming out are perfectly delicious – the gold and white of the buttercups and daisies is very superior…

The 'bedding out' was a very important annual routine for that part of the garden visible from the drawing-room windows, and in other letters Elizabeth described the operation, with the creation of the 'Pyramid', evidently a central display, perhaps of Canna lilies or other tall and sculptural plants, a Victorian concept now relegated to formal beds in municipal parks or roundabouts.

In April 1861 Elizabeth's brother William's daughter Elizabeth Caroline married the Rev. Robert Everson Harrisson; Elizabeth's daughter Louisa was present – no doubt at Steventon where William was Rector – and Elizabeth wrote to her with the usual catalogue of Dane Court news:

My dearest Lou,

Many thanks for your nice long letter of today, by the time you get this the wedding will be over and I hope happily and that nobody will have caught cold, if the weather is like this I don't see how anybody is to help it. I pity Uncle William more than I can say – there is only one thing worse than a wedding and that is a Funeral, but such things must be, only the seldomer the better, they will all miss Caroline very much, I am only glad that she has been spared to have a happy single life for so long and I am sorry Lady Jane Hope is so poorly, you do not say what is the matter with her. When the wedding is over she will be able to be mentally quiet as well as bodily, and I dare-say that is what she wants. [Lady Jane Hester Hope, widow of General Sir John Hope, was, or was to be, the third wife of William Knight]. Ernest and his lion arrived yesterday evening happy and well, I shall have no peace till it is gone, it flew at a hen yesterday and killed it in a twinkling, and sucked its blood with a low growl, and grinning teeth, little ass. It is only 4 months old, and it is not an African lion, but only an American one, or Puma, it likes Ernest and licks his hand and his head all over, it lives in the Owl house close to the barn. Walter and Ernest both go to Chawton tomorrow, the latter only for one night or perhaps two, on his way to the RN College Portsmouth – we shall be dullish 3 here till the 30th, I rather wish but only for the rheu-matism that we were going tomorrow. Papa and I went to Church yesterday – Ernest was much prized by Mrs Barker and all the Twiggs, he shook hands with the Governess mistaking her for Mrs T., for which I daresay they shut her up all the rest of the day – he went to see the old Harveys on the way home, to their great pleasure. Poor old Harry is worse and confined to the house, his breath is so short. Mr Leggatt says he may go on so for years but may die very suddenly... here comes Ernest leading his lion, he puts it up in the window-seat (out-of-doors) and it purrs and licks his face and his head all over and rubs it-self against him – he is more like Arthur in head and figure than anybody else. Our nightingale in Mount Pleasant is all we have heard as yet. The strawberry wood is too lovely to mention, Oxlips in every shade of gold have appeared all over it mixed with primroses. Caroline and I picked the most gorgeous bunch of them for the Drawing-room on Saturday and we have got a fresh basket of roses – this is as it should be... Goodbye, my dearest Lou...

Elizabeth's attitude to family weddings was rather strange, but consistent. There is no evidence about her reaction to the weddings of her daughters Fanny, Marianne and Florence; but she lamented when Marianne's daughter Blanche became engaged in the late 1870s to an entirely suitable young man called Anderson:

I can't write much [she wrote to Louisa] as I have already written to Blanche and to poor May, the sunshine of whose life is sadly dimmed by Anderson. I am very sorry indeed for it and hope it will make them all very happy – I have expected it of course for a long time – there seems to be nothing to recommend it except his being a very good man which is of course the first of things but does not doo instead of everything else …I am dreading Marianne's letter tomorrow I am afraid she will feel hurt at the very little I was able to express at Blanche's engagement – I am more reconciled to it today from Derby's nice letter to Papa in praise of the man, it is only on his and Marianne's account that I hate it – she will be such a loss to them, I never can be glad that any girl should marry who has such a happy home…

She was no doubt pleased when her sons married, though she did not attend their weddings, as far as we know. Of course, her brother William's position was a particularly sad one – in 1848 his second wife Mary and the three little daughters of that brief union were all carried off in an epidemic; his dependence on the surviving daughter by his first marriage must have been the more complete, at least until he married for the third time.

However, this is to anticipate chronologically the events of the family history; Elizabeth's family was at last complete with the birth in 1842 of Lionel Knight, more than twenty-two years after the birth of Edward Bridges. Five daughters and ten sons, with a large domestic staff, dogs, cats and canaries, not to mention pumas and other outdoor pets, must have filled Dane Court to bursting point, and created a cheerful and noisy confusion with continual goings and comings and endless activities.

The Rev. John Morland Rice, Fellow of Magdalen College, Oxford. The most scholarly of the family, his career was checked by the injuries sustained after a fall from his horse.

Marianne Knight, Elizabeth's younger sister. She survived all her siblings, dying in 1896 at the age of ninety-five.

Elizabeth Rice with her daughter, possibly Louisa.

Charles Augustus Rice, RA.

John Plumptre.
The Plumptres were neighbours and friends of the Rices; John
Plumptre was the suitor of Fanny Knight, much approved of by
Jane, but finally rejected as almost too good to be endured.

Lady Knatchbull, née Fanny Knight, Elizabeth's older sister and
Jane Austen's niece and correspondent.

Lady Knatchbull, née Fanny Knight, in her old age when her judgement had become warped by Victorian prejudice and the onset of senility.

One of the vessels in which Edward Bridges Rice served.

Edward Bridges Rice RN, the oldest of Elizabeth's children. A first-rate sailor and an uxorious husband.

Elizabeth Rice with her husband Edward. He became paralysed from the waist down as a result of a fall in his seventies.

Madame Sarah Rice, mother
of Edward Royds Rice. She
liked to wear white, even as
an older woman, and was
never without her white bonnet.

Earnest Rice RN.
A fanciful studio portrait.

The family of John and Florence (née Rice) Wright /
Osmaston in 1887. Elizabeth and Edward Royds Rice had a
family of the same size.

Cecil Rice, 72nd Highland Regiment. A veteran of the Crimea and the Indian Mutiny, and 'a regular cheese', according to his brothers and sisters.

Fanny, Countess of Winchilsea, in her widowhood; oldest daughter of Edward and Elizabeth Rice.

Walter Rice, RE. Caroline Cassandra Rice.

Dane Court, in Tilmanstone, Kent.
From a watercolour, probably by Fanny, Countess of Winchilsea,
Elizabeth's oldest daughter.

The Children

1   Edward Bridges

The lives of the fifteen children of Elizabeth and Edward Rice are well-documented in family letters, although of course there are enormous gaps. They comprehend a period which was very active in military and imperial terms, as well as in domestic politics, and in many of these activities the Rice family were involved. But in a study such as this, of the uneventful life of an unremarkable woman, these great events can only be mentioned as they impinged upon the careers of the different family members. Yet the brief accounts of the careers of the members of the Rice family which follow, indicate the wide range of their involvement in the historic occurrences of the century.

Edward, the oldest of the Rice children, was born in October 1819 at 'blessed Godmersham', a nativity which in his mother's view endowed him with an especial grace. He never had any doubt as to his destiny, to be a sailor, although his parents would have preferred to keep him at home, as the heir to his father's property. But by the age of eight or nine he was at the Royal Naval College at Portsmouth, and thenceforward his career progressed slowly but steadily, echoing that of his great-uncle Admiral Francis Austen, to whom he bore a remarkable resemblance, in physique, character and abilities, to the rank of Admiral and KCB. In September 1838 the family at Dane Court had a visit from one of Edward's senior officers; Edward was at that time in HMS *Rodney* in the Mediterranean under Captain Hyde Parker. The resultant letters give a happy picture of domestic life at home, and must have made Edward not a little homesick to read them. The officer in question was the Hon. Henry Keppel, a younger son of the Earl of Albermarle. He wrote to Edward:

> Your kind letter of congratulations on my promotion I found awaiting my arrival in England but have delayed answering it before that I might have the pleasure of doing so from Dane Court. We have just had prayers and I am now sitting in the drawing-room which is the prettiest room I think I ever saw. Mrs Rice is on the sofa reading and Miss Rice doing the same in the chair opposite, but as they are both to see this, I shall make no re-mark on them. I am only astonished how you could have submitted to follow my advice and remain so long away from such a home. Your brother Morland is home now for the holi-days, he is exactly what you were when we first met. The greatest pet is a darling little sister you have not yet seen, Caroline, she is just that delightful size and age that she never ought to grow any bigger but that is the case with the whole family and any alteration in any one of them would render the whole less perfect than it is...

Elizabeth added her contribution, crossing Captain Keppel's letter:

> I have read Captain Keppel's letter [she wrote] and kept it a week because the packet does not sail until the 15th. You have no idea how we

all liked him and how sorry we were when he
went away – he arrived on Friday just as Papa
was gone to St Albans [home of their neighbours the Hammonds] about 3 o'clock and I
was putting the drawing-room to rights before
putting my things on to go out – Mr George
Oxenden happened to be staying here – he
and I and Fanny took him out walking – it was
a lovely hot day and we sauntered about the
garden and wood and sat on benches and
talked and though rather shy at first he very
soon got quite intimate with all of us and
played with little Caroline in the most good-
natured way you ever saw, ran all about the
flower-beds with her after him, and planted
flowers in her little garden, scratching out the
dirt and stones with his hands and poking
holes with a wicket to put the flowers in – we
happened to have a large dinner-party that day,
Guilfords, Oxendens, Hammonds – the next
day he drove me in my ponycarriage to
Walmer, and he hunted about everywhere for
Newfoundland dogs, as he wanted to buy two
– the Duke of Wellington is there, so we
walked to the Castle and he left his name and
some of the servants told him of a famous dog
which he got at last and brought home with us
– he gave three guineas for it – quite black and
very handsome – he did not seem to care
about shooting, tho' it was the 1st of September – and liked driving with me better, so Papa
and Mr George Oxenden went out shooting –
there are very few birds and very wild, and
they only killed six brace between them – we
enjoyed our drive of all things, and talked an

immense deal about you and how high an opinion he has of you – he told me a great many anecdotes about you and said he was determined not to go to sea again without you. On Sunday we walked to Updown and Betteshanger after Church and we had a very pleasant cheerful dinner at which he ate an immense deal of roast beef and plum pudding …The next morning Morland drove him to Margate to go up to town by a steamer and he told him as they went along that he had never been at any place in his life that he was so sorry to leave – or where he had felt so completely at home. I am so glad he has been – how frightful he is! – I quite laughed sometimes when I was looking at him and wondered how he could be so hideous.[1] …Captain Keppel seemed to think you would certainly be here by Christmas – only think of the delight of it!! …How I shall think of you! do you remember coming into my room in your sailor's dress and tail-coat – just the last thing to see how you looked before leaving, and do you remember the people drinking Midshipman Rice's good health…

There was one small and unexplained hiccup in this exemplary career which is worth revealing, as it illustrates the tolerant and kindly attitude of both Elizabeth and her husband. Some time in late 1839 Edward Royds Rice wrote to his son:

---

[1]Family portraits of Henry Keppel do not indicate exceptional ugliness; but he was very short, under five foot. Queen Victoria was fond of him, and called him her 'little Admiral'.

I am writing under circumstances of great anxiety and uneasiness in consequence of a letter from Mr Woodhead [their banking agent, who continued to act for Edward throughout his career] enclosing an account of your drafts upon him last year and this present and requiring me to pass the balance as I had promised him to do, I told him two years since not strictly to confine your Bills to the amount of your allowance of £50, but to honour your drafts trusting to your prudence not to exceed that amount more than you could help, but from this account which I have now received it appears that in 1837 the amount of your Bills was £68.9s.4d, – in 1838 (including two Bills at Portsmouth amounting to about £19) your expenditure was £107.9s – and in the months of Jan and Feb only of this year he says you have drawn for £78 – and he wrote to me in the hope that you have sent me some explanation of this as he thought there must be some mistake ...however should he be mistaken and should they be correct he says it might be attended with very unpleasant circumstances to you if they were not honoured. I have therefore directed him to do so, I have never had anything yet that has given me more pain and anxiety than the fear that you have been imprudent – your good conduct which I hoped was uniform has been the greatest source of comfort and happiness to me under many circumstances ...and I am unwilling now to think you have done wrong though I fear you must have acted imprudently, I fear you are not aware or do not sufficiently consider how impossible it is for me with 12 children and the many expenses I have therefore necessarily entailed upon me to meet all the demands I have if your expenses and those of others exceed what I can reasonably expect, indeed, my dear Edward, I do not wish to write unkindly to you on this subject, but it is necessary for your own welfare as well as for the sake of your brothers and sisters that I should point out to you the necessity of avoiding imprudence, even if I had more means of meeting it, it would be your duty not to exceed your allowance more than possible but the fact is I cannot afford it. I beg you will send me a candid explanation and tell me the whole of the case. If you have been induced to lend money never do so again, you cannot afford it and if you could you had better give £5 than lend ten – by lending you lose your money and ultimately your friend also, Mr Woodhead spoke to Captain Keppel who appears perfectly at a loss to account for this …I hear you had been in the habit of giving money to the men which Mr Shidwell got back for you. I shall be anxious for your answer, you may trust me with entire confidence and you may depend on my wish to act as kindly as I feel affectionately towards you – it would be a great misery to me to have to do otherwise…

Elizabeth appended her share of the sheet:

My dearest Edward,

Your Father has given me his letter to read and I am sure you will feel the kindness of it as well as that his refraining from writing to Captain Parker on the subject which he has been advised to do, but he is very unwilling to place you in an uncomfortable position in any way, and would rather trust to you to explain the reason for this apparent imprudence which I trust you will do immediately... for neither of us can bear to think that you have willingly done wrong, I am afraid you do not sufficiently consider the very great increase of expense that his being in Parliament entails upon him and with no increased means of meeting it – besides this, Henry and Morland become more expensive in every way each half-year so that any unexpected demands upon him not merely distress him at this time but are the cause of serious anxiety as indicating a tendency to extravagance which must bring great misery upon all of us, I am sure my dearest Edward you will feel this and endeavour in future to be as careful as you possibly can...

In view of what appeared to be shocking overspending over a long period of time, these letters are remarkably gentle in tone, and show a great unwillingness to suspect any real culpability on the part of their son. Both Elizabeth and Edward senior must undoubtedly have had in their minds the habits of the latter's brother the Rev. Henry Rice, who was still a trial to their mother. Could his tendencies to gamble, squander and generally to live beyond his means have been inherited by his nephew? Tantalisingly there is not a particle of evidence or explanation to account for this apparently unique outbreak in the early career of young Edward. Thereafter his life seems to have been a model of the behaviour appropriate to his rank and the social conditions of his life. A naval officer, in those days, however high-ranking, who had small private means (he could scarcely survive at all without any!) was by no means wealthy, or even in easy circumstances; and Edward Rice, even – or perhaps especially – as an Admiral, had real difficulty in maintaining his establishment aboard, where he had heavy mess expenses, and an establishment to maintain at home for his family. Certainly, it is clear from his letters Edward in later life enjoyed spending money, buying presents for his wife and rugs and china for his house, but between them he and his wife kept meticulous accounts, and avoided running into debt or indulging in unnecessary extravagance.

Edward served in the Chinese Opium War, the Burmese War, the Crimea, and in the Mediterranean as Second-in-Command of the Mediterranean Fleet which kept an eye on the Turks and the Russians during the period in the 1870s where European politics were dominated by what was known as 'the Eastern Question'. He spent a period in Malta as an efficient Admiral Superintendent of the Dockyards, at Sheerness in charge of the Steam Reserve, in addition to numerous other appointments. A detailed account from an official at Gibraltar to the First Lord in 1854 describes a particularly daring and successful action when Edward was Captain of HMS *Prometheus*; he was sent off to the Rif coast (on the North African coast) to deal with pirates who had destroyed trading vessels and captured a British brig. He sailed in to the cove where the pirates lay with complete disregard for their continual fire, destroyed their boats and recaptured the British vessel, returning without loss and to much commendation.

In 1864, when he was forty-four, Edward married Cecilia Harcourt of Nuneham Courteney; he had wooed a number of ladies in the course of his rather infrequent leaves, including his attractive cousin Norah Hill, daughter of Cassandra Knight, Lizzie's younger sister; but in this marriage he found complete happiness and the support and affection his nature required. One son was born to the marriage. Cecilia was one of the three daughters of Canon Vernon Harcourt, former Rector of Bolton Percy, near York (his father had been the Archbishop of York); he had recently inherited the house and estate of Nuneham Courteney from his older brother. The younger of his two sons was Sir William Harcourt, the distinguished Liberal politician, who held high office under Gladstone, including the post of Chancellor of the Exchequer. During Edward's frequent absences at sea, Ceci and her son Henry paid long visits to Dane Court, particularly during the summer months, where Henry had the benefit of the company of uncles and aunts and cousins. When he was about nine years old, he suffered a severe leg injury at school, which was evidently badly handled and which gave him trouble for most of his life. He spent a great deal of his boyhood laid up with this injury and never went to school thereafter, being educated rather haphazardly at home. His uncles were of the opinion that he was mollycoddled by his mother, and that the association with uncles and boy cousins was wholly to his benefit. Certainly Ceci, then and later when Edward was retired, had the reputation for fussy and overprotective preoccupation with his and her own health. But she enjoyed her visits to Dane Court, and had a happy relationship with her parents-in-law, particularly perhaps Edward, to whom she would read the papers. She was able to join her husband in Malta, living in state in the splendid house which had been a palace of the Crusader Knights, but when he was with the Fleet, she lived quietly at Hampton Hill, their home in Hampshire, pouring out daily letters to her husband.

Edward's letters to his wife were even more frequent and detailed, and gave a very full description of every aspect of his activities, with a commentary of his views on the current international situation as well as pen-pictures of his colleagues and other dignitaries he met in the course of his duties. They carried their fair burden of complaints of ailments and discomforts, longing for her and home, criticism of the inadequacies of the 'Service', (particularly the Lords of the Admiralty), their failure to provide him with a proper flagship, give him promotion, send him home, etc. But Edward in fact loved being at sea, was a first-class sailor with a very open mind about the innovations of steam, ironcladding, torpedoes, etc.; he was of a very sociable disposition, and enjoyed the companionship of his fellows on board and a great variety of people on shore, in Greece, Turkey and elsewhere, all faithfully and fully recorded in his letters to Ceci. As acting C-in-C in the Mediterranean he had a more than formal relationship with the Greek royal family, and called the Queen a 'kissable woman'. He was slightly less fond of her sister – they were both daughters of the Russian Czar –married to the Duke of Edinburgh, but flirted happily with her too when she was on board with her husband. He, the second son of Queen Victoria, was Captain of HMS *Sultan* and therefore under Edward's command, and they became good friends, Edward portrayed him as a most likeable person, generous and sensible, an enthusiastic musician and an able sailor.

In 1878, soon after Edward relinquished his Mediterranean command, Edward Royds Rice died. Although Lizzie retained possession of the house, her son assumed ownership and responsibility for the estate. Although Lizzie spoke lovingly of his care and consideration for her, she also remarked on his 'man-of-war moods' when he was brisk and overbearing, and commented ironically on his protestations of poverty: 'E. and Ceci went away yesterday,' she wrote, 'he got through a great deal of business and I believe was satisfied on the whole though he thinks at least he says of course he is going to be ruined as people always do when they have got much richer than they ever were before...' Like other members of the family, she considered Ceci mollycoddled him excessively 'E. is quite well now that Ceci is not here to smother him in Shawls and encourage him to eat and sleep all day long, he is tearing all over Elvington and Street End now to settle whether he shall try to buy it...'

Edward did build or buy a house in the neighbouring village of Elvington, but after Lizzie died in 1884 Edward and Ceci eventually returned to live at Dane Court on which Edward spent a great deal of money, refacing the pleasing stucco with brick and carrying out other improvements. He spent a tranquil and pampered retirement there, surrounded by a very large number of his kinsfolk in and near the village of Tilmanstone, and died in his sleep by the fire on his eighty-third birthday.

The long letters which he and Ceci exchanged in the latter half of the 1870s form a large part of the Rice collection, and those he wrote give a vivid and detailed account of many aspects of naval life, as well as an equally vivid impression of his own personality and predilections.

2   Fanny

The oldest daughter of the family, Frances Margaretta, was born in 1820 and in spite of a history of frail health in her youth, lived eighty-nine hearty and energetic years. In July 1841 she was at Walmer with her mother, her brother Edward and two of the younger boys, Charles Augustus and Cecil, aged thirteen and ten, hoping to benefit from the good sea air. Lizzie wrote to daughter Louisa in her customary bracing style:

Many thanks for your very pleasant letter of this morning, so much do I enjoy it that I sit me down instantly to answer it having little or nothing to say – Fanny is in bed with the Rheumatism, Edward sitting beside her – Augustus playing at cricket in Bax's field with 10 other boys and Cecil somewhere about the Goodwin sands in Mr Woolaston's boat. I admire my own position in a great chair by the fire in a safe room greatly the most. Poor distressed Fanny got a chilter in the Pony carriage about a week ago which produced first toothache then stiffness and now this roomatiz I greatly fear. I have sent to the doctor and will add his opinion when he comes, she was much better before this provoking cold, however, she has no cough or pain in her chest or side she had two leeches on her gums last night which have done her teeth good. I am sorry Uncle Charles and Morland have given up their Isle of Wight excursion. [Charles Knight, Rector of Chawton], though it would have been such fun, however I dare say they would have been drowned... How happy you both seem to be at nice old Chawton [Chawton House, at this time occupied by Edward Knight junior and his family]. I knew you would like it and everybody in it, so do I and I wish I ever went there. It is a great comfort knowing people are alive, but it does not do nearly so well as sometimes seeing them – is Eliza as big as Florence and has she got as immense a face? [Florence was the most recent Rice baby, the fourteenth, born 1841; Eliza was the first child of Edward Knight junior's second wife Adela Portal, born also in 1841.]

I am her godmother, and meant to give her a handsome present but Aunt Adela gave Florence one instead which did just as well so now I shan't. Augustus and Cecil bother me nearly every night to let them keep watch on the beach with the Preventive men. Sometimes I do and sometimes I don't – when I do they put on their rough Trusties and Glengarry caps and walk up and down till 3 in the morning – there is nothing in the world they enjoy so much – if it rains they creep under the men's oilskin cloaks – they like having them very much, especially as they generally take out beer and sandwiches to regale themselves at intervals. I went to call on Mrs Garrett the other day, and had a long chat with her – she is a little tight maidy-looking woman with a short blunt snub nose I rather hated her – Garrett was at home, we were talking about the Queen's visit here last winter and how little she cared for bad weather etc. etc. and he said, 'Why, I was out on duty one morning and it was blowing pretty well a Northerly gale and I saw the Prince come out of the Castle Gates and presently Her Majesty joined him and hooked on to his arm and he towed her along to windward for close on an hour.' I have found out a thing to say to beggars when you want them to go. Edward told me of it and I tried it on an impertinent monster who came to the windows demanding alms the other day with great success. He was beginning to tell a long story about an old sailor, suffering shipwreck, and very grievous, etc. etc. and I said, 'Come, come, my friend, none of this. Top your broom and sail large, will you.' He_stopt directly and sailed off grumbling daggers at me. We are pestered to death with them here and can't make them go or care for any threats of being taken up... So Dr McArthur has just walked off with his guinea and says Fanny has got rheumatism certes but nothing else, she is to take a colchicum draught tonight and another tomorrow and he advises her to have her tooth out and I strongly advise her not – she is always disposed to have teeth out, and a very bad plan it is – it hurts very much and it costs very much and makes another ache directly. We shall be sorry to go away from here, it certainly is the healthiest of places and has done Fanny worlds of good...

With the terrible toll of young people of all classes taken by tuberculosis at this period, the family anxiety over Fanny's health is understandable. Again, sometime in 1844, a family party visited Kissingen, a spa in Bavaria, in search of improved health, and to enable Papa to take the waters. The party consisted of Lizzie and her husband, Edward, Fanny and her younger sister Marianne with Wyver the Dane Court butler and Charleton, probably Lizzie's maid. The trip was not an unmitigated success, though Lizzie squeezed much entertainment from its vicissitudes, and her letter home gives a picture of what travel was like before the advent of the railways.

We staid one day to rest at Frankfurt [she wrote to Louisa] and set out on Wednesday morning at 7 – 4 in one carriage, 3 in another, for Lohr (where we were to sleep). Fanny and Marianne were both quite ill all the way and could enjoy nothing, poor fellows, we even doubted whether we should be able to get them there at all – we came with Voituriers so we had to rest and bait their horses every now and again which was all the better for the sick girls. We rested two hours at Schappenbourg where the King of Bavaria has a beautiful summer palace all the Royal family were there, so we could not see the inside of it but we careered about the outside and heard a lovely Band play for an hour and looked at a very curious old Church full of relics and images and other vile abominations – the poor girls all the time in bed at the Inn – the fact is that poor dear unfortunate Fanny has got another boil plaguing her to death and she is now in bed with it – of course the pain of travelling over rough roads in such circumstances was very great, and made her quite ill and our great fear was that she would be laid up before we got here. We left them with Edward and Wyver at Schappenbourg and went on ourselves two hours before them to Lohr to have rooms and beds ready for them to get into as soon as they arrived. The Country was beautiful, such a magnificent Forest! It took us two hours and a half to get through it. We borrowed pillows from the Inn at Frankfurt to lay Fanny on and their carriage was fortunately an easy one – ours was that rough that my very bones ached and I am still pretty stiff but quite well. So the next day we jolted off from Lohr at 11 so that they might lie abed as long as possible and baited at a place called Himelbourg which we left at 6 in the evening and arrived here soon after 9 – we are put up at a Lodging House opposite the Hotel de Russie, and are comfortable enough, but the place is stupid I think and not very pretty and there is nothing to do but walk up and down the gravel walks between rows of trees and see other people doing the same – they meet for this entertainment at half-past-five in the morning – we have only accomplished getting out at ½ past 6 as yet – a band plays from 6 to 8 in the mornings, and evening. Fanny is not to drink the waters till this inflammation has quite subsided. We have got a German doctor …and I am horribly afraid of his starving her – he says she may eat 'a little tinsoop and boil plums and bread.' Papa has begun the waters and they disagree with him much which I suppose is the proper thing. He looks very pale and sleepy and hates it. Marianne has had a bilious attack – we have repented a hundred times ever having brought them – but I hope things will get cooler soon. There are not many English here but quantities of foreigners of sorts – I never thought until I found myself getting so far away from home how I hated that part of the treat, I long so to hear how everybody is – my little darling baby, I keep longing to see and kiss all day long, and all the dear little others – give my very best to all of ye – I hope you and Morny are happy and pleasant and Walter and Arthur tolerably good… How does my border do? I am happy to say that Wyver and Charleton detest their 'living' and look back with unfeigned regret to their 'wholesome joints of roast mutton and sweet vegetables and good sound Beef' – greedy toads – I am very glad now that Wyver came – I hope that he will nearly starve!

Fanny did not marry until she was turned thirty, although she was noted for her good looks. She had a brief engagement to a son of neighbours, the Hammonds of St Alban's, Wingham, which was soon broken off amidst some embarrassment and ill feeling. Fanny's chosen partner was George Finch-Hatton, 10th Earl of Winchilsea. nearly thirty years her senior, and an old student friend of her father's. They were married in the early spring of 1850. He is distinguished by one or two mentions in the letters of Jane Austen; once in August 1805 when Jane was staying at Godmersham and she visited Eastwell, the home of the Finch-Hattons, with some of the family. 'Fortune was civil to me in placing Mr E. Hatton by me at dinner [i.e., George's father]. George is a fine boy, and well-behaved…' George was then a youth of fourteen. In September 1813 Jane was again at Godmersham and she wrote, 'We hear a great deal of George Hatton's wretchedness. I suppose he has quick feelings but I daresay they will not kill him. He is so much out of spirits however that his friend John Plumptre is gone over to comfort him…' One suspects the rejected lover, for in October Jane Austen reported, 'There is no truth in the report of G. Hatton being to marry Miss Wemyss. He desires it may be contradicted.' Two weeks later, he paid a call at Godmersham – 'I saw him, saw him for ten minutes; sat in the same room with him, heard him talk, saw him bow, and was not in raptures. I discerned nothing extraordinary. I should speak of him as a gentle-manlike young man – eh! *bien tout est dit…*'[2] Someone must have been praising him to her in extravagant terms; she was never prepared to be overly impressed by members of the aristocracy solely on account of their rank.

In 1814 George Finch-Hatton married Georgiana, daughter of the Duke of Montrose, and they had a son (Lord Maidstone) and a daughter. After she died he married Emily Bagot, who died childless in 1848. On her tombstone in the churchyard of Ewerby Church in Lincolnshire, which adjoins the Victorian Gothic mansion called Haverholme Priory which George rebuilt in the 1830s, is the saddest and most dispirited epitaph:

> When the knell for the dying soundeth for me
> And my corpse coldly lying,
> 'Neath the green tree,
> When the turf strangers are heaping
> Cover my breast,
> Come not to gaze on me weeping,
> I am at rest.
> All my life, coldly and sadly,
> The days have gone by,
> I who dreamed wildly and madly,
> Am happy to die,
> Long since my heart hath been breaking,
> Its pain is past.
> A time hath been set to its aching,
> Peace comes at last.

In spite of the disparity in their ages, Fanny's marriage was a very happy one; she was genuinely devoted to her husband, and loved his cheerfulness and good humour, and

---

[2]Jane Austen, *Letters* (no.45, p.160; no.84, p.331; no.87, p.351; no.89, p.362); Chapman [ed.], OUP.

his eccentricities and enthusiasm. All the family liked him, although they were less admiring of his violent political prejudices. He was an arch Tory, and a fanatical anti-Catholic; the latter prejudice led him to fight a duel with the Duke of Wellington in 1829 when the latter brought in the Catholic Relief Bill. Even though his political opinions and affiliations were different from those of Fanny's father, Lord Winchilsea was able and more than willing to exert what influence he could for the benefit of his brothers-in-law. In 1852 Fanny wrote to her brother Edward:

> Lord Winchilsea will do anything he can for you, I only wish he knew what to do, I hope the present Government will remain in for some time that he will be when you come home! He is sitting opposite to me now writing an appeal to the County saying it all very loud and exactly as if he were making a speech and appealing to me every instant to help and approve so that I can hardly write. Now he is rejoicing in a fling at Sir Jas. Graham – it is the comfort of one's life to have anybody always with one so constantly cheerful and happy – he sings loud over his bills and accounts tho' he has not near enough money to pay them with.

The rather brief marriage (Winchilsea died in 1858) produced four children, three boys and a girl; a greater part of their existence was spent at the home in Lincolnshire called Haverholme Priory which they shared rather uneasily with Winchilsea's older son Lord Maidstone and his wife and daughters. Some months of the year were spent at Eastwell in Kent, near Godmersham, a beautiful house whose situation was a good deal pleasanter than the rather bleak countryside of Lincolnshire.

All the family felt the benefit of Fanny's marriage, and the Haverholme house was always full of sisters and brothers, cousins and aunts. The brothers particularly would spend part of their leaves with Fanny, and Morland, who suffered a severe fall from his horse in his final year at Oxford would spend months at a time recuperating with Fanny.

Fanny's widowhood lasted over fifty years, and her activities are not recorded in any detail, but were many and varied. She was a more than averagely good amateur artist, exhibiting once at the Royal Academy – she spent some time during her honeymoon visit to Seville copying a picture by Murillo which is still extant. Like many of her female contemporaries, she took a great interest in self-help medicine, particularly homeopathy; she did not herself aspire to the heights of hypochondria indulged in by her daughter-in-law and the latter's mother Lady Susan Harcourt, but she was always ready within the family to impart advice and instruction.

Fanny enjoyed the company of young people; a friend of her son Murray at Eton, Reginald Brett – later Viscount Esher, a distinguished public figure, recorded a holiday with them at Nairn in Scotland:

> Lady Winchilsea, their mother, I looked upon as the kindest and most true-hearted of women. Whether this were true or not, she was brimful of sympathy and of real affection and love of youth. 'Go out for walks with your hostess,' wrote W.J. [William Johnson, a master at Eton, better known as the poet, William Cory] to me, 'and talk to her thoughtfully but freely; she will trim the luxuriance of your fo-

liage and make garlands of the snippings just the same. She is like me, a true lover of beauty and youth, and thinks the sentimental part of life as real as the jolting in the ruts of business.' I spent some very happy days at Geddes. To W.J. my hostess wrote thus of my visit – 'So much mutual love and admiration, so much youth and beauty and music with so little that was otherwise than beautiful and sweet was rarely seen. To me it was a continual feast. I walked with the children in the lovely woods of pine, climbing mossy steeps covered with ferns and heather, and each looked more beautiful than the other. Henry had his gun and Murray and Reginald hunted the dogs and found and carried his game. You should have seen them gathering round a poor fluttering pigeon, and then sitting with the dogs on their knees and their arms linked round each other, with Evelyn in happy admiration, and the soft wind made the gentlest of rushing sounds in the pine-heads above...'

I was glad to return to Eton in September. Lady Winchilsea occasionally wrote to me, tender poetical letters asking for accounts of my friends and of the glorious autumn sunsets. To please her I used to go into Poets' walk and watch the red gables of College grow redder in the sunlight, and the river catching the colour as it rolled under the walls, die again into yellow and greys as it floated away past the elms of the playing-fields to the meadows beyond...

It sounds a very Victorian idyll, sentimental and rather unreal, with the beautiful widow cast as a benign goddess or Muse, half mother figure and half love object in the style of mediaeval chivalry.

Fanny outlived her two older sons who both died before they reached the age of fifty; Murray, by then the 12th Earl, died without an heir, and Harold, the youngest son, a bachelor, died at the age of forty. The third son, Henry, thus became the 13th Earl, and his descendants maintain the succession. Fanny lived latterly at Hatton near Sevenoaks, and was reported in the diaries of Helen Rice, one of the daughters of Charles Augustus, as descending from time to time on the colony at Tilmanstone, full of vigour and cheerfulness, sometimes sweeping one of her maiden sisters off to Grasse for the winter months. She died at the age of eighty-nine in 1909.

3   Henry

Henry was Lizzie's second son, whose arrival in 1821 was so warmly welcomed at Godmersham by his grandfather, Edward Knight. His story is all too quickly told. In a family of good-looking and good-humoured sons, he was reckoned one of the handsomest and liveliest, although no pictorial and very little literary evidence survives to exemplify the claim. He was destined for the Army and was sent to Sandhurst. He gained a commission in the 72nd Highland Regiment (the Seaforths), and was not at first sent overseas. From Portsmouth in 1840 he wrote a cheerful chatty letter to his sister Fanny, exchanging information about 'beautiful pieces of music', in which they were both interested. (He played the flute, and was involved with finding music for the regimental band). He described a party he attended which contains one of the rare mentions of Jane Austen, and singularly unimportant it is!

Last night [he wrote] I went to a quadrille party at Mrs Arnold's, the old fellow that used to live at Dover and whose husband is second-in-command here, they were very civil to me and talked a good deal about Dover of course. The rooms were very hot which made it very myst for dancing. I had a very agreeable partner most of the time, however, what didn't get hot (which ladies never ought to do) so that I liked it tolerably well. My nice partner was a Miss Johnston; short, very good hair, black eyes, nez retroussé (or ée, is it masc. or fem.?) not to say snub, mouth – I don't know, and a very pretty foot; you like to hear all these particulars, don't you? she is sister of a friend of mine at the RNC of that name, and daughter of Sir Henry Johnston, a pleasant little covey what lives at Bath; they knew the Honeywoods very well, and my Johnston said as 'ow the H'woods like you very much. I said that you were amazingly partial to Louisa Honeywood, as she appeared to be the one that Johnston liked most. [The Honeywoods lived at Elvington, a village neighbouring on Tilmanstone.) You ask me to tell about Bouveries; never did a party afford less to tell about, it was as stupid as a dolt the whole time; the party consisted of Adml. B. and his missus and a few old naval officers; no moosic, except a toon played by old Mrs Bouverie, which was poor stuff, good old fellow, she did her best, you know... Mrs B. said that Aunt Jane was an old and Valleyed friend of hers, which of course I 'was very glad of...'

Henry was at home in January 1842, shooting blackbirds to the horror of his sisters, especially when he later ate them for dinner 'poor things,' wrote Louisa, 'I can't bear such lovely "songsters of the Grove" being shot.'

Some time in 1845 the regiment was sent overseas, at first to Gibraltar, a pleasant posting. By 1848, Henry was in Barbados. Barbados, that 'pearl in the English crown', had been a colony since the days of James I, and a source of fabulous wealth for its English sugar planters with their armies of African slaves. Far from being the resort of luxury tourists and sun-worshippers as it is nowadays, the island was regarded then as an intolerably hot and unhealthy place, another 'white man's grave' on the British Imperial circuit. The handful of letters that survive are full of family news, hopes of promotion – for himself and his brothers – births and deaths, and the tedious, uncomfortable life in this unhealthy posting, enlivened by swimming and the occasional cricket match. The heat was very trying:

> We are enjoying the hottest part of the year just now and at this moment I am gasping for breath ...my ideas are constantly on the verge of suffocation and I can only write short sentences at a time and at long intervals which are employed in struggling for fresher air, and bathing my hands in eau-de-Cologne.

In November 1848 Henry succumbed to the 'fatal sickness' which was killing more British servicemen than enemy action, cholera. A fellow officer wrote to Henry's father:

> ...You will have received my melancholy letter of the 28th ultimo, I now finish my sad duty, by telling you that on the same day, at 20 minutes to 4, your son, and my poor friend,

breathed his last, he was buried the next morning with the usual military honours at 7 o'clock, and rests by the side of 12 other officers carried away in one short year, by this fatal sickness... I believe I told all else in my last letter, all that care, skill and attention could give was bestowed on him and well he deserved it by his amiable, resigned patience – his nurse, a good brown woman was very unremitting in her zeal and a Highlander from his company by name Benton was equally so. I mention these matters feeling that they will be interesting to his family of whom he always spoke with the warmest affection... I hope the fever is abating somewhat, but alas, the change is not so rapid or manifest as we had hoped the encamping of the troops would have made it, we lost 2 men yesterday and in all 42 of the regiment and 4 officers have died since the 5th of October...

Lizzie wrote to her son Cecil on July 1849 on the occasion of his leaving home to Join his late brother's regiment, the 72nd Highlanders. He was just eighteen years old. Lizzie had a firm Christian faith not blurred by sentimentality or wishful thinking, but strengthened by her clear-sighted and practical intelligence. She was well aware of the importance of Christian principles to support her young sons going out into the world, and her letter is a model of clear, kind and caring advice. That all her children were not only conforming and practising Christians all their lives, but evidently strove conscientiously to regulate their everyday lives according to Christian precepts must be largely attributed to her guidance and example. Her description of Henry as a veritable saint in shining armour is no doubt overdrawn, but understandable in the circumstances.

> I should have liked to talk to you before you leave home, my dearest Cecil [she wrote] but I think I had better write as I cannot trust myself to speak on the subject which is uppermost in my thoughts now that you are going to join his Regiment, our dear, dear Henry. I hope and pray that you will try to follow his most excellent example – you have seen how he was loved and respected and the reason was not only that he was amiable and kind-hearted naturally which being his disposition was no merit of his, but because his religious principles were excellent and that he was never ashamed of endeavouring to act up to them – they enabled him to resist bad example and temptations which you will be exposed to as well and which nothing but religious principles can save you from yielding to – he did not care for being ridiculed or called a saint or a Methodist, he persevered in the right course, and how soon was he called upon to rejoice that he had done so! if when he was on his death-bed he had had as so many must have I fear (especially in that profession exposed to temptation on all sides) an idle profligate life to look back upon how different his end would have been...! The Saviour whom he was not ashamed to serve and to confess before men, supported him in that aweful hour... Try to be like him, dearest Cecil – he was kind and unselfish and gentle, but firm and unyielding in what he knew was

right and untiring in doing his duty in the Regiment – as Captain Boyle said in one of his letters. You will have a bright example before you, and the thought of him will be a safe-guard to you and a passport to the goodwill and regard of all who loved him. I have the greatest confidence in your intentions to do right but you are young yet and perhaps you are hardly aware of what strength of principle it requires to keep in the right course... do not be tempted by fatigue or business to neglect your daily prayers – you may not find the comfort in them at first that you will do as you grow older – if indeed you are spared to grow older, but it will be doing your duty and when sorrows and misfortunes come as come they must you will find the benefit and comfort of it – I do not want you to answer this letter I am only writing because it is what I should have said and besides I know how disagreeable it is to answer a letter of advice, but I know you will attend to it and sometimes read it to put you in mind of my anxious wishes and hopes for your happiness here and hereafter, and now God bless you, my dear dear Cecil, and give you strength to act up to your duty... There is one thing more I meant to have said and that is to advise you to devote some part of every day to useful reading something that will improve your mind and add to your stock of information – a well-informed soldier is a fine character and not a very common one, and perhaps after a little while you might like it...

Many years later, in April of 1862 or 3, a younger brother of Henry's, Ernest, then a gunnery officer aboard HMS *Hero*, came in to Barbados and stayed there a week or ten days before proceeding to Trinidad; 'the heat of this place is feefo,' he wrote, 'and they say Trinidad is much worse, how I shall exist I don't know.' He found time to seek out and visit his brother's grave, and gave his mother a detailed description of his enquiries and the successful outcome of his mission; how he had to seek out some person old enough to recall the time when the 72nd was stationed on the island, and how he had found a lady who did indeed remember, and remembered in particular Henry as the officer who had saved herself, a little girl, and her mother from falling out of their cart when the regimental band had caused their horse to shy; and how 'Captain Rice had been the nicest, quietest, religiousest young man in the regiment, and was the friend of all the poor people, white and black, in the place.' Ernest had found the grave, in a quiet church-yard, flanked by the graves of two fellow-officers who had died, one two days before him, and one three days after. Ernest concluded his account with a somewhat cryptic remark, 'I could tell you a great deal more, dearest Mama, but I am not quite sure it would do you or my Father any good.'

4   John Morland

John Morland, born a year after Henry, was intellectually the most gifted of the ten Rice sons, and seemed to have the greatest potential to reach the heights of whatever profession he decided to follow; though his father, in a letter to his eldest son when Morland was still a schoolboy, expressed doubts as to his application and dedication to succeed in his ambition, which at that stage he had declared was to be a lawyer. Maybe there was a natural indolence in his disposition which was compounded by his later disastrous accident which was to put an end to his ambition. Morland, unlike his older brothers, was sent to Eton, and in due course, in 1842, he won the Newcastle Prize, a notable award which two of his sisters recorded in their diaries with a wealth of capital letters, exclamation marks and excited repetitions. He chose to go to Merton College, Oxford rather than the usual destination of Newcastle Prizemen, Trinity College, Cambridge, as a Postmaster, or Exhibitioner. Here, on the eve of his final examinations, he was thrown from his horse and sustained head injuries from which he never completely recovered, and which destroyed any hopes he might have had for a brilliant career in public life or in the law. He was granted a degree, and his academic standing must have been high, for he was immediately appointed as a Demy (a half Fellow) and then a Fellow of Magdalen; here he remained for seventeen years, acting as Bursar of the College, happy and probably rather idle years, full of good fellowship and undemanding existence. The Bishop of Armagh, Archbishop Alexander, who was his contemporary at Oxford, bore witness to Morland's social graces at this period – 'the most brilliantly clever, delightful fellow I ever knew', and always referred to him as 'dear Morland Rice'. He wrote regularly to his brothers overseas, entertaining and lively letters, many of which survive, and he paid long visits to the Winchilseas at Haverholme, fishing and walking, very popular with the children and a general favourite. Fanny was not uncritical of his idleness and tendency to hypochondria – she confided to her brother Edward:

> I do wish he had some quiet regular duty to do, I don't like his wasting these best years of his life in idleness nor do I think it good for his health. I don't think he could do much but

if a small curacy would present itself I think he wd. take it and though it might tie him down a little at first I think it world be so good for his mind to sober and settle it and feel himself useful and following to a degree his vocation that the good would counterbalance the evil – as it is I am afraid he will get into desultory self-indulgent habits which are not right in this uncertain life – there is a great difficulty however in finding any thing to suit him – people want curates to do two duties every Sunday always which he could not do – he is useful now at all events at Godmersham with poor dear Cakey and Grandpapa...

Morland had taken Holy Orders after graduating, and was able to be useful to his uncle Charles Knight at Chawton, as well as at Godmersham where his grandfather found him gentler and more sympathetic than the youngest Knight son, still unmarried, Brook John. He was a great support too to his own father at Dane Court during the stressful tines of political campaigning. As a priest, and as more often than not the oldest of the sons still at home, as well as an intelligent and well-educated man, he was much in demand for advice, support and spiritual consolation in times of family bereavement.

In 1864 – in the same year as his brother Edward – he married; his bride was Caroline York, whose father was the incumbent of the parish of Wighill, in Yorkshire; it was probably no coincidence that the father of his brother's bride, Canon Vernon Harcourt, was still at that time the incumbent of the neighbouring parish of Bolton Percy; some years later their younger brother Ernest was to marry Caroline York's sister Laura. On his marriage, Magdalen College presented him with the College living of Brambercum-Bolseth, near Brighton, and there they remained for the rest of their lives. They had no children, but he continued to pay long visits to his relations at Dane Court, Haverholme, Godmersham and elsewhere. He was never able to carry out fully his parochial duties, particularly after he suffered another head injury when he hit his head on the low lintel of a cottage he was visiting. He would conduct services, but never preached, though he was said to be very skilled at extemporary speeches to his parishioners. Ceci Rice, on her visits to Dane Court with young Henry in the absence of Edward, found him very supportive over all her problems, her 'fusses' and her decision-making; he was occasionally disconcerting, she confided, as a fellow guest.

Habits of ill health had made him irritable at times, and no doubt consciousness of his intellectual superiority made him intolerant. She commented on his disagreeable habit of rustling his newspaper when crossed or displeased! But general opinion described him as 'brilliantly clever, charming and attractive', with a large share of the family conversational gift.

It was Morland who originally owned the portrait of Jane Austen as a young girl, once ascribed to Zoffany; it was left to him by a colleague and old friend at Magdalen, Dr Newman, whose stepmother, a great admirer of the novelist, had been given the portrait by Colonel Thomas Austen, Jane's cousin. Neither Dr Newman nor Morland had the slightest doubt that it was of Jane Austen the novelist, whatever subsequent opinions may have been.[3]

---

[3]Much research has been carried out in recent years on the authenticity of this portrait, notably by the owner, Henry Rice, the present writer, and Ms M. Marsh, whose conclusions can be found in the JAS Report for 1985. Although the JAS and the National Portrait Gallery have yet to be persuaded to accept its authenticity as a portrait of the novelist, there is now a general acceptance of the established tradition.

In the summer of 1897 Morland was with Ernest and his family at Portsmouth for the Naval Jubilee celebrations, Ernest at that time being in command of the Dockyards there. Towards the end of July his niece Helen Rice who was also there as a guest of her uncle and aunt reported that, 'Uncle Morny was ill in the evening – a slight attack of pleurisy – and everyone rather anxious.' The next day he was reported to be 'a wee bit better', but later he was declared to have 'pleuropneumonia and everyone anxious about him.' So in the midst of dinners and parades and regattas, his health fluctuated until, on 5th August, he died, at the age of seventy-four. His wife, a sweet-natured and forbearing woman, had died four years earlier, and both lie buried in Bramber churchyard.

5   Louisa

Two daughters followed John Morland in successive years, Louisa in 1824 and Marianne in 1825. Louisa, who never married, was to be the longest-lived of the family, dying in 1916 at the age of ninety-one. She was the chief companion and helpmeet to her mother, while her younger sister Caroline Cassandra, who also remained unmarried, was the devoted attendant on her father. Louisa had the reputation of having a large share of the family wit and conversational brilliance, a characteristic they were proud to associate with the comic genius of their Aunt Jane; but it must be admitted that Louisa's surviving letters show little evidence of this, neither the ironic quirkiness of some of her mother's comments, nor the impulsive liveliness of the letters of her closest sister, Marianne. Excerpts from just one of her letters written to her brother Edward when he was on the China station in 1852 illustrate this pleasant but clumsy and platitudinous style and reflect a fairly conventional and unadventurous approach to life:

My dearest Edward [she wrote] I hate to think how long it is since I have written to you someone else is always writing so then I don't – I only hope no letter will come from you soon saying in mild terms what a beast I am. I often think of so much to say to you that it seems to me as if I had written. Another great drawback is that Papa always wants to know how much anybody writes and will only send one letter, and if I think there is any chance of his or anyone's reading what I write I fall back rebuffed but I am bound to admit all that is selfishness. Papa, Mama and Marianne I have just left in the drawing-room... the Plumptres, Mrs and Cecilia Coote with her little eldest boy called here the other day – the way in which they loudly made some remarks about Matilda [a Plumptre daughter recently deceased] astonished me more than I can say – to one of us I can talk about Henry – but to mention his name to strangers I could not do – still more in the cheerful loud way they do, it is I believe from an excess of goodness, but acting I should think on dispositions without any strong feelings – or deep ones. I think you must often long to have one of us to talk to about him... it makes me miserable but I can't for a moment wish it made me less so – I believe you and Morny talk about him when you are together – I don't know why I can't, but I can't to Morny, or very seldom... Morny went... to Godmersham to take Uncle Charles's place with Grandpapa [Edward Knight] who is as well as usual but always getting weaker. Uncle John does not do well for him – he is not good or gentle and next to Uncle Charles he likes to have Morland better than anyone… There are next to no birds this year – to Papa's horror – though almost everywhere else (except Knowlton) there are an immense quantity. It has been a very unusually dry season and the birds have run away from here and Mongham and Studdale, to where they find more cover and probably more food. Lord North was at the Regatta Ball on Monday at Dover to which we went and he said they had plenty of birds but I saw as Mama and I drove yesterday to call on Lady North, that they had some very good fields of turnips and fresh clover. It was not reckoned a good ball – but was all the better for being thinly attended. Marianne and I do not dance polkas and valses we find it almost impossible to pick and choose who we will and won't dance with when you know many people, but I think Monday's was the first Ball where we really danced none – tho' we danced very few at the Canterbury cricket one – you can't think how all people dance it – almost all at least – the most exaggerated way you can think of, it takes you entirely round your waist etc. – directly people find you don't really mean with them they gradually say what they really think about it and how right they think you are (making however always an exception in favour of themselves of course) which convinces me how much better it is not. I had not been to a Ball for so long till this year in which I have already been to three that it is easy to establish a character for never dancing valses etc., but it makes a Ball rather stupid – the Quadrilles are so few and far between. It is more becoming (which is a consideration) not dancing them certainly, to us at any rate. We know a great many of the Rifles – so many of them are Kentish – no particular lovers are rampant at present – unless Colonel Buller who goes on at intervals at Marianne when he sees her – I don't know whether he is flirting or really liking her – but I hope she never will him – he is oldish – but I am sure rather bad and unprincipled which is much worse. I know a very nice (ha-ha!) officer at Canterbury who was supposed to like me and did I think, I met him at Goodnestone first at dinner – he is Adjutant of the 65th, Mr Ewan, very quiet and gentlemanlike, and nice-looking, but Papa and Mama don't mean to ask anybody here from Canterbury – and no one lets you like poor people... Dane Court gets prettier every year certainly and it has been a lovely summer and how we have longed for you – I never walk about home without thinking about you and how lovely it wd. be if you were at home – and then I hate so thinking of the two years to come that I push it out and keep up a sort of delusive idea that you will come sooner and oh dear how I wish you could – what a first-rate commander you must be by this time – how I should like to spend a day – or a month – on board the *Hastings* and see you Commanding – when you were in sole command I should have liked it best. – I wonder how the Austens are – what a pity Mrs Austen doesn't come home – you must be

very tired of them all except Uncle Charles
…there are a great many pheasants which are
expecting to be shot soon – meanwhile they
look very pretty feeding in groups at the top of
the avenue about sunset these autumny evenings – yellow branches begin to appear, or
more than begin now, and showers of brown
and yellowish-white leaves fall and shower
every morning over the grass and avenue and
look so bright and beautiful in the sun and in
the chequered shade of the Lime Walk where I
go sometimes Marianne too every morning
after breakfast …the new £25 grey does a great
deal of work very well but without any fore-
legs I hear – Papa likes him very much and
says if he had any he wd. be the best horse he
ever had. Simpson (the new steward) is tall
and bony and Scotch – means to be civil and
has a pleasant grave face – a very nice-looking
wife and 2 children – he walks fast and seems
to know about things and Papa likes him…

It is amusing to note how Louisa's pronouns and grammar
disintegrate when she embarks on the dangerous subject of
the intimate modern dances. Her descriptions of the
changing seasons at Dane Court are vivid, as are such
descriptions in most of the family letters, but in general
slight incoherence is a characteristic of her style. The
photographic studio portraits of the middle part of the
nineteenth century are inevitably statuesque and wooden,
and the portraits of all the Rice girls are singularly heavy
and lacking in animation. The long pale faces are not
helped by the unbecoming hairstyle then in vogue, a
middle parting from which the straight dark hair is pulled
down across each cheek and drawn back into a bun behind,

the expression is invariably grave and the costume plain, dark and serviceable, Louisa, however, did not lack suitors; we hear of a few, and no doubt there were others we know nothing about. In April of 1850, for example, Marianne reported that 'Louisa... saw Wyndham Portal the other day in London for the first time, she got red and he looked foolish, luckily she was alone when he came into the room.' This would imply perhaps a rejected proposal from a young man who was possibly the nephew of the two Portal sisters who had married William and Edward Knight junior. In the course of another letter to Edward in June 1850, Louisa recounted the activities at Dane Court in the summer season, including merry encounters with visiting 'beaux':

> This is a lovely-ish day in June at Dane Court
> – a hot sun (for us) and a cold north breeze;
> breeze I mean to sound less a good deal than
> wind – smelling very sweetly of syringa and
> clover – all the syringas are in full bloom in
> the shrubbery and the sanfoin fields are red –
> and being cut in some places... Cecil has just
> looked in at the window with a rifle (yours, is
> it?) in his hand Bose walking by him...
> Temple Harris is staying here... he came
> Thursday and means we think to stay some
> time – some people have no idea of being
> turned out as soon as they generally are here –
> Papa not having been at home he has not
> found out that people here are always expected
> to go in 2 days at the longest... Marianne and
> Temple have just gone out riding there has
> not been much for him to do – nothing yet –
> it poured so with rain till Saturday evening –
> he is funny, rather clever, very slanderous,
> doesn't shoot or play at anything and looks

very ill and is at Christchurch and reads novels all day... About a month ago Uncle George Hill brought Norah over from Ireland to Godmersham... she is the prettiest as well as the nicest girl of 14 I ever saw... she always looks pretty and never thinks an instant about it... I wish Caroline was like her but she has been improved lately by her Confirmation – she was confirmed at Goodnestone by the Archbishop – she is a little taller perhaps than when you went and much the same in other respects – she alters in looks more than any girl I ever saw – sometimes quite plain, sometimes quite pretty – so I suppose she will grow into something between the two – I go on missing you – I hate you wasting among the Austens – though I love well dear Uncle Charles... Sir Robert Ferguson came and stayed here a few days at Whitsuntide. Mr Slaney was asked and couldn't come and sent some verses to me instead. Do you remember Sir Robert Ferguson? an old dry sandy stiff cross spiteful good-natured Irishman who scarcely speaks 2 words in an hour. Part of Mr Slaney's verses said –

> How very provoking
> To tarry here croaking,
> As the writer unhappily made is,
> While polished and merry,
> The member for Derry
> Is saying soft things to the ladies.

with a note explaining that it meant Sir R.F. at the bottom – all which insult as I consider

Morland read out to the poor thing who laughed and twisted about and turned it off and hated it – 'polished and merry' ha-ha, you would have roared at the verses, one part said:

> Now the world will consent
> That the maidens of Kent
> Are the nicest of numberless nice,
> And none I believe
> Will think I deceive
> In saying the fairest is-Rice!

there! I am dying of laughing at my copying out that part – as the most complimentary – but really it was the most ridiculous too. We have had cricket here of evenings lately. How I wonder if you are promoted – I won't waste words on it – but if you a'nt – why trials are good so I find them… it is so late, near 5 and I meant particularly to go up into the village to read to poor horrid Mrs Bean – in a consumption, poor thing, mother of all the Beans. A sheep was stolen Saturday night and Harris and Narborough D'Eath are on the scent I believe – David Neves who is only just out of prison (where he had been for two months for poaching) is strongly suspected. [He] had the impudence to come down to play at cricket the day he came out – and was sent off 'with a flea in his ear' by Papa – and so I daresay picked off a sheep in revenge…

The brothers canvassed the girls' prospects anxiously between each other – with Father's financial situation apparently increasingly precarious, and with such a very large family to settle in a limited range of suitable careers, it was a matter of some importance that the girls should be advantageously disposed of; by 1852 Morland reported regretfully that 'there is every prospect of Lou and May ending their days as maiden aunts [they were aged twenty-six and twenty-five at that time]. Caroline is taking the wind out of their sails already.' The parents were equally anxious to find suitable and if possible prosperous husbands for the girls, and there were many visits *en famille* with at least a partial motive of widening the girls' circle of acquaintance and 'raising' possible suitors. There were many visits to London and to the different Knight establishments at Godmersham and Chawton, to Fanny's homes at Haverholme Priory and Eastwell Park, and further afield to Chicksands in Bedfordshire where the Russells lived, to Scotland and occasional holidays abroad. In 1865 Louisa, now in her forty-first year, was faced with a difficult decision when she received a proposal of marriage from an unidentified Captain D. She appealed to Fanny for her advice:

> My dearest Lou [wrote Fanny in reply, from London], I did not get your letter till I got back last night from Bramber, how I pity you having to decide that sort of thing in such a hurry – but oftener than not such is the course of proposals. I should calmly wait a little and see a little better than you can in such a hurry what you feel and act accordingly. I don't think much advice on such occasions is desirable unless it is necessary to try and persuade the poor victim not to marry a villain which is not your case – all I shall say is that in my opinion as a rule people are far better and happier married than not and I think if you

really like Captain D. very much and approve
of him – taking all I can gather about him – it
would be the happiest and wisest thing for you
to accept him – but as I said before I should
wait a little and enquire about him and his
Family as he leaves you time it is no bad
compliment to him to take a little time to refuse him and if on the other hand you accept
him he will be consoled for waiting... I am
sorry Captain D. is not fine enough to satisfy
one's family pride but after 40 one is expected
to give up something or not marry at all and I
think the latter is very often an unhappy alternative, of course I am supposing as seems the
case that he himself is likely to make you
happy and fond of him... do write to us when
you can and say what you keep feeling and
thinking and hating and liking and seeing...

Marianne too wrote to Louisa reporting that they had had 'a
very good report' of Captain D. from a Dumfriesshire
friend, though as he had thought the enquiry related to the
possibility of Captain D. joining the Conservative Club, the
report perhaps had limited relevance. In any case, Captain
D. was rejected. So, what with suitors being too old or not
coming up to scratch or 'not sooting', and what with not
being allowed 'to like poor people', Louisa settled for the
unmarried state. To what extent pressure was exerted for
her to fulfil the important role of her mother's companion
and assistant housekeeper it is impossible to guess.

Elizabeth suffered from a good deal of ill-health from
time to time after twenty-four years of incessant childbearing, mainly of a rheumatic kind. She hated the damp airs
and cold winds of East Kent, comparing the climate
unfavourably with her 'native country' of Godmersham,

barely twenty miles away to the west, but more sheltered and salubrious. She never complained, for her spirit was as robust as her constitution was frail. Letters report that she bore her headaches and face-aches and rheumatic discomfort with stoic cheerfulness (though she was very reluctant to allow the dentist to remove a tooth!). Caroline reported in a letter to George in 1852 that Mama had seen a specialist, Lowcock, in London:

> he absolutely forbids salads, cucumber or anything else that is worth having in summer. I told him he had destroyed my one hope of earthly happiness and he went laughing away to enjoy his own salad at home. Isn't that like Mama?

Elizabeth was in the habit of rising early and ordering her household before the day was well started for most of the family, but increasingly she handed over the finding and replacing of servants and other domestic chores to Louisa.

Louisa was very fond of children and was regularly in attendance at her sisters' confinements, especially those of Fanny and later of her youngest sister, Florence. Later, the growing children would visit Dane Court and Louisa would enjoy the role of devoted aunt. There are great nieces surviving who still remember her and her sister Caroline Cassandra as eccentric old ladies in their home at South Court, on the Dane Court estate, squabbling happily with each other about health and draughts and diet, and delighting in the proximity of so many members of the family.

6   Marianne

Marianne, Louisa's great companion, seems to have been lively and emotional with a strong humour which was often quite caustic. For example, in a letter to Louisa, who was away on one of her frequent 'sickbed' visits, Marianne described a visit from a neighbour:

> I was just creeping out at 5 when I was over-taken by Lady James and Sarina driving here to call and had to come back with them and sit till half-past six in and about the garden arbour with them – and Sir Walter who appeared – they were arrayed in summer muslins and Sarina is the almost only girl who looks less ugly in a hat than a bonnet. Lady James looked less dug-up than usual and was very affec-tionate, and entered with warmth into my praise of India muslins…

Marianne's letters were often impetuous, emotional and a little incoherent, especially those written when she was young. She ended one letter to Edward in Hong Kong – 'I think I have written a very bad letter – sorry – it is very difficult to write as far as Hong Kong!' A fine example was written to him in about 1852, when both he and his younger brother George were serving in Burma, where Britain was engaged in one of the series of wars in that region:

> how I do utterly hate your being such an im-mense way off [she exclaimed] and in those vile hot climates, I cannot express – I really do think you ought not to stay out there to injure your constitution and I hope and trust you

will not do that, for the sake of promotion – I want you very much indeed to get your promotion, and know it is of consequence to you, but nothing is of such importance as health, if you are 40 post-Captains, it would not make up for a liver complaint – and a ruined constitution – even if you were a younger son, and depended on your profession, I should think it much better not to stay out there if it was bad for your health, but you are the oldest you know, and the staff of the family, and for everybody's sake you ought to take care – so I hope and beg and desire, my dearest Wood, that if you find you keep on not being well, you will settle bravely (for I know you would hate giving up the chance of promotion) to come home before the two years are up – I know all the difficulties and trials (as hard to bear in their way as knaves and blockheads and hard work and climate, etc.) of living at home, but I think with several of us together, and with walks to the pointing post, etc. we could get on very nicely – Papa really wants very much a son at home, and you of course are the one that ought to be there, and you shall – I daresay that everybody would say that I am an ass, but I don't care, and steadfastly, seriously, I advise and counsel you to come home and recruit your health and be a comfort to your parents and sisters. There is a very nice Miss Miles with £60,000, who will do very nicely for you, so make haste. I like you to write rougeish letters when you are rouged, I know by experience what a comfort it is to pour forth venomous sorrows it works off half their

sting – write one to me full of rouges – I am
very rouged at your being so far off and have
been crying most of the morning with rage
and grief at the thought of your staying two
more years – don't do it – it will be cruelty to
animals if you do... Come home – I cannot
write about anything else...

Such a letter was inspired not only by her affection and
longing for her absent brother, but by the restlessness and
boredom of an active young woman idle at home with her
brothers all engaged in stirring activities elsewhere.

In 1850 Marianne's cousin Edward Knatchbull
Hugessen, the eldest son of Lizzie's sister Fanny, proposed
marriage to her; in spite of dangerously close kinship and a
strain of physical frailty in Fanny Knatchbull's family – four
of her children died before they were forty, only three of
the nine survived her – Marianne's parents did not forbid
the match, and Fanny herself urged it with enthusiasm.
Marriages between cousins were common at that time, and
there were many within the families of this history. But
they left Marianne to make her own decision. Edward was a
year or two younger than his cousin, perhaps a fatal
impediment! The Rice girls were said to have a predilection
for elderly suitors. Marianne rejected his proposal, but
evidently did not close the door completely; when Edward
Knatchbull went off on a tour of Italy in the early summer
of 1851 accompanied by his cousin Morland Rice, he was
still much in love with Marianne, and not without hope
that she might change her mind. But on 20th May he wrote
to his mother from Naples – 'how astounded you will be to
hear that I am engaged... I now wait for your approbation
and consent...' His new love was Anna Maria Southwell,
the daughter of a clergyman, Rector of St Stephen's in St
Albans, who was travelling on the Continent with his wife

and daughter for the sake of his health. Edward continued to his mother:

> when I came from England... I firmly be-
> lieved that nothing on earth could ever make
> me love anyone but Marianne... at the same
> time I have never felt confident... that she
> would ever love me – I cannot tell how it hap-
> pened but by little and little my dearest Anna
> grew upon me... 'if there was no Marianne
> what a beautiful wife this lady would make
> me,' and then, how long I had loved her and
> how little I had been rewarded for doing so by
> any return of affection... you will show this to
> Marianne and tell her her prophecy has indeed
> come true, that I should fall in love with
> someone that I should meet abroad... yet I
> begin to think that my love for her has really
> always had a great deal of a kind of brotherly
> feeling in it – I ought to write to M. but I can-
> not – do tell her all and say I shall always be
> very fond of her, but will never tease her
> again.

It was a little awkward to be with Morland, not that there could be any real resentment. He concluded, 'whatever happens I must separate from Morland soon now because I must be near her as much as ever I can – I have money enough to pay his expenses, I hope he cannot really be called ill-treated.'

It is pleasant to learn that good relations were main-tained between the Edward Knatchbulls and Marianne and her family. After Anna died in 1889, Edward Knatchbull caused his children some resentment by becoming engaged only five months after her death to the twenty-five year old

Ethel Walker. She was the daughter of Colonel Walker of Crawfordton, Dumfries, a neighbour of Marianne and her husband at Maxwelton, where without doubt Edward had first met the young lady. In spite of his family's disapproval Edward married Ethel on 3rd June 1890, and it was from Marianne's house that the event took place. He had a very distinguished and interesting career as a politician and writer. He was Member of Parliament for Sandwich from 1857 to 1880 and held several offices; he was a Justice of the Peace and a Privy Councillor and was raised to the peerage as the 1st Baron Brabourne in 1880. His major claim to our interest is his editing of Jane Austen's letters to his mother, as well as other letters then available.

Marianne's chosen partner, when she married in 1857, was the son of old neighbours and friends in Dover, Sir John and Lady Bayley. Emilius was a clergyman of Evangelical views, a man of strong and dependable character who became a great supporter and adviser to the whole family, to the extent that Edward Royds Rice appointed him as one of his executors. He was known universally as Derby, because a horse called Emilius won the Derby the year he was born. The first years of their married life were spent at Woburn, where Emilius was vicar. They became very friendly with the family of Lord Charles Russell, a younger son of the 6th Duke of Bedford by his second wife, Georgiana Gordon; he had taken over the running of the estate, a little to the chagrin of his senior half-brothers.[4]

---

[4] Lord Tavistock, the half-brother of Charles Russell and heir to the Duke, wrote to his brother Lord William Russell in December 1832: 'Charles has now the management of everything; the shooting, stable department and the invitations, and it is curious to see how completely he rules my Father. He seems to do everything very well, with the exception of being a little too selfish and arbitrary.' (Georgiana Blakiston)

Marianne wrote an entertaining account of a picnic with the Russell ladies and children in the early days of her marriage – she wrote to her mother at Dane Court:

My dearest Mama,

Many thanks for your nice letter, but I am sorry, very, you wrote when your head ached, I had much rather you didn't, a few lines from somebody would appease me. There has been a good deal of electricity in the air the last few days… and I daresay it affected your head. I hope it is better – it rained almost all night but it is still hot. We went at one to the Charles Russells and had luncheon – Lady Charles and all the girls and governess had luncheon (their dinner) in the schoolroom – she is the most hearty talkative good-natured good-humoured person you ever saw, never stops talking; Clara the eldest, about 18 is rather a good-looking girl without being the least pretty, tallish, and pokes her head – regular features and good profile – Gertrude I told you about she is the most sturdy, maidish looking wonder, honest and blunt like Lady Charles, only not good-looking, which Lady Charles must have been, and is now. Elisma (?) the third, about 14 or 15, is the image of Lord Charles, quieter than the others, pale and lady-like looking, Isabella, 4th, they call D – she is a very nice little thing about 12 or 13, rather nice-looking, pretty rather, and a nice-mannered affectionate little fellow. They seem all nice girls and Gertrude a wonder rather – all luncheon-time they all talked very loud and fast in a variety of harsh swift voices they were all very civil and friendly to me not at all shy, and very soon got quite as if they had known me all their lives and followed me about talking – the youngest, George, a baby of 2½, came in with his nurse and sat on her lap and spooned up his food and said all sorts of dickey dickey docks at the instigation of his Mama and sisters who are all immensely fond and proud of him. The girls all waited upon Derby and ran round bringing him pudding and sugar, etc. I went out to look at the garden and then came home as they were to set off for their picnic at half-past two – we came back here and at half-past three drove in the pony-car to the wood at Bean Brickel (Brickhill?) where we found them all and Mr Coe – and after a good deal of settling we fixed on a place and Lady Charles and the nurse spread out the food and the girls and all the rest lighted a fire and did about and talked and yelped – Lady Charles brought a chair for me and at last we fell upon the food and eat strawberries and cake and Tea and buns – it rained the whole time hard except for about ½ an hour whilst we ate – a woman came up directly and was very insolent and stood there the whole time and wouldn't go and said she would call her husband if we didn't pay her something – we had taken sticks out of the hedge and I wished so Papa was there, and still more when the man came just as we were all setting off and said he would 'make you folk pay' and walked slowly round the donkey cart that brought the nurse and baby and food for names – he stood studying 'Charles James Fox Russell' for a long time and then kept walking round our pony car on which there is only a crest – then he walked up and turned Lady Charles and her girls out of the wood where they were standing waiting for their brougham – Lady Charles thought all the woods were the Duke's, but there is a Mr Cob that some belongs to, and the woman said her husband rented it off him, so that really I suppose they were in a way right, but they were so insolent that of course they got nothing – when everybody was out of the wood where the man was standing, Derby walked up the bank and into it where the man was and walked slowly about to see what he would do, I thought he would fly at Derby and kill him, he looked such a fierce wretch so I sent John up to be ready to help but he I suppose saw Derby looked fierce and walked away without speaking. I only wish you had seen the Russell girls in the rain – I shall never forget Gertrude, sitting on a camp-stool, her black silk gown (they are all in mourning for Lady Robert Seymour) pulled over her knees, and a very short sort of crinoline petticoat, none of the girls had any white petticoats on, long white legs with loose white stockings, very thick ankles with soft black boots, her legs crossed and her head back drinking out of a ginger-beer bottle, Lady George sat busy keeping little George dry under her cloak… it is near 10 so I must leave off – I hope somebody will write to me often and say how you are my darling Mama – I cannot bear not knowing – goodbye dearest Mama best love to all, I am ever your most affect. Mne Sophia Bayley.

Another of Marianne's letters, to her sister Louisa, describes the wedding of her cousin Georgina Elizabeth Knight to Frederick Pretyman, which took place on 31st August 1858 at Godmersham. Georgina was the daughter of Edward Knight junior and his first wife Dorothea Knatchbull. It is interesting that Morland Rice had courted his cousin, and actually became engaged to her, and finally withdrawn, which had caused some ill-feeling as well as grief and chagrin to the jilted girl. The fact that Morland had consulted Aunt Adela, Edward Knight's second wife, and Georgina's stepmother, with whom Georgina was not a favourite, turned the knife in the wound. Georgina's marriage was happy but of short duration, as poor Georgina died in 1864, possibly in childbed, like so many of her contemporaries.

Marianne wrote to her sister:

> L. Knight [possibly her Aunt Louisa Knight] wrote a good account of the wedding with some suggestions of mine, so I let myself off that, as it was altogether an uneventful one, tho' there are always things one sees that can't well be writ – and I had a letter from Morny begging I would write to him and tell him the chief features, which I did two or three days ago wishing he had asked me before he left home, as one cannot write the same things twice over – well. I am so delighted at the better accounts of Papa and Mama – I trust Papa will not forget how important it is to be careful – and also Mama must remember that the autumn damps and colds are to be met, and rheumatic times draw on. I think the house at home must be too cold for her to come down early… I think so of home and see

so well everything, the heavy sparkling dew in
Mama's garden at prayer-time, the sunny
stones and our bright warm shining gardens,
and lingering bits of Graham Moir jasmine.
Georgina is married and likes it very much. I
have a real dread of writing things from the
swift way that every remark and sentiment
flies round the family and brings one in Guilty
– so I was careful in writing to Morny not to
make any remark about Georgina etc. that I
didn't want to get round to Aunt Adela, as he
really can't help saying things – I wish poor
fellow (ha-ha) that he didn't always adopt a
rather contemptuous way of speaking of
Georgina – it does not become him in their
relative positions, and considering all she has
gone through on his account, poor girl –
Uncle Edward I am afraid has not at all
forgiven him, from a little conversation I had
with Georgina once about it. I know Morny so
well, that things that he does and says don't
make me think ill of him – but one can't wonder at Uncle Edward. Aunt Adela is so anxious
to prove that he never cared for her, that she
tells Uncle E. things with exaggerations that of
course make it worse. Please don't say a word
to Morny or anyone. I think the thing that
rankled most in Georgina and hurt her most,
was Morland's talking it all over with At.
Adela before it was broken off – instead of
their doing it between them – enough – let
bygones be bygones – and I am very glad indeed that G. is safely and I think happily
married. I am very fond of her, and we were
great friends. Mr Fred… is delighted with her

and immensely fond of her, and really anxious
to do all he possibly can to make her happy –
and she is the sort of steady unchanging girl
that having once begun is sure to go on getting
fonder and fonder of anyone who likes her.

Colonel Pretyman is quartered at Dover.
He knew darling Henry very well and thought
me the image of him... said he was quite star-
tled when he saw me – not knowing the least
who I was, he knew me by the likeness – we
all grow like him, I believe – Aunt May said so
too. He praised him so much and said he was
the nicest person he ever saw in his life and
that nobody ever knew him without loving
him. I thought Papa might like to ask him to
shoot – he is very ugly and very pleasant and
cheerful and good-natured – they are very
amiable people I think, they love their old
Mother to distraction, and take such care of
her – she is a nice large expanded carrot – everybody liked her. At. Adela was very smart in
strong pink flounced silk – and yellow tussore
with lilac – very fat and very good-natured and
shy – she nerved herself into suddenly calling
G. 'darling' and kissing her in the house in a
sudden frenzy of joy at her going away – but
they neither of them pretended to care for
leaving each other – which sooted. G. said
very often she was very glad – ha-ha – she
looked less pretty than I expected in her wed-
ding-dress but very pretty in her go-away
which was very nicely made and the sort of
simple rich pretty that becomes her better
than full dress... I don't think I ever saw
Georgina quite cry – tho' tears filled her bright

eyes now and then – she was as matter-of-fact and of course-ish as if she had been married very often. That is the sort of thing I did not say to Morland – and the grave way that she always from the first called him Frederick was so like her – don't you know the grave way she winks her eyes and rather sticks out her chin and says things – her face looked so nice and delicate and pretty and she is a very good girl I think. Yes, it makes me angry Aunt K's [Fanny Knatchbull] inveterate prejudice about Portals and she is the last person I should have told about 'red-faced one' which Derby heard in the train the day before the wedding and Uncle Charles told Aunt K. don't tell anyone else – I haven't. I like her very much, she is a very nice girl I think, very affectionate and altogether nice. People think her very plain I mean Uncle Charles, Aunt May etc. she is plain certainly, but I don't think so very, she has got a nice expression and a very nice look in her eyes when she smiles – I saw At. K. hating them all – with no reason, for they are very nice children, all of them and very nicely behaved and brought-up it appeared to me, Charlie is a nice little boy, but hideous. [All this refers no doubt to the young family of Edward Knight Junior and his second wife Adela, Portals on their mother's side, and therefore tainted socially according to Fanny's increasingly prejudiced view. The 'red-faced one' would probably be the oldest daughter, Elizabeth Adela, born 1841, and little Charlie was at this date twelve years old.] ... [Georgina's] evening silks – 2 – were much too much trimmed at the top to please our taste – a heap of lace and ribbon bows lashed on in a berthe shape – that is the fashion – my blue silk which I am good-naturedly going up to look at – I can't find it – Mary is gone out in the yacht [doubtless her maid] but I know it has got blue satin ribbon rather more than an inch wide gathered round the top and two rows of blonde or lace sewn on in a sort of berthe shape with bows of blue satin ribbon put where I have drawn them – what is your silk? How horridly sorry I am that you will all be gone when we go to Walmer… we mean to have our horses if we can, and to have ridden constantly over to home – but I can't risk Mama or Papa to be there then – if, as I suppose it is, it is not healthy. Ah me! I had a horrid fall in the yacht on Monday, down the ladder into the cabin – the Cook happily caught me and prevented my head from banging against the wall, I fainted from the shock and then was very sick, and my legs were very bruised but no hurt to signify and I felt it less afterwards than I expected. Mary had a much worse one head foremost over a pail in the kitchen, flat on her nose and face, on the stones, marking her nose and face and bruising them dreadfully. She sails forth in the yacht to support Derby, and I hate the yacht and go but seldom except to luncheon when it is quite still. Now we are going to rob fig-trees – my cheeks burn like flames and my back aches horribly with writing all this so I hope you will duly appreciate it… the babies are quite g– I want you to see baby she is the most

> perfect of sweets to me... We were so com-
> fortable at the rectory (Chawton) and liked
> our short visit so much. Uncle Charles and
> Aunt May are so comfortable... You write
> fearfully seldom – I wish you would oftener.

Derby soon left his parish at Woburn to take charge of a parish in the Bloomsbury area of London, providing another base for visiting family, perhaps not quite so smart as their other pieds-à-terre. Later he moved to St John's, Paddington, which must have been another tough and demanding parish. Many years later Derby inherited through a female relative a title and estate in Scotland, and became Sir Emilius Laurie of Maxwelton, with a home in Scotland which became another popular rendezvous for members of the family. Children arrived speedily, first Blanche, and then three sons, Claude, Wilfred and Cecil. Marianne after her marriage was always desperate to keep in touch ('write, write, write!') and concerned about people's state of health, particularly her mother's, express-ing herself firmly and forcefully on the subject. She made cogent comments on her relatives, though not uncharitably. Brother Edward visited – some time in the early 1860s:

> poor fellow, I hope Norah will not sadden
> him, he said rather bitterly that he daresayed
> he could do without her – somebody else that
> is nice is what to turn his thoughts...

Fanny Winchilsea was in London, and her son Murray was unwell. Derby and Marianne had been to sit with him:

> I am glad... that she is not thinking of going
> tomorrow it would kill Murray I think, he is
> no more fit to travel after being in bed all day

yesterday than he is to be thrown into the Serpentine and ought not certainly to have moved from Haverholme so soon – his cough is loose and not bad – but his voice has rather a bronchitic sound at times – which needs great care... dear little Murray, I think he is certainly much the nicest of them – tho' Henry is very nice – Evelyn much the least nice – in short at present I can't say I like her much poor little thing, she is so selfish and spoilt. I hate having written that as I should hate anybody having written it of any of mine, but having said it to Fanny I don't so much mind and she knows it... This is Sir John's birthday, [her father-in-law] and we dine at S. Lodge. Lady Bayley wrote to beg I would be 'very smart' which I can't be having got no new evening gown at all – but I shall wear my blue silk and diamond cross and try and invent something flaunting and vulgar for my head...

A fifth child must at some date have been born to Marianne and Derby; for in 1874 we learn in a letter that Elizabeth wrote to her son Ernest that the child had died.

I am so unhappy about dearest May [she wrote] I cannot bear to think of the misery she is enduring and Derby too, they were both so wrapped up in their little darling Arthur – the impossibility of the blank ever being filled up makes it so hopeless to say a word of comfort – no blank ever is filled up that death makes...

All Marianne's letters that survive are full of brief and vivid vignettes, such as her summer picture of Dane Court:

it is a lovely day Louisa at Dane Court. The limes are now in full blossom and today for the first time smell satisfactorily, waved about by a strong soft swishy very warm S.W. wind – a sort of day of which thousands have passed over our summer noses, and on which arrayed in our striped lilac prints we sat out and watched cricket in the 40 acres…

Or her comment on a visit to the village:

I walked yesterday to ask after Mrs Barwick, and didn't go in as they were all having tea in their Sunday gowns with enormous brooches with photographs of their husbands in their collars – about as big as small looking-glasses – she was not so well, and asked for jam, which Mama sent her – poor thing, I never thought she would get well – she lies in bed and has long fits of pain…

Even her last letter in 1909, taken down by her daughter Blanche from her bedside, and sent to her beloved sister Louisa, has the authentic touch of oddity:

My darling Louisa, Goodbye, do not be too miserable about me – or wish me to stay here – it is not likely that we shall be parted for long, and think what it will be if through God's mercy in Christ we are together where there is no more pain. I cannot help that thought being prominent with me. It is not odd but quite true that when I think of you now I almost always think of us walking about in Mama's garden with our bows and arrows

with nosegays tied at the top of them, and a red paeony which we pretended was ill, and had a doctor for! Goodbye darling, your most affect. M.S. Laurie
Dictated to Blanche.

7   Caroline Cassandra

Caroline Cassandra, eleven years younger than her sister Louisa, was a very different personality. There are several indications in the family letters that she was as she grew up a bit of a problem – as, for example, the hint in Louisa's letter quoted above that Confirmation had 'improved' her. Her niece Marcia wrote of her that she was 'somewhat of a puzzle and even a trouble to her family. She required a wider scope for talents which remained undeveloped, and had ambitions of which she herself was scarcely conscious. She should have had a university education, and might well have become head of a College.' As Marcia herself was one of the earliest female undergraduates at Oxford, and became headmistress of a well-known girls' school, she spoke as an authority. The boys discussed with their usual fraternal frankness her character and appearance as she grew up, and her chances in the marriage market. She was rather short in stature, and Morland remarked that her nose appeared to be growing at a disproportionate rate in comparison with the rest of her person. She was her father's constant companion, and his favourite daughter – Marcia wrote, 'she centred her love passionately upon her father, and upon her brother Walter, and to far too great an extent for her subsequent happiness upon Dane Court itself.' When their mother died at last in 1884, and Dane Court was cleared of its surviving inhabitants to make room for its new owners Edward Bridges Rice and his wife Ceci (who did not in fact occupy the old home till some years later), the experience for Louisa and Caroline Cassandra was a traumatic one, even though they were moved to an attractive smaller house only a short distance from their old home. Walter, their brother in the Royal Engineers, wrote to Ernest from Dane Court on the eve of his departure from it for the last time:

> My dear old Brod,
>
> I am off tomorrow morning by early train. I shall wave my hand to our dear old home, as such, for the last time. It is sad, but my dear old brod, there is so much for us all to be thankful for – homes over our heads etc., when others are deprived sometimes of every comfort on earth by the death of their relatives – so I refuse to be otherwise than brave – but it is rather a wrench when one comes to look back and forward. I have just been up to my mother's grave and send you 2 or 3 flowers taken off it, to put in your Bible and shew me when we next meet. The girls bear up well – they are most to be pitied – but are interested a little in their South Court arrangements, furnishing, etc. They stay here till the 19th of May then they both go to May [Marianne] in London and then to Bramber (home of Morland) and then I suppose to South Court. Morland and Car remain on a bit. Fanny comes over 13th to portion us all out some of Mama's things – dearest Mother, how thoughtful she was of all of us – no one quite knows what are her things and what are Edward's – but hers will be very few – and not much to divide between us – and as I shall not be here I daresay I shall get something I don't

care the least about but Dane Court being gone I don't much care about anything else. Edward has been very kind indeed I believe to the girls – and Ceci too, without of course being gushing – she will be glad doubtless to have a general 'go in' at the house when we are all clear off. They won't live at Dane Court for a long time – Elvington at first – and then do a good bit to Dane Court when he can raise the money, so for months if not years D.C. will have a caretaker in it and the rooks will caw and the birds sing and the wind howl round the empty house.

Thursday evening, United Services Club. Here I am and didn't I hate going. The two girls, I pity them very much, they are so crushed and miserable and worn and I quite hated leaving them this morning – Dane Court looked perfectly lovely yesterday evening as I stood on Mount Pleasant and looked around…

Although there is little in Caroline Cassandra's letters to indicate literary or intellectual interests, she was the only member of the family in that generation to leave any record of family history; these consist only of miscellaneous scraps and notes concerning the history of Dane Court, the life of the family and the early life of her father. Some notes were dictated to her niece Marcia in her old age. It is possible she may have intended a more coherent record, but all that survives is these fragments. In her middle years she became engaged in charitable work in London, becoming one of the 'Grey Ladies' of Deptford; Marcia recorded:

there she found herself. Her work in
Deptford, then a dreadful place, was really
remarkable, so much so that she was a constant anxiety to her superiors. She was quite
fearless, and penetrated into places where no
women had ever ventured. In spite of protestations she continued this work, and she made
herself, quite unconsciously, a strong influence in the place.

8   Florence

Florence Mary was the youngest of the five sisters. Born in
1841, with three brothers and six years dividing her from
Caroline Cassandra, and three years between her and her
younger brother Lionel – the last of the flock – she may
well have found herself, if not solitary, at least in an isolated
position in the family. The three brothers immediately
older than herself, Walter, Arthur and Ernest, were no
doubt boon companions to her in their childhood, but all
three soon left home to Woolwich, Mr Paul's School at
Shooter's Hill, and the Royal Naval College at Portsmouth
respectively. She received little mention in surviving letters
– from an unparticularised member of the nursery world,
she became good little Flossy, who danced attendance
devotedly on her mother in the absence of her seniors, and
began to grow into a 'tall miss'. From the single letter
written by her in the collection, one can observe that she
shared, indeed exceeded her sisters' tendency to overt
expressions of piety; the passage throws a light too on the
temperamental problems suffered by Caroline Cassandra,
with her reputation for being 'difficult'. Florence was
writing to Louisa from Haverholme Priory in January 1859,
where she was looking after the children in Fanny's

absence. After passages devoted to health and nursery matters, she added:

> Yes, dearest Louisa – I think we must all feel – as each New Year comes round – how much more and more we need to 'redeem the time' we have lost because 'the days (that is, practically, our own lives and hearts) are evil' – there is only one way – to keep on praying more and more earnestly for God's holy spirit even at points in which we find that notwithstanding all our prayers – we seem to lose rather than to gain it. We still ought always to pray and not to faint. Sometimes I think if dearest little Cam could see into all our hearts and see as I am sure she would see in mine that we have as many temptations and as many (or even more) falls to be miserable about as she has – she would be able to feel that a constant and determined inward struggle and warfare is not inconsistent with outward cheerfulness and activity in 'life' and 'family' matters and society – and even that the latter is a positive duty to aim at – I only say this as a mere suggestion – we none of us can know what are each other's inward feelings – but what, after all, an immense comfort and blessing it is that we are all as fond of each other as we are and can pray for each other as I know we all do – there – I have said my little say…

Clearly all the Rice daughters suffered to a greater or lesser extent from the disease so common amongst prosperous Victorian young ladies, compounded of hypochondria, (together with a certain amount of genuine ill health) frustration, emotional or intellectual or physical, or a combination of all three, and enforced idleness. The religiosity which is so alien and strained in its sentiments to most modern readers was of course the common currency of the period, but the sense of guilt which often pervades it seems almost ludicrous in relation to these blameless lives; it reflects either the anxieties caused by their innermost thoughts, or a sense of lives wasted and talents not put to the best use.

Florence married at an earlier age than her sisters; she married John Wright (1831–1901) a widower ten years her senior, whose first wife had been Emily Plumptre, a granddaughter of the John Plumptre who had wooed Fanny Knight and who had married Catherine Mathilda Methuen of Corsham. Emily had died in childbirth in 1860, leaving four children; the distraught widower had immediately set off on a journey of eight months through Scandinavia, Russia, Persia and Syria, 'often on horseback with little but a money-belt of gold sovereigns and a five-barrelled revolver'. These travels resulted in a book called *Old Ali*, describing his adventures. On his return he lost no time in seeking another wife, and married Florence early in 1862. They were to add another eleven children to his family of four, eight boys and three girls, Arthur completing the family in 1885.

John Wright's father had been Francis Wright (1806–1873) of Butterley in Derbyshire, a wealthy evangelical and charitable ironmaster and coal mine owner. He had a strong and enterprising character, and,

> besides building or restoring 27 churches and numerous schools and hospitals, he built in 1846–49 a handsome but idiosyncratic country house near the village of Osmaston; there was

a railway 300 feet long in the cellars for distributing coal, and all the chimney flues drew downwards to a large isolated stack at the rear of the house, thus leaving the flat roof uncluttered (this innovation proved unsuccessful so a normal roof and chimneys had to be added later). He showed some perspicacity in leaving the family business to his younger sons, in whose hands it prospered, but Osmaston Manor and a considerable fortune went to his oldest son John... John was, however, less successful in financial affairs, losing most of his money in unwise ventures and having to sell the Manor in 1883 (eventually in 1967 it was demolished as a white elephant by its new owner). After an interlude at Pau in the Pyrenees whither he drove with Florence and his older children in a four-in-hand, he settled at Hawkhurst in West Sussex, but nostalgically took the name of Osmaston in lieu of Wright for himself and his numerous family.[5]

Louisa continued in her role of support and nurse to her married sisters in their confinements or other crises, and her report in January 1864 gives a rather lurid description of such a visit to her sister Florence:

I had a painful night in head face and chest and same today but now towards evening my face is easier... it is violently enflamed and swelled – head bad – You can fancy the desperation of our state here – three maids in bed

[5] Henry Osmaston, *Foresters and Imperial Servants. The Osmaston Family*, The Commonwealth Forestry Review, March 1989.

yesterday – by my having Basil in here with his cot to sleep last night – we were both of us awake and he in my bed good but vivacious till 3 o'clock I shd. think and I had to get up and steam my chest and keep laying him down as he rose up to watch me, and ended by crawling out, at last in despair with pain and tire I laid him firmly in his cot as I had done unsuccessfully before and we each went to sleep – he was such a little darling – the new wet-nurse has come and baby has taken to her quite well… Floss has risen up better luckily but is of course weak and it was to save her that I had Basil. Did she tell you of Emmie [Emmie was the youngest of Emily Plumptre's children, now about four years old] hitting the wet nurse's baby on the head when she was left alone with it by chance yesterday? it shrieked for help – it was quite ill all day with a great swelling – she had been longing to hurt it and took the first opportunity and was horribly frightened when she had done it – I think she did it for curiosity to see what it did – poor little thing, it was laid on a basket (for convenience for a minute) in a shawl…

In September 1864 Florence and her husband came on a visit to Dane Court with two of the older children. Elizabeth reported, 'Floss… looks very poorly and burst into tears as soon as she came into the room. Aunt May hurried her off 'to take off her things' and she soon recovered poor dear and has been cheerful since…'

In September 1876 Edward's wife Ceci was staying at Dane Court with their son Henry, aged 11, and her letters to her husband, always very long and detailed, give much family news. She reported:

> Saturday Florence Osmaston and Basil arrived. Morland says he has written to you and he has I daresay told you of the change of name, I think it is a pity, it is more respectable to keep one's own name, whatever it is, and Wright is not bad enough to have any reason to change it – Florence is much better than I expected though she is very thin and able from indigestion to eat very little, and she has an irruption on her face; she dines with us but has breakfast upstairs and luncheon with your mother, and is downstairs a good deal, went to Church on Sunday morning, and walked a little in the afternoon; Basil is a nice boy now, nice mannered and unselfish, still ugly as to his nose and mouth. He is at Mr Bramston's house at Winchester, and going back there tomorrow.

Basil duly departed for school, in tears, and the proud mother of Henry reported that he 'went off to get the kitchen maid to cut him eight sandwiches which he (Basil) stuffed into his greatcoat pocket, he is quite changed since you saw him here, a really nice boy…'

Florence was evidently recovering from illness, but Ceci reported continued improvement, though it does seem that there was a psychological element in her condition – 'she goes out in your Father's old carriage, about the garden and wood, and she seems better in spirits, and I believe likes him (J.O.) much better' – a curious comment on a married relationship of upwards of fourteen years!

> Your Mother [continued Ceci] came and sat a
> little while yesterday afternoon partly talking
> about Florence, she has such an odd drawn
> look about her upper lip at times, which your
> mother had also observed, and which I told
> her I thought must be hysteria, and that that
> was what she perhaps had – it seemed quite a
> relief to your mother to think it was that, and
> she said she should write to the doctor F. is
> going to see and ask him…

A paper entitled *The Osmaston Memories* records family recollections of Florence and John and of all their children, too detailed to enumerate here. The youngest son, Arthur, described his father as a man of strong constitution and a firm and inflexible character, an autocrat and an intolerant fundamentalist Christian; but he was a devoted family man and loved and was beloved by his family, as long as they conformed to his views. After the collapse of his fortunes and enforced money-saving stay in France, he settled down on his estate in Sussex, Hawkhurst, and expended his energies in creating gardens and plantations there.

The younger children and grandchildren remembered Florence as a gentle, quiet, invalidish person, almost obsessively religious; she had been physically lively and active in earlier days, and was still a witty and entertaining conversationalist – a family trait. Much of her energy and influence latterly was exercised in healing the differences which arose amongst the family, particularly between father and sons. After John Osmaston's death (he died while conducting family prayers) the stricken widow lapsed into a state of permanent mourning and isolation. Her daughter Violet was married to Benjamin Nicholls and lived nearby at a house called Brownings with her young family. Florence required the family to come and live with her at

Hawkhurst, a move attended by some inconvenience to them, particularly to Benjamin, who had in consequence to make a long cycle ride every day to his farm, and to go to the trouble of letting his own house to tenants. The death of a younger daughter, Olive, who declined into melancholia after the death of her father, and succumbed to pneumonia six months later, contributed to the atmosphere of gloom and isolation in which the little grandchildren spent the early years of their childhood. One of them wrote:

> Here my childhood was spent, not with my mother, but with nurses. We scarcely saw her. In the early years the house was run as a house of mourning. Grandmamma spent much time on the drawing-room sofa, having her head stroked whenever possible. Everything was geared to Grandmamma's wishes and mode of life. She saw us once a day, brought down to the drawing-room after tea. Both my brother and sister suffered from severe nutritional disorders unrecognised – nothing was known of modern dietetics. No one was invited to the house except relatives; but these did come fairly often and I began to recognise and be slightly acquainted with the younger uncles when they visited, who were always welcomed and appreciated. So too, were the families of the 'Indian' cousins, Bertram's and Lionel's, who on their parents' rare visits from India, came to stay.

In November 1906 Ulric Osmaston, Florence's seventh son, spent a few days at Danefield in Tilmanstone with the family of his uncle Augustus Rice. (Augustus had died the previous year, leaving his widow and three unmarried daughters.) Helen Rice reported in her diary about his 'Collins' – in which he described his gloomy home, with poor Aunt Floss, Violet, Ben and their children in varying degrees of ill-health and depression – 'with what an atmosphere of gloom Hawkhurst must be pervaded! No wonder Olive was nearly out of her mind and had melancholia, poor thing.' Ulric attempted to liven things up at Hawkhurst – 'What? no papers, no *Punch*, no company?' he exclaimed. Although his family used to say of Ulric that he was more of a Rice than an Osmaston, perhaps because of a light-hearted entertaining quality and a gift with his pencil of caricature, Helen Rice wrote that when he was in London and took her to see 'Miss Hook of Holland' he brought with him a bullfinch in a tiny cage, 'who amongst ten thousand would do the like, except an Osmaston!' He and one other brother, the more forceful Cecil, joined the Forces, the oldest, Basil, a gentle and self-effacing bachelor, became a farmer, but the other brothers all spent their active lives in India, Ceylon or Australia, particularly as Forestry Officers in India, where they became renowned as naturalists and conservationists.

Florence died after a fall in 1910, at the age of sixty-nine, relatively young in comparison with her long-lived siblings. An aura of melancholy seems to shroud her memory, compounded of physical debility, mourning and obsessive religiosity; it is as if the vigour and humour that might have emerged and persisted in her were drained away by the large dominating presence of her husband, keen-eyed, black-bearded and autocratic.

9   George

George was Edward's junior by seven years; his career in the Navy followed that of his brother to a certain extent.

They were fortunate that from time to time their paths crossed and even ran parallel on occasion: for a period they even served in the same vessel. George's temperament and character, as far as one can judge from letters, was rather different from Edward's. He was less outwardly stoical and more emotional, lively in company, and clamorously devoted to his family and home. He suffered much from homesickness, and a remark in one of his brother Henry's letters in 1848, 'I feel quite sure that his quick promotion will put an end to his dislike of his profession...' implies that in the early years at least he did not much enjoy sailoring. In 1844, when he was seventeen, he was in HMS *Inconstant* under Captain Fremantle, stationed in Kingston, Jamaica, and about to be sent to Vera Cruz in South Mexico, a move he regarded as out of the frying pan into the fire.

> Fancy 6 months at a place like that [he wrote to Edward then at Plymouth] I should not care so much but I am afraid we shall get no letters all the time we are there or at least very seldom which I cannot bear the thought of – you know well what it is, not to hear from home for a long time.

He enquired eagerly for news of the family – Mama had just produced her fifteenth and final child, a son, Lionel, and 'dearest Fanny' with her tendency to be delicate, was tenderly asked after. George grieved for the death of 'poor Uncle Henry', their great-uncle, the third brother of Jane Austen – he had died this year at the age of seventy-nine. George thought nostalgically of springtime in Kent.

> Are the rooks building? and are there many there? would that I was at home to watch

them – this is the time of the year that I loved in England. Lovely fresh mornings with birds singing and little lambs capering about all of which I suppose will be when you get this letter or soon after. I hope my father has been fortunate in lambs this year – I wish I was riding our farms with him today instead of Atlantic billows…

In March 1850 George suffered another disappointment in missing meeting his sister Fanny at Lisbon. She had married the Earl of Winchilsea as his third wife, and they spent part of the wedding trip in Seville. George's ship HMS *Arrogant* arrived at Lisbon twelve hours after Fanny and her husband left for Gibraltar. George's grief at missing her at Lisbon was quite frantic, and brings home to us the heartfelt longing some of these young men must have experienced, exiled from home for very long periods of time in conditions often neither comfortable nor stimulating. He described in terms of hyperbole to his sister Louisa,

my painful feelings and the bitter rage and disappointment which I am still feeling – we went into Lisbon for a few hours on the 13th of March to get our letters and pick up our new Captain – and you can guess the rest! …I am certain I have never been so disappointed in all my life… I am so glad for Gusty [his brother Charles Augustus, in the Royal Engineers, who saw Fanny and her husband in Gibraltar] lucky fellow that he was to have seen both Edward and Fanny – and I have missed them. La, my love, I turn pale when I think of it… Well, it can't be helped… I have made up my mind to sorrow and disappointment.

George went on in this letter to describe life on board – hard work when they were short-handed – and some gruesome accidents when seamen fell from aloft on to the deck – '...We have just buried our poor shipmate. It was quite calm and the hollow plunge into the sea sounded all over the ship. Poor fellow, he will be forgotten by tomorrow by many.'

It was not long before George was home for a period of leave before preparing to join his brother Edward in the Far East. Their destination was Burma, which had for some time been causing trouble to Britain by sending invading armies into Assam in N.E. India, and by hampering the activities of British traders in Rangoon. This at least gave Britain the pretext to commence the annexation of Burma, which, starting in 1824 with the First Burma War, continued at this period up to 1853 and was completed with the annexation of upper Burma in 1886. Edward had sailed in HMS *Hastings* as lieutenant under his cousin Captain Frank Austen, son of Admiral Frances Austen; the latter's brother, Admiral Charles Austen was to join the ship as his flagship later at Suez. George was to follow in a smaller vessel, the frigate HMS *Fox*. At Portsmouth waiting to sail, he was busy collecting music for the ship's band, and demanded copies from his sisters. He also enjoyed such social amusements as the port offered.

Another Lovess of mine has just been alongside to see me [he wrote, and continued rather unflatteringly] or rather two Lovesses, Misses Byng and Vincent, they having come all the way to Spithead to see me and ask me to dinner – but I would not go, to their chagrin, ha-

ha! – Byng you know of, Vincent is a cousin of hers who has been staying here for some days and has fallen in love with me, poor thing! I know you like to know what she is like, so I shall tell – well, she is very like a pale fox with its nose bent very much down and with languishing eyes and an oval mouth – I really think you must see what that is like, it is a very good description of her – and yet she is not ugly. Her mother is a very fat Mrs Charles Bailey – who has been able to sing at some remote period but now only thinks she can, and screeches most vilely all the evening.

George mentioned that they had 'a very young set of Middies. There are eighteen of them under 17…' Their life was hard and their prospects dubious, in service overseas – many died of disease. They were dependent too on the attitude to them of their senior officers, and George was evidently one who was kind to them and took an interest in them, perhaps recalling his own periods of unhappiness at the same stage. Young Prince Ernest of Leiningen, the nephew of Queen Victoria through his mother, the half-sister of the Queen, who had been with George in *Arrogant* was determined to accompany his friend in *Fox*.

I heard from Prince Ernest two days ago [George wrote] he was then in London on his way to join the Queen and Prince Albert – they have sent for him to come and settle about going in *Fox* – I wrote to him at Balmoral to push him up and make him come.

Morland reported to Edward that:

George's friend Prince Ernest of Leiningen left the *Arrogant* because George did and came home to ask the Queen to let him go with George in the *Fox* – so he joined her yesterday and sails for the East tomorrow. He must be rather a brick I should think to like leaving Balmoral and grouse-shooting for a Midi's berth in a baddish old frigate going to the East – all along of friendship…

During the spring of 1851 George and Edward were often together, serving on the East India Station based at Trincomalee, or on the China Station, at Hong Kong and elsewhere in that region. Edward was acting captain of their uncle's flagship HMS *Hastings* for much of the time, as the captain, their cousin Frank Austen, was in Madras with his wife, (his Uncle Charles's daughter Fanny) who was ill. The companionship of his brother, as well as the comfort provided by Uncle Admiral Charles Austen's home on shore at Trincomalee, made this a pleasant time for George. George wrote long letters to his brother Cecil, a soldier serving in Halifax, Nova Scotia, describing this agreeable, if temporary situation; he concluded one letter:

Well, old Chisel, …I think you will like it (Halifax) very much indeed – or rather you will like the sleighing, skating and Moose shooting in the Winter, and the Picnics in the Summer – I mean the public ones. You will find that I am pretty generally known among the Halifax gals. Some of them are very pretty and nice and of course you will fall in love with them – I will send you a letter of intro-duction to some very great friends of mine named Hill – they consist of several very beautiful daughters with no money so don't marry any of them – a Father who holds the exalted rank of a Dockyard clerk – and a nice old Mother – if you get there before my letter, round you go and call on them – I am sure you will be well received. They taught me to dance – an accomplishment at which they are stunners so don't forget Mary Hill.

Over the next twelve months or more George cruised about the wide oceans comprising the British Naval 'China Station' from Madras and Trincomalee to Rangoon, Singapore and Hong Kong. He had been transferred from *Fox* to a small brig, *Lily*, and as the Captain had been invalided, George was put in temporary command, which was hard work and expensive, as he did not draw commander's pay, nor expenses for the cost of entertaining local dignitaries.

I find that being First and Captain and 'Protector of British Interests' is ruinous work – all sorts of officials and gents come on board to see the Captain and I have of course to serve out the corresponding refreshments... I would not care if I was pulling the Commander's pay and Battel into my pocket or even if there was any chance of my remaining in my present place... I don't care how soon the new man makes his appearance for pleasant as it is being Commander and being in such a situation, my pocket cannot stand it – I am beautifying the brig a little, and I flatter myself she looks rather the cheese...

At this period his letters portray a rather dispirited George, overworked and frequently unwell. The references in the letters to headaches, insomnia, 'attacks' (malaria or dysentery, perhaps) tell their sorry tale of the debilitating effect of the climate and conditions on even strong young constitutions. Loneliness and lack of home news played their part too – he wrote to Edward at Trincomalee from Amoy:

> …our Mail arrived yesterday and I was taken down a peg or two by not receiving a single line from anybody – I have not heard from home since I left *Fox* and am beginning to get rather anxious for a letter… I am terribly lonely here – there is nothing to do except for me – and I am sorry to say I am losing a lot of my energy. I have been losing strength ever since leaving Singapore – and now I can scarcely get myself to turn out in the morning. We are all suffering from coughs and colds now – I have a very bad one, but I hope it will soon go. It is pretty cool here out of the sun, but the effects of the sun are terrible – I cannot stand it a bit, which is something new for me for I have hitherto braved the sun pretty well, I hope you are quite well and have quite got rid of all your boils – and the dear old Admiral – I hope he's quite well, how I should enjoy another sight of his face.

In the course of these letters George referred frequently to his uncle Admiral Charles Austen, always with warm affection as 'the dear old Admiral'. He was much concerned with the Admiral's health, which was not good, and in fact necessitated him taking leave in April 1852 in Calcutta as the guest of the Governor-General, Lord Dalhousie, actually after the commencement of operations against the Burmese; in this first phase the Admiral had led the naval contingent in the operation which resulted in the fall of Rangoon. Charles Austen's condition cannot have been improved by a family tragedy which befell him at this time, the death of his son Henry as a result of an accident at the Cape. Henry Austen had started his career in the Navy, and had served as a Volunteer (a rank somewhat similar to midshipman) under his father in *Bellerophon* at the siege and capture of St Jean d'Acre in 1840 when he was fifteen years old. But three years later he is found as an ensign in the 81st Regiment of Foot, in which he rose – by purchase – to the rank of Captain, transferring to the 73rd Regiment. In October 1851 the regiment was at Grahamstown in Cape Province, and here on 21st October Henry died as a result of a fall, at the age of twenty-five. That there was something mysterious and possibly disreputable about the accident is suggested by George's remarks in a letter he wrote to Cecil on 24th February 1852:

> I know you have of course heard of poor Henry Austen's death at the Cape under such melancholy circumstances – it has been a dreadful blow to the good old Admiral and it will be long before he gets over it entirely – it was a miserable death to die, certainly – I am very sorry that he did not die in action for his parents' sake. I saw him at the Cape when we were coming out. None of the officers of the *Rupert* have written a line to the Admiral about it – and all his information has been gathered from the papers. It is odd that the Colonel has not written, I think, don't you?

Soon George found himself, greatly to his satisfaction, involved in action against the Burmese in his little *Fox*, mainly engaged in attacking forts and stockades in the Irawaddy River, all described in great detail in his letters home. While very excited to be part of the action, George was horrified by the slaughter, and by the terrible toll taken by sunstroke and cholera. With unconscious prophecy, he wrote, 'War is dreadful – we ought to invent some horrid machine that would frighten people without killing them.' George saw his Uncle Charles at Rangoon in May, 'I fear that you will find him much altered in appearance unless he improves...' he wrote to Edward, 'I cannot help feeling anxious about him...' In the course of operations about this time, George suffered an injury to his hand, evidently a bullet wound in the wrist; the wound seemed to mend quite well, but he had to be content with non-combative duties in the background for some time thereafter. However, reunited with Edward, he was able to take part in the assault and capture of Prome, up the Irawaddy, where he and Edward both earned commendations for gallantry and leadership; shortly after this, George fell seriously ill with dysentery, and was despatched to convalesce to Maulmein, a more healthy place on the eastern side of the Gulf of Martaban, where he was very comfortably housed in a private home of a British family, including some pretty daughters. Here he seemed to be regaining his health and wrote long letters home, including an account of the death near Prome of Admiral Charles Austen.

> You will have heard of our great loss in the death of our dear and gallant old Admiral Uncle Charles Austen. He died near Prome of Cholera very suddenly the day before I arrived there – I was not so very much astonished as I had been dreading something of the sort ever

since he entered the river but I was terribly shocked. He was beloved by everybody that knew him and he had so endeared himself to such of the Army as came in contact with him that I saw several officers shed tears when they heard of his death. He was without exception the kindest-hearted and the most perfectly gentlemanlike man I ever knew. How sorry dearest Mama will be – his remains have been conveyed to Trincomalee for burial – his family are there, and I quite expect it will kill his poor old wife…

Barely a month later, Charles's older brother Edward Knight, the father of Lizzie Rice, died, peacefully as he had lived; thus there survived of Jane Austen's five brothers (six, if one does not exclude poor George, who was defective, and never mentioned; he had died in 1838) only Francis, who died, full of years and honours, in 1865.

George's letters were full of interest in his current surroundings, and plans for the future, but by the New Year, his health had so much deteriorated that he was on his way home 'overland', i.e., not round the Cape but via the Red Sea and the Mediterranean. He was so ill that doctors in Alexandria doubted that he could survive the last stages of the journey. Members of the family described his arrival, in early March, at Southampton, 'in almost the last stages of decline'. The account of his arrival at Dane Court, where he 'walked slowly and gently upstairs to the green room, leaning hard on Morny and Gusty' remind one of the account in *Mansfield Park* of a similar arrival of the sick Tom Bertram, where his mother is shaken out of her customary state of indolent indifference to exclaim to Fanny, 'I am so shocked to see him, that I do not know what to do…' George's last days – he died only a few weeks after his return – were documented in great detail by his sisters, writing to Cecil, the brother, along with Charles Augustus, closest to George, and at that time far away in Nova Scotia. It was a very Victorian scene, family clustered round the bedside, the consolations of religion gratifyingly evident, last words spoken and the beloved features tenderly described; a scene which, were one to read it in a novel by Dickens, one might presume to be idealised and unreal, but in this case absolutely authentic. Lizzie's letter to Cecil is very characteristic of her directness and strength of feeling and her Christian hopes – as always, sympathy and straightforwardness without undue sentimentality are her hallmarks:

> My dearest Cecil [she wrote] I cannot leave so many letters having been sent to you without a line from me and yet I hardly know what to say. There is no use in avoiding the subject which engrosses all my thoughts and there is no use in writing about it to add to the sorrow which I know too well you have been and still are feeling. It will be long before you can realise the dreadful fact that our darling George is gone from us for ever, even to us who saw it all, it seems like a dream! From the moment that we heard he had arrived at Southampton, it seemed like a frightful dream! seeing how ill he was! seeing him arrive in almost the last stage of decline, the 3 weeks of agonising hopes and fears, the pain of body and mind he underwent, and finally the closing scene of peace and almost happiness which he said he felt, forms altogether such a retrospect as nearly to break one's heart with grief and sorrow for what we have lost and never can see

again in this world. I know we have very much to be thankful for… that he was permitted to come home at all is a thing to be sufficiently thankful for and the comfort is great to me little as it signifies now… [he] was surrounded by all he loved most in the world and whose love for him he was well assured of – dearest darling George – how can I ever bear to think that the rest of my life must be passed without ever having the happiness of seeing him again. I am indeed very miserable, my dearest Cecil, and so I know are you, for you loved him as much as he did you and that was not a little as you would have felt if you had heard him speak of you in his last moments; his bodily sufferings were very great, poor darling, it nearly kills me to think of them even now when all suffering for him is over for ever, but what made us by far more miserable was to see his unhappiness and anxiety about his own salvation. This made us wretched but as you have been told all his fears dispersed and by the wonderful influence of God's Holy Spirit upon his mind whilst he was as we thought lying for several hours quite unconscious, he awoke quite happy, ready and anxious indeed to die and feeling as he said assured of forgiveness and eternal happiness – it was a scene never to be forgotten by all who witnessed it… How we felt for you dearest Cecil with no one to talk to or enter into your wretchedness, poor Edward too, he does not even yet know the sad news – Morland has been waiting at Portsmouth the last 10 days and hoping the *Hastings* would come, but she is not come yet

– do you know that though I have been writing this to you I still can hardly believe it, I look up and see all looking just the same, the rooks he used to be so fond of watching, the trees all coming out, the garden wood full of primroses everything seeming so happy and spring-like, and full of recollections of him and he himself gone from it all. I try to comfort myself with the thought, and so must you, dearest Cecil, that he would not if he could come back again – we ought not to weep for him but for ourselves – I cannot write on any other subject so I shall say goodbye...

10   Charles Augustus

Charles Augustus, born in 1828, formed with his older brother George and his younger brother Cecil a middle trio of the ten Rice brothers. The two survivors of this group were close friends all their lives, and there are entries in the diaries of one of Charles Augustus' daughters of the welcome visits of Cecil to their home in Tilmanstone, where he would sit in the kitchen in the evening, smoking cheroots and recalling his experiences in the Crimea and in India to his enthralled audience of nieces and his admiring brother. Augustus (he was always called Gusty by the family) did not have the exciting military career of his younger brother. His niece Marcia wrote:

Augustus stands apart in many ways from the other brothers of his family. His physique was weaker, his temperament less buoyant, his spiritual qualities earlier developed. He had a strong individuality... he had never good health, and his career in the Royal Engineers must have been a disappointment to him. Living for years in the Dane Court village of Tilmanstone he had great call both for patience and for long suffering in his daily relations with his parents and his sisters, so great was their reliance on his wise judgement, and so incessant the sisters' claim on his time and companionship.

Augustus was sent to Woolwich and gained a commission in the Engineers; his experience of overseas service was more limited than his brothers', periods in Corfu and Gibraltar – in the latter place he had more luck than George in seeing his sister Fanny and her new husband. But quite early in his career his health broke down, though there is no information as to the nature of his ailments. He spent time in Malvern with his sister Louisa, drinking the waters and undergoing a popular treatment there which seemed to consist of being wrapped in towels soaked in ice-cold water! At the outbreak of the Crimean War, there were four of the Rice brothers at the scene of action, but apparently Augustus' role was a passive one – he was on sick leave, which he spent aboard his brother Edward's ship *Leander*. The treatments for his condition, whatever it was, do seem to have been bizarre.

Much of the rest of his service seems to have been spent in Dover. The only letter which has survived from his pen was written to his sister Louisa, and describes his arrival at Dane Court from Dover one lovely evening in May 1861, to find the house abandoned by its usual residents and undergoing a rigorous spring-cleaning. Like his mother and all his family who ever mentioned Dane Court in their letters, he rejoiced in its beauty and tranquillity:

My dearest Lou [he wrote] On Tuesday at
two o'clock I drove home in my short coat –
called on the poor old soldier at Ashley in my
way in obedience to orders received from
Good little Caroline, found him weak, infirm
and very poor, they miss the dinners from
Waldenhan twice a week sadly – I got home
about 4, having been over to Purchase [a
neighbouring farm] ...I hobbled up into the
woods to the Goose below the Grotto. It was a
lovely afternoon and everything was far too
lovely for description. The shades of evening
had fallen early on the terrace walk where two
half-grown young rabbits supped on young
grass and daisies – as I approached they sat
erect and motionless till I got pretty near and
then discovering suddenly that I was a peram-
bulating monster they dived into the bluebells
which carpet the wood, to the consternation of
several blackbirds whose nests I immediately
found hard by in the evergreens, all along the
walk was a glorious damp smell of bluebells
and moss. There was not a breath of wind,
thrushes screamed from the large oaks in the
middle of the wood, and nightingales far and
near. The cows were slowly walking in to be
milked as they have done for the last 40 years
with Dawkins in his shirt-sleeves and a long
crooked stick in his hands. In the eleven acres
it was quite hot and sunshiny still, and quantities of cowslips scattered abroad on the
emerald sward – single rooks walking about
for unwary worms and overfed young rooks
sitting expectant with quivering wings waiting
to receive their nauseous portions. Your wily

wood-pigeon cooed in the distant grove waiting the departure of the punctual Gooseling [i.e., Gusty himself] to descend and feed heartily on aspiring peas – Ramsgate sat silent and glaring, crossed by a line of thin blue mist over which might be seen one white sail, betokening the becalmed mariner – the white and red lilacs outside the grotto were coming into blossom and the grass grown rank and tall – the inside of the grotto looked sad and deserted, but lovely enough, with a wren, as of yore, creeping in and out of holes in every direction, pretending its nest was everywhere but where it was – little knowing that I had known where its nest was twenty years before its great-grandmother was laid in the same hole. The primroses and anemones have yielded to bluebells, orchis and red robins in rank profusion – yes, Lou, you and May and old Floss know two or three things of all this better than I can tell you – but the actual experience of it was too lovely, though the desertion of the place made it sad – 'and so 'twill be when we are gone, The garden wood will still go on…' I had tea in the old schoolroom and then went out to the stable and smoked outside sitting on a stable chair. The noises had subsided into silence broken only by a nightingale in the garden wood and Mount Pleasant and now and then a stifled caw from a somniferous rook. A white mist rising in the pony meadow and long meadow afforded a fine chance for smells of earth to reign abroad which Tawny was inhaling with satisfaction after the day's work which he never fails in getting – all the other ponies and horses have their shoes off to rest but Tawny is too old and worn to be allowed any indulgence and so he sleeps in his boots to be ready to work early the next morning.

…I went into your room and was edified at the sight – I wanted to choose a room to sleep in as they were all upside down, but yours was upest side down of any of them – piles of mattresses and white basons in the middle of the room, a looking-glass knocked down on its face, no carpet, and hopeless confusion reigned. I retreated rapidly, sickened at the sight, to try Mama's room – this was arrayed in sepulchral white sheets tied all over. Everything gave a dim aspect painful to behold – away I went to the first passage room and finally settled on that to sleep in – about 10 I was disturbed by maidish shrieks and going out stick in hand discovered two stupid housemaids frightened out of their wits by a rat which they had seen – they did not dare come down the garret stairs to shew me where it was – I should think from their state of alarm that the reign of the rats must be absolute in the family's absence …I was valeted and waited on by several maids and Charles, the latter went away at seven the next morning for a holiday …so the house is left to itself save Laundry Kitchen and two Housers, William and John. The evergreens are sad to behold – all cut down and the stables exposed to view – my knee you will be sorry to hear is worse than it was – I do too much and cannot help it whilst here on duty – I must see a Dr when I go to London which I shall likely do the 1st of June in my way to Anthony[6] for a fortnight to stand godfather to Miss Caroline Carew... C.A.R.

The only other manifestation of the literary talent of Augustus was a novel, published by Hatchard's in 1876; it was called *Boy Mill*, and was illustrated by Fanny Winchilsea's daughter Evelyn Templetown (née Finch-Hatton). It is a lively tale, attractively told with a great deal of humour, and draws very closely on the backgrounds and characters with which the author was familiar. The hero is the only son of a wealthy and aristocratic family, whose estate owes much to Augustus' knowledge of Eastwell and Godmersham; he is at Woolwich Military Academy, of which Augustus writes with personal knowledge; and when the young man goes to sea – as the result of a dramatic duel with a highly improbable dénouement – Augustus is able to draw on his knowledge of naval matters derived from his naval brothers, just as the scenes in Sydney Harbour must owe a debt to his brother Lionel. His heroes and heroines are conventional, though the former – there are three of them – are well differentiated; the young men are above all manly, courageous and high-minded, their chief faults impetuous temper quickly aroused by insolent and 'cowardly' behaviour, and a tendency to a Darcy-like grimness of demeanour, concealing, of course, admirably noble and unselfish motives. The girls are spirited, but innocent and ignorant, and liable to fall into depression and near-terminal illness under adversity. His best characters are the 'lower orders', whose dialogue is clearly drawn from

---

[6]The home, near Plymouth, of the Pole-Carews; many of the Rice brothers were friendly with the sons, and were frequent visitors to Anthony.

Augustus' own recollections of family servants. As an
example, in a conversation between Harry Elmhurst, the
'young master', and the coachman Daniel:

> 'By the bye, [says Harry] how has Hippo-
> potamus turned out? My Father gave a long
> price for him.'
>
> 'Wal, Sir,' (Daniel invariably prefaced his
> answers by 'Wal, Sir') 'Wal Sir, the horse do
> well enough he ride cheerful, and he look
> cheerful, but he dry gummy, Sir.'
>
> 'Dry gummy, what does the fellow mean?'
> said Harry to himself, scarcely able to help
> laughing.
>
> 'Oh, he dry gummy, does he, Daniel?
> That's a pity.'
>
> 'Yes, Sir. When my master give the horse a
> gallop and bring him in warm, he do dry very
> gummy, and takes deal of elbow-grease. How-
> somever, Sir, he's a uncommon good 'os to
> 'ounds, Sir.'

And again,

> 'I hear your old Tabby is dead, Daniel, how
> came that about?'
>
> 'Wal, Sir, the cat she took on to poaching,
> and I thought it best to get rid of her before
> she came to a vilent hend, Sir.'
>
> 'Certainly; did you shoot her, Daniel?'
>
> 'Wal, Sir, Mr Gerout, he come out to the
> stable one morning, and we put her into the
> stable cistern, poo thing; and when she come
> up one side, I fetch her spat, and when she
> come up the nother side, Mr Gerout, he fetch

her spat, and she was soon drownded, poo thing.'

The two characteristics evident in the letter quoted above, a detailed observation of the beauties of the countryside and a self-deprecating ironic tone, are both exemplified in the novel; he describes his heroine, Alice, as having 'once fallen in love, but finding there was a chance of its being reciprocal, she had fallen out of it again as quick as possible.' His amusing account of the row of tongue-tied young naval officers at the dinner table of the Governor-General of New South Wales smacks of reported experience, and the names given to the ferocious aunts of the orphaned Heathcote children, 'Battle', 'Murder' and 'Sudden Death' must surely be a family joke.

Augustus' account of the Battle of Meanee in February 1843, in which Sir Charles Napier and a modest force defeated a huge army of 'Belochees' (Afghans) and thereby enabled the annexation of Sind (giving rise to the General's witty telegram home, the single word 'Peccavi'), is very graphic and detailed; the pen of the soldier is evidently at work. The scenes of carnage he describes recall Cecil's accounts of the taking of Balaclava. The description of the death of Charles Heathcote in the arms of his friend Edward Vernon recalls in its recording of every detail the death of George at Dane Court, and is over-sentimental to modern taste.

But it drew many a tear from his contemporary readers. Edward wrote to his wife Ceci in November 1876:

> I have been reading Augustus' book *Boy Mill* and like it – he has a great power of writing sad things well – the death of C. Heathcote for example – and he puts in clever touches of character without dwelling on them – and ex-

plaining – I think he should not have called Hurstwood 'the Abbey' and then said it was built as a dwelling house in Henry VII's time but perhaps that is being hypercritical – I am so glad he has preserved William's sayings in Daniel – I hope the mixture of old Daniel at Godmersham and William at Dane Court will prevent W. finding himself out. He had Chawton and Uncle Edward in his eye too very much in all his descriptions with a mixture of Godmersham and Eastwell. Sir William Hope is quite enough like Keppel for a picture. I wonder he could put Harry Elmhurst in so completely as to name – short and ugly! too which he is! His sketch of the Captain of the Marines and Master-at-Arms and Boy Mill together made me laugh and are not too much overdrawn. The death story of Heathcote made me blow my nose at least to say no more – altogether a very nice book… I think there is a little too much poetry at first.

Augustus retired from the Army early, with the rank of Major, and soon after, in December 1875, he married his first cousin, Adela Mary Margaretta Knight, at Chawton. Adela was one of the five daughters of Edward Knight junior and his second wife, Adela Portal; all five daughters bore their mother's name as well as their own personal names.

Possibly some mild discouragement was encountered over this marriage, more on account of kinship than the Portal lack of gentility which was rather a bugbear within the family. In Augustus' novel he remarked with mild irony – 'I will not here detain my readers with a subject so prosaic, and as many would say, so undesirable, as a love-affair between cousins…'

Elizabeth told her son Edward, who had sent her a telegram as soon as the ceremony at Chawton was over, that the servants had enjoyed Punch and a plum cake to celebrate, and that Augustus had left wine and cake to be distributed amongst 'the Old Villagers'. She had half-feared that the highly-strung Augustus would panic at the last moment 'I had no idea that Augustus would go through it all so well, and in fact I was prepared all day for a Fly tearing up to the door with him in it pale and mad!'

Augustus was forty-seven years old, his bride only twenty-five. They settled first at South Court, a stone's throw from Dane Court, and on their small property kept cows and poultry. Augustus became, after his father's death, an indispensable support to his mother and sisters. After Lizzie died and Louisa and Caroline Cassandra moved into South Court, Augustus and his family moved into another house in Tilmanstone called Danefield.

He had three daughters, and one of them, Helen, kept diaries for several years, from which we learn of their contented and lively existence, surrounded by friends and cousins, aunts and uncles, and with many interchanges of visits between relations further afield, particularly the numerous married members of the Knight family.

Augustus was never very prosperous financially, and the diaries are full of cheerful contriving, sales bargains and the triumphant acquisition of a few shillings from the sale of produce or home-reared pets or chickens. In spite of the lack of robust health, Augustus lived to the age of seventy-seven, dying after a long and crippling illness in 1905.

11 Cecil

Of all the Rice brothers, Cecil was reckoned by his siblings to be 'the regular cheese'. His daughter Marcia confessed it was difficult to write about him without affectionate filial prejudice, but she quoted the opinions of many relations and friends to testify to his numerous admirable qualities.

> My father [she wrote] was very tall, and all his life had a wonderful figure and carriage, an ideal specimen of a soldier, moving with freedom and ease, a notable figure, his upright, soldierly bearing and commanding stature making him conspicuous in any assembly. Like many other of his brothers he was very good-looking, with the rare attraction difficult to define that the Rice brothers all possessed. My father had this to a marked degree, but was entirely unconscious of the fact. He was by nature happy, enjoying his neighbours' society, courteous and friendly, modest and unassuming and interested in others rather than himself, and most certainly he was universally respected and loved.

Cecil followed his brother Augustus to Paul's School, Shooter's Hill, a school which prepared boys for the Army. He remembered the journey to the school, in the carriage to a point on the Dover road where the London coach could pick them up and deposit them at Shooter's Hill, and the freezing cold in early winter mornings when the smaller boys could never get near the fire, and suffered terribly from chilblains. Cecil proceeded to Sandhurst, where, when he passed out in 1848, he was awarded the Sword of Honour; unfortunately that year for some reason the actual sword was not forthcoming, and Cecil received four volumes of the works of Milton, handsomely bound and inscribed. His chagrin was considerable. Cecil joined the 72nd Highland Regiment, and there survives an amusing letter he wrote to Louisa from a posting in Alderney, in which he describes the provincial gentilities of the islanders. The date was July 1851, and Cecil was twenty, with much of the scathing snobbishness of his age and class:

> ...Are the gooseberries getting ripe, and have you got green peas ready to feed on? I ask that because such things are not to be had here, you might as well try to get a dish of minced ferrets as of green peas... Oh, I hope someone will write and tell me what... Dawks [the Rice butler] thought of the Exhibition,[7] did he like it and London or was he disappointed at not finding all the things made of gold. The Alderney people are capital fun, the greatest snobs you ever saw, they think they are as they call it 'exceedingly genteel'. If one girl meets another in the street, she says always 'Good-morning, Miss' or if there are more than one, 'How do you do, ladies?' and they invariably call all gentlemen 'Sir'. – 'If you please, Sir, may I ask for the sugar', 'Oh, thank-you, Sir'. These are the aristocracy of the place, and have made their fortune in the village, how I can't conceive. The head one of them all is the Judge of Alderney, a man of the greatest importance. I went to an evening party at his house a few nights ago. 'Tea at 9' as he called it in his note and he was right enough there

---

[7] The Great Exhibition at the specially built Crystal Palace in Hyde Park, which opened in May 1851.

for a more outrageous tea-fight I never witnessed, men with short trousers well strapped down, and Ladies with very dirty nails who wore short black jackets and large white gowns and belaboured one unfortunate pianoforte which I should think from the sound of it must have received many very severe lickings lately, and when the supper came, it was ten times better fun than ever, most of the gentlemen no sooner got into the room than they left the ladies entirely to their own devices, and proceeded to get drunk in a corner alone, superintended by the village doctor and his brother-in-law who to my horror proclaimed in a loud and cheerful voice that his name was Rice and that he had a brother in some regiment (corporal of Pioneers, I have no doubt) who might perhaps being a namesake of mine be also my intimate friend. I was delighted to be able to tell him as civilly as I could that I had never had the pleasure of hearing of him; in the meantime, the girls, who seemed to have had no food for some days, fell to like so many cormorants, my friend, rather a pretty girl, a Miss Sandford, bolted two large glasses of jelly and a plate of strawberries and cream in no time, and finished up with two very large thick beef sandwiches, refreshing herself between the attacks with champagne. How she got home I can't say, but I have seen her since then, and strange to relate she is quite well. I wrote a long account of the party to May a few days ago, but I forgot to tell you about it... I laughed all night at it and dreamed of nothing else when I went to bed... There was no dancing at the Judge's party, only conversation (much more refined, my dear Caroline) and pianoforte. I tried the first but failed miserably, I began at one girl and said, 'Have you lived long at Alderney?' Girl, 'Have I lived long at Alderney? Oh, yes,' 'Do you like it?' 'Do I like it? Oh, no.' 'Do you ride much here?' 'Do I ride? Oh, no.' I was quite vanquished then and retired quickly, and at the pianoforte I was rather worse off, three girls together having almost bellowed our ears to bits, pulled up, I suppose completely blown. I began to thank them and praise their song, but I found they were rather insulted and discovered that there were nearly seven pages more yet. However at supper we made it all up, I plied them well with victuals...

His next posting was to North America, where his brother George had been before him, though in the other Service, and had left memories and impressions amongst the community there. Before the news of George's death blighted his enthusiasm, Cecil wrote home with descriptions of the life there, and his activities in an area almost as strange as the Far East, with its intensely cold winters and endless impenetrable forests of fir and pine. He had hoped to go out into the forest to shoot deer accompanied by an Indian guide:

I know a capital Indian that was to have come with me, his name is Brasil, pronounced as if it was French, we were to have gone about 50 miles in a steamer and there struck off into the forest and when we got to a good place made a camp of boughs of trees and lived in it for a week or ten days, I think it would have been capital fun, there were to have been two of us and two Indians, one of the latter to hunt with us and the other to take care of the camp, cut firewood, cook, etc. They are wonderful fellows, no Englishman can go into the forest alone, it is so thick you can hardly walk in it, and in about ten minutes you get so thoroughly bewildered that you can't find your way to the place you left. Many people who have been foolish enough to go shooting into the forest and have left the beaten track, have wandered for days and found after all that they have gone on going round and round and not got a mile from where they set out, and many more have not come back at all, but these dodgers know quite well always where they are, it is a regular gift they have, you might walk one blindfold through the forest all day long and the moment you took off his bandage he could tell exactly the direction he came from, though of course not the distance he had come. They always know the points of the compass, and can take you for miles and miles where no man has ever been before and don't lose themselves a bit. I can't imagine how they lived before roads were made through the country, there could not have been much in this province of anything but wood, so thick that it is very difficult to push your way through – the thickest cover in England is a joke to it, except in the parts where the very high trees are, and there though the undergrowth is not so thick there is a sort of (I scarcely know what to call it) deluge of fallen trees crossing one another in such heaps that going along in it is climbing more than walking, but it is very nice indeed, and very beautiful and still and odd…

It was early September, and winter was coming on.

The winter will soon be coming on again now, how quick the time goes, I rather dread this winter, it comes suddenly in the middle of November and you never see a thing after that except glaring snow until the end of April or beginning of May, which is beyond a joke particularly as you are all this time freezing away with the thermometer fifteen or twenty or sometimes even thirty degrees below zero, that being 64 below freezing point, rather chilly that, Lou, eh? I really can hardly believe it till I see it. I wonder what would become of you and May if you were to live in such a temperature as that for a week, you would have no noses left, I should think. The poor sentries frequently get frostbitten, one man last year who got drunk and staid out was fruz dead in no time, poor fellow. I hope the Monkton crops have turned out well. I hear the harvest altogether has been a bad one this year in England. I am sorry to say the Yankees have had a good one which will enable them to bring corn cheap to England. Curs. I can't bear them, I hope to goodness our Government are not going to be such mean asses as to knock under now about the fisheries. 'Reciprocity' is all nonsense. It is no use for our colonies to be able to fish within three miles of the American coast or in their bays where there is nothing to catch, whereas in our bays there are millions of fish which if we had it all to ourselves, would immensely augment the value of the provinces of Nova Scotia and New Brunswick.

Cecil's attitude to the 'Yankees' was quite common at this period, and one sees it in more distinguished writers than Cecil, for example in the works of Charles Dickens or Fanny Trollope.

Cecil's other surviving letter from North America was written from Prince Edward Island, Nova Scotia, in the spring of 1853, cheerfully unaware of his brother's death.

...the same fix again, my dearest Lou, Mail going out, t'other one late, so it is a chance if this doesn't go before I get a word or two from home, which I hope this post will bring me as the last one which came in just two hours after I had written to you last month, failed in that respect, but no news being good news I presume all was well at home at the time of the Packet's departure and I sincerely hope the same salubrious state of things still continues... So, Lady Maidstone has got a son I see, I am sorry for it, it puts my friend Murray quite in the shade, I had set my heart on his being an Earl, but now I am afraid he is sold. [Lady Maidstone was the wife of Fanny's husband's son by his first marriage, who had hitherto had only daughters; the little boy who thus became the heir to the heir to the Earldom only lived until his eleventh year, so in fact Murray did eventually succeed to the Earldom.] There is nothing to be done here except skate and go out fishing which sport is carried out by dragging out a sort of house on runners (not footmen but the things a sleigh runs upon) for a mile or two out to sea, on the ice, which is easily done as the runners being shod with steel, it goes on ice so 'glib' as they say here! that a horse can take it along at a smart trot. The house is made of wood, and is something like a large bathing-machine without wheels, it has a fireplace in it, and a box for coals and wood, also it has a false bottom, that is to say some of the boards in the middle take up, and having removed them you proceed with a large axe and a spade to cut a hole in the ice which is in some places three feet thick or more, and in others only a few inches, then having arrived at the sea which is beautifully clear you proceed to let fall several pieces of string about 2 feet long with bits of red cloth, tin, or anything gaudy or glittering attached to them, and immediately instantly several fish appear and rush frantically to destruction for the moment the deluded wretch comes in sight of the fishermen, i.e., the officers of the garrison to whom the house belongs, and who are sitting on small stools round the ice hole close to the fire, each with a fish spear about six feet long in his hand, dart upon him, and spike him before he can wink his eye. In this way smelt (they are mostly smelt) are lured to a violent end and very seldom escape...

By the summer of 1854 Cecil was with his regiment in Limerick; the Crimean War was raging, and Cecil hoped to be sent out to the 'seat of war'. But in his letter to Louisa of November 1854 he was not very hopeful:

> ...we are not likely to go out anywhere for some time, and certainly not to the seat of war – if the regiment does go out, I shall very likely, if I get my promotion soon, have to remain at home with the depot as all the regiments going out now leave their four juniors of each rank behind, so you see my chance of honor and glory at present assume a mild shape... Yes, you are right in supposing I should not think it very safe my dear Lou to write anything to you I didn't wish to be made public. Your letters certainly have an unpleasant knack of laying about on sofas and chairs; however at present I have no secrets that I know of to propound... this is a terrible stupid place, there is nothing to do except shoot snipes and as I never can get away from barracks till 12 or 1 o'clock and the snipes live a long way off, I have only been able to go out once since I came here... I am as hungry as a demon having had nothing since breakfast. I can't afford to eat luncheon it costs a shilling which would be eighteen pounds in a year and with a glass of beer (4 pence) six pounds a year more so I eat about 4 pounds of meat at breakfast which carries me on till 7 o'clock, which arrangement though slightly perhaps à la boa-constrictor is the most economical and in reality the most wholesome one to pursue. Try it and if you find yourself very hungry about 2 o'clock smoke a pipe of Cavendish. I do. Has anyone heard about Astley in the

Wars? I am very glad that Robert Portal was not hurt, and Lewis was well out of that blundering, mad charge.[8] Did you read the account of the 93rd receiving the Russian Cavalry quietly in line, the first rank kneeling with their flank companies wheeled back to prevent their being ridden at in the flank. They are a splendid regiment, certainly. I don't suppose there is another like them in Europe. The dinner-bugle having sounded, I must say goodbye…

Cecil, just promoted Captain, was indeed left behind in Ireland when his regiment was sent to the Crimea, but almost immediately he was sent out with a small draft from Dublin, to help reinforce the regiment, depleted by the Battle of Balaklava and by the depredations of a savage winter. J.B. Priestley noted their need while extolling the incredible courage and fortitude of the over-stretched British troops:

The Battle of Balaklava on 25th October (1854) was initiated by the Russians who came out of their Sebastopol defences to attack the supply base of the Allies at Balaklava. The approach to it was covered by the Turkish contingent, in redoubts; and in support of them, directly defending the town, Sir Colin Campbell's Highlanders, and the Light and Heavy Cavalry Brigades, both considerably below strength. The Russian forces were far

---

[8]The infamous 'Charge of the Light Brigade'. Lewis was Lewis Knight (b.1833) son of Henry Knight and his first wife Sophia Cage; he was in the 17th Lancers, and reached high rank later in his career. Astley was Richard Astley Knatchbull, Fanny's third son (1832–1875).

more numerous and included their finest cavalry, a great weight of horsemen. They routed the Turks and captured their guns, which Raglan deeply resented because this loss of guns would suggest a notable Russian victory. However, the Russians were now swarming towards Balaclava and its scanty defences, and there now occurred three events that made this battle famous –

The first was the stand of Campbell's Highlanders, formed only in 2 lines – 'I did not think it worth while to form them even four deep,' Campbell said afterwards – who coolly faced and then broke up a massive thundering cavalry charge, a triumph of cold courage and musketry skill. This was the origin of the 'thin red line' a phrase used so often later.[9]

Priestley goes on to quote the *Times* correspondent, Russell:

If it is considered that the soldiers who met these furious columns of the Czar were the remnants of three British Divisions, which scarcely numbered 8,500 men; that they were hungry and wet, and half-famished; that they were men belonging to a force which was generally 'out of bed' four nights out of seven; which had been enfeebled by sickness, by severe toil, sometimes for 24 hours in the trenches at a time without relief of any kind; that among them were men who had within a short time previously lain out for 48 hours in

---

[9] J.B. Priestly, *Victoria's Heyday*; Heinemann, 1972.

the trenches at a stretch – it will be readily admitted there never was a more extraordinary contest maintained by our army since it acquired a reputation in the world's history.

He quoted also from a book called *A Voice from the Ranks: a Personal Narrative of the Crimean Campaign by a Sergeant of the Royal Fusiliers* which gives a truly horrifying description of conditions in that brutal winter:

…The Commisariat had completely broken down. All that was wanting was someone with a head on to put things straight. – All was higgledy-piggledy and confusion. The cavalry horses, that had cost an enormous amount, sank up to their knees in mud at every step, until they dropped exhausted; and all the way from the camp to Balaclava were to be seen dead horses, mules and bullocks, in every stage of decomposition. And our poor fellows – who had fought so well at Alma, Balaclava and the two Inkermanns – were now dying by hundreds daily.

The army was put on half-rations – half-a-pound of mouldy biscuit and half-a-pound of salt junk (beef or pork); coffee was served out, but in its raw green state, with no means of roasting it. No wood or firing was to be had, except a few roots that were dug up. Men would come staggering in to camp from the trenches soaked to the skin and ravenously hungry, when a half-pound of mouldy biscuit would be issued, with the same quantity of salt junk, so hard that one almost wanted a good hatchet to break it. The scenes were heart-rending.

The whole camp was one vast sheet of mud, the trenches in many places knee-deep; men died at their posts from sheer exhaustion or starvation, rather than complain, for if they reported themselves sick, the medical chests were empty. And amidst all these privations the enemy kept peppering away at them...

To such scenes Cecil arrived at Balaclava in late December 1854; with welcome breaks at Kamara, he remained there until the spring of 1857. Two of his letters survive, one of them of the greatest interest and importance. The first was to his sister Marianne on the eve of the attack on Sebastopol in September 1856, a mixture of domestic and military information; the incidence of the dreaded cholera, the difficulty of finding a horse, and the encounters with or news of friends and relatives who were also serving in the Crimea. He had seen Somerset Ward, who was married to cousin Norah Hill, and Ernest Knight, the nineteen year old son of Uncle Edward; he was to die of cholera within a few months; Maxy Hammond, a younger son of one of their neighbours, was to be killed in the fighting for Sebastopol the next week. Meanwhile, in the lull before the renewed outbreak of hostilities, his great need was books – a small testament, a French dictionary and a 'plain cookery book' were some of his requests, as well as 'cheap railway publications'.

Five days later, Cecil described the taking of Sebastopol in great detail in a long letter to his brother Edward. At the end of a long day which involved marches of as much as eleven miles as well as bloody fighting, firing from the Redan – the parapetted fortification protecting the town – seemed to have stopped, and Cecil sought permission from

General Colin Campbell to go out and bring in some of the wounded, and in particular to seek for the body of his friend Maxy Hammond:

> ...the General gave me leave at once and as I was going away said quietly, 'By the way, Rice, as you are going out just take a look at the Redan and let me know if it is really deserted, don't compromise yourself, you know, be careful.' I said, 'All right, Sir Colin, I'll go and see,' and thought to myself at the same time, 'Here's a nice go. The only way to know any better than I do now who is in the Redan is to climb up into it and if the Russians are there they will nobble me before I am half in and if they are not I have a very comfortable chance of flying up in another powder magazine.' However off I went of course having obtained the co-operation as I was instructed to do of ten volunteers from each Highland regiment. When we got well out in front of the salient angle, the scene was more awful than I even expected, crowds of dead men of course, and quantities of wounded. However, we pushed on to the ditch, but there I found only one man with me, a Private of the 93rd. Most of the others thought we were only come out to get the wounded, and they were all scattered about giving water to the poor thirsty fellows and helping them up. I thought it was perhaps better to go as quietly as possible and the 93rd man was a very plucky fellow and said, 'I'll go with you, Sir, come on.' So we dived into the ditch which was of course also strewn with poor fellows, and then began to ascend. It was

really a very difficult climb with even no one to knock you down all the time and when I was halfway up my foot slipped back and the 93rd man got on first and pushed through an embrasure one moment before me and shouted out, 'I am Peter Mackay of the 1st Company of the 93rd and I am the first man in the Redan!' We found some guns left there, lots of muskets, swords, etc. and of course dead bodies both English and Russian. I took the man's bayonet and scratched his name and mine on a brass twenty four pounder and we each secured some trophies to take back and some other men and some 93rd officers who had in the meantime come up to get some things too and out we bundled again glad enough to get away having done all that we were ordered to do. I hunted about for poor Maxy but never found him, though his body was found at daylight by his own men when they came down. The rest of the night we spent in bringing in the wounded men and officers, and as soon as we knew for certain that the Russians were gone we made lots of large fires in the 5th parallel and put the poor fellows down by them, sherry and water and brandy etc. It was a bitterly cold night and they were nearly frozen. We had not been out of the Redan a quarter of an hour when up went the magazine with another bang like the first. [Earlier in his letter, he had described numerous violent explosions caused by the Russians blowing up installations before they retired.] The town was by this time on fire in lots of places and looked beautiful and the magazines of the different batteries all about blew up at intervals. The explosion of all was one on the left called the black battery. The shot and stones and earth fell all round at a radius of at least half a mile the shells bursting all the time in the air, altogether the scene was more terrible and more beautiful than anything I can conceive. Of course there will be *Times* correspondents and *Illustrated London News* all about it, but the only fellows who really saw it well were the Highland Division, we being in the advanced trenches. I wish I had time and paper to tell about it better, but I haven't so goodbye. We marched home here (Kamara) and arrived yesterday about half-past one. I never in my whole life was so done up. We had been 35 hours hard at work and had marched 19 miles at least, 11 there and eight back. Altogether we have very great cause to be thankful that we are safe. If the 72nd had had to attack the Redan alone, as was intended, supported by the other three Highland regiments, we must have been almost annihilated, but I hope we shall never have any more such work as that to do as such sights are not seen every day. Poor Maxy...

According to the family, Cecil got little credit for this exploit of bravery, humanity and initiative; Sir Colin Campbell was for some reason out of favour and was soon to be replaced; his report, which included favourable mention of Cecil – which Sir Colin told him he hoped would be 'of use to you' – was never published or alluded to. Another officer, in the 93rd, was given the credit for being the first Englishman in the Redan on that night of 5th

September 1855. A postscript to a letter written in November by Edward Knight, the father of poor Ernest, perhaps refers to this neglect, 'I am sorry for Cecil's disappointment' he wrote, 'how ill old dawdling Simpson has used him!' (Simpson was the General who had succeeded Lord Raglan, recently deceased, as Commander-in-Chief.)

This period cannot have been the happiest time for Elizabeth. The heart-rending death of her son George revived memories of the loss of Henry, and it must have been a matter of no small anxiety that Cecil on land and Edward at sea were facing danger at the heart of the conflict, with Midshipman Ernest also facing the enemy in the Baltic and even Augustus at risk. A letter she wrote in July 1853 to Louisa and Marianne is rather dispirited; they had just left Dane Court to visit their sister Fanny Winchilsea at Eastwell Park:

> My dearest L. and M.
> I have nothing to say except that I miss you both so very horridly I cannot help writing to say so – I went to both your rooms and mowled down again just as the slow Carriage came back from the Station. I am glad you were in time wh. I was afraid you would not be when I heard the one o'clock bell ring abt. ten minutes after you were gone. It is very sad and …without you, worse I think than if I were more alone. The poor boys were tired out and headachy and went to sleep for an hour or two, and then got up and found the lark dead and a young Hawk come for Arthur from Harris with which he is delighted. A Goodnestone party arrived about ½ 2 and stayed till now – 5 – Aunt Louisa, Harriet Bridges and Charlotte – we have been walking

about and just as they drove off Admiral and Harriet D'Aeth walked in – now they are gone and I wish I knew how you both are… It has rained here a good deal… my best love to dearest Fanny, I am so in hopes to hear a better account of her, I suppose all the fine folk are pouring in, I pity poor Matilda without a friend. Aunt K. [Knatchbull, her sister Fanny] and I shall probably read pocket books after dinner in the Library in the 2 green chairs…

Cecil had a relatively short respite in England after the rigours of the Crimea, for by September 1857 he was on his way to India. His service in that country consisted of two tours of duty, divided by a home leave and a period in charge of the Regimental depot in Aberdeen; the first period was full of military activity, as the Indian Mutiny had broken out in May 1857, and Lucknow was not to be relieved until November of the following year. As James Morris wrote in the *Pax Britannica* trilogy (*Heaven's Command*, Penguin) – 'the rising grumbled on in guerilla skirmish and punitive hunt, until the summer of 1859.'

Although the Mutiny was very much confined geographically, and the rebels limited mainly to the Bengali Sepoys, this 'most horrible of Imperial Wars' aroused passions of hatred and disgust leading to acts of reprisal almost as barbarous as the hideous episodes which gave rise to them. From this time thenceforward in India,

in the aftermath of the tragedy [wrote Morris] the worst national streaks of intolerance and chauvinism showed themselves; the restraining authority of Lord Canning, the new Governor-General, merely brought him the contemptuous title of 'Clemency Canning'.

The British saw the war as a straight fight between good and evil, and the savageries of the rebels, though they could hardly be exaggerated, were shamelessly exploited. Contemporary accounts are rich in gloating detail – every sepoy a crazed barbarian, every Englishwoman raped before mutilation. In memoir after memoir the Indians were pictured as faithless and brutal ingrates – 'niggers' as they were now often called, who were animated by no normal instincts of mercy and kindness, and showed no sign that they might ever, even in God's infinite mercy, be capable of redemption.

This attitude is manifest in letters Cecil wrote home in the early months of 1858; Cecil was a hardened warrior, but he was new to the subcontinent, and he arrived there at a time when passions were at their highest pitch, and British troops were galvanised by a lust for bloodletting and vengeance. The later letters he wrote during his second tour of duty in India are in marked contrast.

Cecil wrote to Lou in February 1858 from Deesa (about 300 miles north of Bombay) describing their plan of campaign to pursue, outflank and destroy rebel forces at Kotah.

The whole of Rajhpootana and Oude are in revolt, and they are a fine warlike set, especially the Rajhputs. Sir H. Rose got into a mess a few days ago and lost a good deal of baggage, a most serious consideration. Fancy in the field, hundreds of miles from any means of replacing it, and this abominable climate, losing one's tents and clothes and means of transport for food, etc.

As in the Crimea, there were numerous cousins serving – Philip Knight, son of Uncle Edward Knight, Brodnax his younger brother in the 72nd Bengal Native Infantry, and Arthur Hill, who was the son of Lizzie's sister Louisa. Sunday was Cecil's day for writing letters, and he wrote nostalgically of home:

> I read the proper lessons and fancy you all listening to old Twigg reading the same in dear old Tilmanstone Church, and Mrs Baxter's fat respectable face coercing small infants and making them pretend they can follow in their books. Remember me to her and say I hope she hears good accounts of Jem.

Cecil's dislike and scorn of the 'natives' was virulent and highly prejudiced and was no doubt echoed by most of his fellows. These young men rarely praised an enemy or the native inhabitants of the countries they controlled except – occasionally – for their fighting qualities and courage. In a letter dated December 1856, he described the pursuit of the army of 'Tantia Topee' and his regret that:

> we didn't kill half or even a quarter so many of the brutes as we should have done if it had been an open plain. That sounds sanguinary you think, I daresay, but upon my word, without being, I believe, a more than ordinarily bloodthirsty party, I rejoice at the death of every regular Sepoy mutineer, as in spite of what people choose to say and write, the

atrocities they have committed are perfectly frightful to think about.

He described how a group of the mutineers in making their escape came upon the British baggage train, some miles in the rear of the main force,

> poor camp-followers of sorts, cooks, water-carriers, grooms with pack-horses, camel-men, elephant-drivers, hospital attendants, and in fact the regular stream of natives, male and female, that invariably straggle after an Indian army. Well, these demons in their flight came upon the poor unarmed helpless wretches and cut them up in the most barbarous manner.

He described too the amazing stoicism with which the captured mutineers met their inevitable execution:

> they go off in a batch, five or six perhaps in a batch, marching in front of the firing party, chattering and laughing as quietly to each other as if they were the ones going to shoot the others. It is truly brutal work and I am sick of it as you may suppose. The sight of our poor miserable wounded servants and follow-ers is enough to disgust one, to say nothing of having to be a sort of head butcher whenever a bunch of mutineers is caught. Why the stupid idiots can't give themselves up I can't imagine, full pardon has been offered to them all…

Cecil was promoted to the rank of Major for 'distinguished service in the field' after this campaign, which included a famous march in pursuit of the rebels described as 'unparalleled in the annals of war' (which was nonsense, declared Cecil):

> but we marched for ten successive nights, thirty-two miles a night, having but little time to sleep by day, and at last ran into Tantia's camp at Chodaoopoor at daylight on the eleventh morning – but owing to the folly of the officer commanding the advance-guard Tantia got away and we lost him and all the Gwalior Jewels which he had on an elephant. I was Staff-Officer to the Brigade and for this very easy campaign was promoted to Major…

The promoted Major soon returned to England and eventually found himself in charge of the Regimental Depot in Aberdeen. By early 1861 this posting was evidently losing its attraction for him, in spite of the opportunities for first-class shooting and other field sports with Scottish friends. Members of his family paid visits to enjoy the rejuvenating air of North Berwick and elsewhere in Scotland; Lou and Fanny were there in 1860, accompanied by Edward, who was currently at Sheerness, in charge of the Steam Reserve, and who had just celebrated his fortieth birthday, an occasion which evoked a characteristic letter from his mother; her instructions with regard to matrimony can only have turned the knife in a tender wound, as his efforts were still unavailing, Norah Hill's defection being about this time, followed by definite discouragement of his interest in one of the Russell girls.

> My dearest Edward [wrote Elizabeth from Dane Court] I would not an any account let your birthday pass without writing a few lines myself tho' I see Caroline is writing and have

no doubt Louisa will too, so I wish you joy
and health and every kind of happiness that is
good for anybody to have and a great many
very happy returns of your dearly beloved
Godmersham birthday, and how many have
passed away to their still happier home since
that day and how many still remain for which
I am more than thankful. But now that you
are forty years old you must marry as Isaac did
and I wish there were as beautiful tho' not so
deceitful a Rebecca ready for you – of all the
Rebeccas I have heard of and not seen I consider Miss Lyttleton the best – I wish tents and
Cattle and heavy bread were all she wanted to
live in and on these days – how much easier it
would be to find wives...

Cecil wrote to Louisa from Aberdeen in March or April
1861; apart from his expressions of detestation for life at the
depot, there is a slightly censorious tone in some of his
remarks to his sister, not unique in his letters to her – on
one occasion she received a scolding from him for failing to
forward an important letter from India. With all his
qualities of humour and kindliness, and a notable lack of
complaint with regard to his own health and comfort, Cecil
had a soldierly preference for order and efficiency.

I am very much obliged to you for both your
nice letters [he wrote]. The last one was very
nearly illegible though, but I believe I have got
it all... How I wish you were not in the habit
of carrying your letters about in your hand all
day and leaving them to the mercy of every
housemaid or houseman or whoever chooses
to read them. I should really like writing to

you very much, whereas now one has to consider really every word that is not quite 'common' to see if it will do for the public and the consequence is the writing is a bore and the letter a stupid cramped lot of stuff. I should like to write heaps of things, I don't say all that to be funny, I really mean that one knows that every letter that one writes home is first handed round the table, and then left about till some kind person buries it in the writing-table or makes it into alumettes. There, so much for all that. I am very much gratified at your having missed me when I went away from home, I missed you all I can tell you, and my little comfortable room upstairs and the evening pipes in the kitchen, and do still, hour after hour. This depot is more detestable than ever. I mean that I detest nearly all the people in it and composing it so much that it will really be a very great set-off against the nuisance of going to India, the mere fact of getting away from these Gordons, Bests etc…

Cecil sailed off for his second tour of India in April 1863 on the P&O steamer *Jidda*. It was an altogether more domesticated affair, with his own bungalow at Mihow and a routine he described as a 'monotonous succession of parades and evening walks, each the same in all respects as the last'. Cecil was one of the few members of the Rice family not afflicted with a degree of hypochondria.

Yes, thank-you, [he wrote] I am a remarkably well person – the heat has set in pretty strong, but it 'don't offer to interrupt me' as they say in Tilmanstone, as long as I don't give the sun an innings more than is necessary which you may be sure I do not. Having given up my tiger-shooting in deference to its warnings, I don't see any advantage in letting it grill me for any more trifling reasons and as there is no duty done in this country in the daytime out-of-doors we can keep pretty clear of the sun in these peacable times if one pleases – and I do please… Now, [he continued] I am going to devour a small cake and eat, I mean drink some sherry which with a mild manilla to follow will constitute the mid-day meal – called in these parts 'tiffin'. Your regular Indian stuffs his gizzard with curry, anchovy toast (a villainous compound much loved in the East) and bottled beer and then goes to sleep, I hope I sha'n't be here long enough to become one – but bad habits are much more easily caught they tell me than good ones. Hot curries are very conducive to enlargement of the liver.

He told Lou there were now forty-five ladies on the station – a great number for an up-country station:

there are three unmarried females in the forty-five and they seem to say I am going to propose shortly to one of them. A young person lately from Cheltenham – sister of the Quarter-Master General of the Division. In case I do and she is agreeable – I might as well describe her – her age I should judge were nineteen – height 5'5" or thereabouts, stout and healthy in appearance – florid visage –

light hair – good blue eyes – hands and about the worst teeth I ever saw in any young party of her age – she is well acquainted with Lionel's Miss Reynolds, and friendly discussions we have had at odd times at Band-Playing and such-like occasions on the subject of that charmer have probably led the sagacious elderly females of the community to the conclusion that I was making advances on my own account. If the poor girl never gets nearer to a proposal than I am likely to be brought to, her matrimonial prospects are very indifferent.

In a letter to his brother Augustus he paints a picture of modest bachelor contentment:

It is eleven o'clock p.m. I have just come from the Mess House where I have had my dinner and played 2 games at Billiards. My pipe is lighted and with a glass of brandy and soda water to refresh the weary scribe (nothing is more heating in a hot clime than writing) I sit me down to scribble. My small dog – a very pretty black and tan terrier of the – ? – kind gnaws the bone of contentment on his mat, and the scene is illuminated by a tall brass lamp burning cocoa-nut oil. The doors and windows are all shut to keep out the damp which is very considerable as we are in one of the paroxysms of an early and unusually wet monsoon – it has not actually cleared up, though it has not positively rained the whole time for twelve days and the whole country is green stodgy and reeking – it is a dark blowy night – looking like November and feeling like July. Many people are howling with rheumaticks (not in my room but in the station generally) I am happy to say I am not. I think the wet weather suits me better than any other, and I am in very flourishing health. I am very comfortable in my new house… This morning I had a great bout at gardening – that is to say potting, as it is not worth while making a regular garden as we shall be gone in a few months, but I have a good collection of flowers in my Verandah in large pots – and the way they grow in this weather is truly marvellous – I have got a creeper in a pot that regularly does its eight inches in height and expands in proportion every twenty-four hours – and a geranium cutting makes a fine plant in a month. Mrs P., the Colonel's wife, is head gardener, and a very good one, but she upset my arrangements a good deal this morning, as she insisted on having her own way in the proceedings – which I couldn't well object to, as she gave me nearly all the flowers and cuttings and knows a great deal about them and I very little. However, they look very nice and cheerful and homeish now. Red geraniums, verbenas, a rose, petunias, pinks, flox, mignonette, creepers, etc.

However, without the excitement of campaigning Cecil was beginning to find life in India tedious, and his thoughts turned increasingly to matrimony:

I will thank you [he wrote facetiously to Louisa] to keep your eye upon any eligible widows you may meet with – without encumbrances as I have no fancy myself to become a friendless, liverstricken starched veteran if I can avoid it. I should prefer a spinster but I fancy thay have a prejudice by no means favourable to your cidevant Indian – whose bilious eye and parchment visage like a worn-out battledore, are not I confess attractive to a blooming home miss, and small blame to her.

Family events preoccupied him more when life in India was uneventful; and there were many events to report from home – their father's fall proved to have much worse and much more permanent consequences than had been expected, and there had been much to report about Lionel's hopes to emigrate to Australia.

…Is he (Lionel) really going to Queensland? by all accounts it is a fine place and if I were not too old to begin afresh, I should like to have a turn at it too very well. He should get himself well started, a house built and his pigs and sheep in order, and then sail home in two or three years and carry out Rose Taylor to milk his cows and sew on his buttons. I am sure it can't be a worse profession than the army which except in this country barely provides its victims with bread and cheese – and if they survive to be general officers with shattered constitutions, presents them with an annuity of three hundred pounds. Whereas if your Queensland emigrant of twenty sticks to his work I should say there was a fair probability of his being able to return to his native land about the time he might reasonably ex-

pect to have become a Lieutenant-Colonel
with as many thousands…

Another major event in the family was the marriage of
Edward to Cecilia Harcourt in the spring of 1864. Cecil
waxed very facetious to Louisa about the description of the
bridesmaids' attire:

> …By the by in your letter …there are allusions
> (as far as I can understand them) to
> 'Crinolines and Bonnets' calculated to pro-
> duce an impression in the mind of an
> uninitiated outsider that those articles, if not
> one and the same portion of the garments of a
> bridesmaid, are by far more intimately con-
> nected than they used to be – How is this? I
> thought it was a mistake at first – and to tell
> you the truth I was skimming rather lightly
> over that portion of the narrative when to my
> astonishment crinolines and bonnets again ap-
> peared on the scene in unmistakeable
> language, as synonymous terms. Am I to un-
> derstand that the upper as well as the lower
> portion of the female figure is now caged
> over? Or is it all one machine? I have been
> told that waists are getting shorter, and more
> desperately short – perhaps now they begin at
> the top of your head and your cage descends
> in one graceful curve – and is hung around
> with cloaks and frocks. How do you see out?
> A place must be left for that – and for food to
> be passed in – When you sit down you must
> feel like a canary covered up for the night.

In a subsequent letter there is a curious link with a passage in one of the letters of Jane Austen, Cecil wrote:

> I see Lady J. Paget is married and I hear she threw over some one else in a very disgraceful way without any notice – to marry Lord Hastings. Is that true? What toads all Pagets are!

It will be remembered that Jane Austen made a very similar comment in a letter to Fanny Knight in March 1817:

> If I were the Duchess of Richmond, I should be very miserable about my son's choice. What can be expected from a Paget, born and brought up in the centre of conjugal infidelity and Divorces? I will not be interested about Lady Caroline – I abhor all the race of Pagets.[10]

By the summer of 1865 Cecil was home from India, stationed with his regiment in Edinburgh Castle. Within a year he had wooed and married the attractive red-headed daughter of Mark Napier, the Sheriff of Dumfries. Frances Napier was eighteen, Cecil thirty-five, so the weather-beaten old campaigner could congratulate himself on his conquest, young, handsome and well-endowed! Cecil remained in the Army only for four years after his marriage, while the regiment remained in Scotland. For two years of that time he acted in command of the regiment in the absence of the Colonel. But on their being ordered once more to India he decided to leave the service; they had by now three small children, and 'he did not think it right to take out his young wife nor to part her from her three little

---

[10] J.A., *Letters* (no.141, p.485); Chapman [cd.], OUP, 1932.

children.' He purchased an unattached colonelcy and settled down to a quiet country life. His wife produced a family of nine children and died in 1884 aged thirty-six, when her youngest child was five years old. At the time of her death the family had just moved to Crieff, and Caroline Cassandra came up to Scotland for a few months to support her brother and his family over this painful and difficult period. But Cecil had a positive and optimistic approach to life, and his practical attitude, dealing with problems in a systematic manner, must have helped him to weather this as other storms.

Cecil's family consisted of five boys and four girls, of whom George was the oldest. Marcia, born in 1868, broke family tradition (and helped to make feminist history) by going to St Hugh's Hall in Oxford and gaining a first-class honours degree in language and literature in 1898. At that time of course neither Oxford nor Cambridge granted women the right to take the degree they had earned, but in 1920 when Oxford at least changed its statutes, Marcia was the first woman belatedly to be awarded her degree. She became the headmistress of a well-known girls' school, St Mary Abbot's, Bromley, and died in 1958 at the age of eighty-nine. She was the family chronicler of her generation, compiling the little typescript booklet called *The Rices of Dane Court*, which collected together all the facts available about her grandparents and their large family; she took down verbatim recollections of her aunt Caroline Cassandra, who was the member of her generation who had made some attempt to record facts and anecdotes about her parents and Dane Court. If her account has inevitable gaps, and is stronger on pious generalisations (particularly in the case of her father, whom she greatly loved, and of her grandmother Elizabeth, whom she, together with her cousin Evelyn Templetown, invested in a romantic aura compounded of lavender water and potpourri) than chronological details, it provides an invaluable base from which to recreate the lives of each individual.

Little is recorded in the family papers of the other children; Cecil Edward was a Major in 1917, the year of his father's death, and had just received a bar to his DSO; his sister Frances Maud was a nursing sister and had also been decorated. Mark entered the Church and had children, and at the time of his death, a few months after his sister Marcia in 1958, was living at Littlebourne, Canterbury, Louisa Mary was then the sole survivor of the nine.

After the death of his first wife, Cecil subsequently re-married; his second wife was Lady Matilda Horatia Seymour, the daughter of Admiral Sir George Seymour. She was a little older than Cecil, and from all accounts was a woman of strong character. Helen Elizabeth Rice refers in her diaries to visits she paid to Kinscote, near East Grinstead, where the family then lived, with the younger girls still at home, sitting cowed and silent at luncheon, and made comments upon the problems of living with a stepmother. Uncle Cecil's visits to the 'Colony' at Tilmanstone were always much enjoyed, particularly by his brother Augustus, (who was a little hemmed in, perhaps, by female relatives); he was always kind and full of anecdotes of his past military exploits, sitting in the kitchen with his pipe or cheroot; but at home he tended to retire to the solitary refuge of his workshop, where he 'turned' little boxes and other objects much appreciated by his relatives. He and Lady Matilda both lived into their eighty-sixth year. In 1907, his niece Helen, evidently short of material to fill the pages of her diary, copied out an extract from a letter her Uncle had just written to 'Auntie', i.e., Louisa at South Court, the recipient and preserver of so many family letters.

...Alice has gone to bed with a bad headache, she has been working too hard, I think, at her

examination papers – writing perfect screeds!!
What a curious age the end of our lives has let
us get a glimpse of – I wonder what the next
generation will see before they die – how little
any of you girls dreamed of Oxford and
Cambridge examinations and how little any of
us imagined that we should be able to tele-
graph to the other end of the earth in an hour
– and now, wireless telegraphy – and flying
machines becoming really possible – I believe
an American has actually made one that can go
twenty miles an hour in a strong wind! – and
these beastly motorcars that rush madly
through the world – look back 65 years when
Augustus and I were at Paul's – no railways,
no telegraph, no steam men-o'-war, and very
few steam ships at all. How we have rushed on
– and I don't think things are a bit better or
pleasanter. When we all went slow no one
wanted to go fast. Labourers could not write
or read and were more contented and better
Xtians I believe – some things are better, people are not hanged for stealing a loaf, and
people are, I suppose, generally cleaner and
healthier an the whole… I look forward with
fear and trembling to what may be the fate of
the country if the socialists get more and more
power, and this brutal Government are playing
into their hands with all their night. No, I
don't forgive C.B. (Campbell Bannerman) or
Winston Churchill. I should like to hang them
both. C.B. well deserves it. He is mainly responsible for the last 18 months of the Boer
War and the loss of thousands of lives – his
speeches as the leader of the radical party tele-

graphed out daily to the Boers encouraged them to go on fighting long after they would otherwise have given in – Good do – I daresay the country will last our time…

12   Walter

Walter was yet another brother whose career was affected by his health; and probably, as most certainly was the case with Morland, his character also. In the diaries he kept in later life, of which one or two volumes have survived, the routine accounts of his variable state of health, his visits, his hunting, golfing and hawking, are interspersed with tortured self-examination and desperate prayers – he felt himself to be a drone, devoting his life to self-indulgence and the pursuit of pleasure. Sometimes his outcries amount almost to breakdown. These crises mostly coincided with bouts of ill health, when he felt himself particularly isolated and lonely. All his interests were out-of-doors activities, and when he was able to indulge in them he was much more cheerful. Sociability was of vital importance to him, and his popularity with family and friends was probably greater than that of his siblings, none of whom were exactly misanthropic themselves! Ceci, for example, found him more sympathetic and understanding about her problems in the absence of her husband than were Louisa or Morland, and certainly less inclined than they were to dictate solutions. His wit and gift of repartee was said to be exceptional, and was exemplified by a story recorded of him when dining with friends. He found himself seated with his back to a roaring fire, and begged to be allowed to change his seat. 'Humph!' said an old General, 'I did not know that young officers could not stand fire.' 'Not at their backs, sir,' Walter replied courteously.

Walter was sent to Woolwich like his brother Augustus, and his letters from there indicate that he found it congenial; he particularly enjoyed the opportunity to improve his horsemanship, and chose the Artillery rather than the Engineers so that there would be more opportunities for riding and outdoor activities. He was mercifully innocent of involvement in a scandal which Morland referred to in a letter in 1852, when twenty-three boys, including Knight and Austen-Leigh connections, were expelled for 'obscene practices'. At the time Walter was at Woolwich, his younger brother Arthur was at Mr Paul's School at Shooter's Hill Blackheath, and they were able to exchange visits and go out together; Arthur attended services in the garrison chapel and was at Walter's confirmation in April 1853. Walter was commissioned in 1854, and probably did not immediately serve overseas, though in the 1860s he served in Sicily and Malta. By 1860 he was serving in Ireland, whence he wrote to his sister 'dearest Carry' a letter describing the rigours of the crossing from Liverpool to Dublin – 'a detestable passage... I was sick the whole time. It is such a nasty short sea that hardly anyone can stand it and 13 hours is a long time...'

Walter's absence from home always caused his mother particular regret; one might suspect that he was her favourite son. Although so many of his letters and diary entries are full of accounts of indispositions and minor complaints and grumbles, he was when at home evidently a cheerful presence, full of high spirits and good humour. He shared his Mother's interest in the breeding of canaries, some of which often accompanied him on his travels. His departure for Ireland drew from his mother a lively letter:

My dearest Walter
Many thanks for so faithfully keeping your promise to write from London, Dublin and

Cork. *I do so hate your being gone and miss you so
dreadfully.* I do not know how to say so half
enough, there is no part of the day that I do
not want you and still half-expect to hear you
whistling or see you coming in. Alas, alas, how
dull it is without you, I am so glad you are
safely arrived through all the storms we have
had here, tho' the passage across the stream to
Dublin seems to have been bad enough – the
sea has done much mischief I am afraid at
Ebbs Fleet... but what I hate more is the old
Scotch firs at the end of the long wood being
many of them blown down and still worse the
two great elms at the top of the hazel walk
covered with ivy are much injured, the top of
one of them nearly blown off! I am so sorry
for that I could cry, they were such beauties....
here comes red-faced Russell (Charlotte, a
friend of Louisa's via her sister Marianne at
Woburn) and sharp-faced Lou back from their
ride to interrupt me which I hate – they are
sipping their tea – I pay no attention to
them...

Walter was serving in Malta in 1864 at the time of his
brother Edward's marriage to Cecilia Harcourt, and he
wrote a rather disconsolate letter to Caroline Cassandra on
2nd March:

My dearest Carry,
It is a sad thing to have to appeal to the columns of the *Times* for news of home – I sat up
till past one last night waiting for the mail but
no letters came and I haven't had one now for
five weeks. I see jolly old Edward's marriage in

the paper and I shall wait till next mail (7 days) for a few particulars which will doubtless arrive sooner or later. I hope it went off all right – by all right I mean that there was lots to eat and drink and not much crying – and that you were well rigged out in your bridesmaids' dresses – lots of people here and at Corfu, Post Captains etc. etc., are very glad to hear of it – some of them wink knowingly and say, 'Ha! Ha! I used to tell your brother he would be caught sooner or later.' Please send me a photograph of Mrs E.B.R....

In this letter Walter referred to 'cousin Hodgson' of the *Resistance*, which had been at Malta *en route* for Athens; he liked him very much, and envied him a very fine cabin. This was probably the grandson of the impecunious Rev. Henry Rice and his wife Lucy Lefroy; their daughter Sarah had married the Rev. Douglas Hodgson.

Walter was again in Malta in 1875/6; another farewell letter from his mother was couched in similar terms as the letter previously quoted, and gives an account of a 'dull Sunday' at Dane Court.

> ...here I sit miserably writing to you instead of hearing your cheerful whistle and voice about the house, alas that it has at last come to this – but our life is made up of meetings and partings and we cannot have one without the other... It is after breakfast now and the party are thus disposed of – Edward dressed for wood-cutting is gone up attended by Ceci and his American axe into the garden wood to cut ivy off the trees – Papa is just come back from seeing the sheep dipped at Suttons and the

Hop-picking and is reading the newspaper by the fire, Louisa is gone into the village to see sick people and Cam settling her accounts opposite to me and asking for 12s. more than the £9 I paid her for sleeve-links for her birthday present. We should have had a very dull Sunday yesterday if it had not been for Edward whose cheerfulness is invaluable and irrepressible – I drove myself to Church alone and walked back and we all had a nice strolling walk together after afternoon service up the 40 Acres into the road by the new white gate towards New Purchase then down the side and in at the gate at the bottom; little Henry went with us and we sat about on benches and when the rest went in Edward and I went into the yard and lingered amongst the poultry and Cows and watched a duck wing cock nearly kill a duck and talked to Richards – we missed you both so at prayers [Gusty as well as Walter], it is so calm and quiet today that I hope you will have a good passage… Papa… is very low and sad but as well as usual. – I saw you waving till the train was quite out of sight and I hope you saw me – I found a very sad party when I got home to keep me in countenance, Lou and Cam both with their eyes swelled and writing last hours to May and Ernest.

When Edward and Ceci arrived in Malta on his appointment as 2nd in Command of the Mediterranean Fleet and Superintendent of the Naval Dockyards, Walter was there to greet them, rowing out with a crew of his Engineers to welcome them before they disembarked. He enormously enjoyed their company and no doubt the considerable enlargement of his social circle that their presence provided; it was probably at this period that Ceci came to know Walter better, and to appreciate his friendly and sympathetic nature. But it was shortly after this that Walter had to return home on sick leave, and amidst the agitated commentaries of the family, was diagnosed as having a damaged heart. It seemed probable that he would have to retire prematurely from the Army; he 'soldiered' on, however, but in August 1880 Elizabeth was writing to him to the United Services Club in Pall Mall, commiserating with him on his imminent retirement.

> ...Your letter was a great relief to me tho' I know well how you will for a time hate leaving the Service, this lessens the pleasure of it to me very much of course, and I hate to think what a trial it is to you, but it will make my home so much brighter and happier to have you always here, I hardly know how to be sorry enough! poor little Cam cries half for you knowing how you hate leaving the service and half at feeling what a difference your being here will make in her solitary life, so you see, dearest Walter, there is much good mixed with the bad –

Walter's retirement did not evidently take place at this time, for later he was stationed at Dover Castle, and did not retire finally, with the rank of Major-General, until 1886, just short of his fiftieth birthday. He relinquished his career with reluctance – 'there is no denying the fact,' he wrote in his diary, 'that a retired bachelor Army Officer has less status and on the whole less to recommend him than any other individual that I can think of.' Thereafter he spent his time amongst or within reach of the 'Colony', at first staying with his sisters at South Court, and then (he reported that maids gave notice and suspected that they – unreasonably, of course – felt he gave them too much extra work) he moved into rented accommodation in Walmer.

Walter was susceptible to the charms of the opposite sex, and numbered many ladies amongst his close friends, but he never married; perhaps initially he felt his health was too precarious to risk offering hostages to fortune in the shape of a wife and family, and later became too set in his ways to desire any change. A certain Mrs Moir was a close friend in his later years, and he complained in his diary for 1887–8:

> Dearest May [his sister Marianne Laurie] is rather officious and dangerous as well – she has been talking all sorts of nonsense about Mrs Moir and me, who are the best of friends – and has succeeded at all events in making me (and I don't know if Mrs Moir) uncomfortable… really it is a great pity that women should be such clacks – Louisa and Marianne, especially the latter are the worst in our family and both 'dangerous' (only of course in the particular way I have mentioned).

Later, in a letter to his sister Caroline Cassandra after his move to Scotland, he wrote:

> I like Mrs Moir very much indeed, she has been so very very kind to me and none of you perhaps know how much good the things she has sent me have done me – if I was quite well I should like to marry her very much…

He would ride round visiting Edward – whose coddling by Ceci he deplored – hunting with Ernest when the latter was at home, smoking with Augustus, attending church, shooting, playing golf on the new course, and visiting all and sundry. He loved all the members of his family intensely, and found it hard to understand how some of them chose voluntarily to live in other parts of the country. But his health was so uncertain in the treacherous weather of East Kent, he finally decided, after a particularly severe winter and spring in 1888, to seek health elsewhere, and found it in the more bracing air of Scotland, in the neighbourhood of Aviemore. His brother Cecil was still living in Crieff, and the Lauries' home at Maxwelton was open house to all the Rice family. Caroline Cassandra, two years older than Walter, transferred the devotion she had lavished on her father to him, and when in his last years – from about 1888 – he moved to Aviemore in Inverness-shire, she spent much time with him, and they explored the Highlands together.

The end came on 26th December 1892, not as the culmination of so much ill-health, but as a result of a wilful act on Walter's part. His niece Marcia described the fatal accident:

> he had been attending the funeral of a Highlander. He had his servant with him, and unfortunately he had a sudden desire to skate upon Loch an-Eilan on his way home. At the time he was staying at Drumintoul Lodge, Rothiemurchus, which may have been nearer the loch than Aviemore, three miles distant. His sister was not then with him. The loch was said to be dangerous, but Walter considered this a Highland superstition. He sent his servant to a cottage nearby to borrow a chair.

But the woman refused. She said the General must not skate upon the loch, and she would do nothing to abet him. Sad to say, he would not listen. The weather was bitter, and he had clad himself heavily and was wearing two thick winter great-coats. The loch was quite deserted when he put on his skates and made his fatal attempt, his poor servant standing on the brink to watch him. Almost at once the ice broke under him. His servant rushed to the cottage for help, which was promptly forth-coming, and a rope was thrown to him. But nothing could have been of avail. He was plunged into deep icy water, and his clothing dragged him down. He called to his servant by name, 'Goodbye, Louis; in one minute I shall be drowned.' And so it was. He sank before his helpless valet's eyes. The shock and grief, not only to his family, but to the whole of Aviemore and the neighbourhood, was pro-found. He had greatly endeared himself to rich and poor by his charm and gaiety, as well as by countless acts of friendliness and kind-ness. He was deeply mourned... By the time his body was recovered his brothers Cecil and Ernest had arrived. It was decided to make the long sad journey back to Kent, that he might be buried at home, in the churchyard at Tilmanstone... relays of Highlanders carried his coffin the two and a half miles from Rothiemurchus to Aviemore station in the centre of the village. A stone to his memory was erected on the site where his body was re-covered by the inhabitants of Aviemore, and a beautiful one-light window designed by Mr

Kemp... has been placed in Tilmanstone Church by his sorrowing sister Caroline.

13 Arthur

Arthur, a year younger than Walter, appears to be one of those individuals whose name is always prefixed with the adjective 'poor'. He was a happy boy playing cricket with his brothers at Dane Court, but was evidently not a great intellect. There was much family discussion about his career; Morland took him off to Eton, where he failed the entrance examination dismally; Fanny remarked on the dangers of the Services for such 'an unsteady little fellow'. The only divergence from the norm that is recorded of him was an excessive religiosity, influenced by the currently popular Evangelism. He would preach in the Tilmanstone village hall or schoolroom, but who listened to him is not recorded!

He had an illness in his boyhood which we would describe as a nervous breakdown. At last it was decided he should follow his older brothers into the Army, and after attending Mr Paul's school he gained a commission in the 72nd Highland Regiment, the regiment of his brother Cecil and his late brother Henry. He was sent to Aberdeen to the regimental depot, where his brother Cecil was also stationed. He was much liked by his fellows and the local families, and paid pleasant visits in the neighbourhood, shooting on the moors and enjoying the congenial company.

But early in 1863, he succumbed to an attack of typhoid, and died in his lodgings in the presence of his brothers Cecil and Morland. As was the custom, his last days were described in detail by both brothers; his state of mind and conscience was of the greatest interest to his family in Kent. It was a solace to know that he died in a conscious state of grace, aware of the love of Christ and confident of his Heavenly destiny. He was twenty-five years of age.

14   Ernest

There is a great deal of material in the Rice family archive about Ernest Rice, comparable in volume and interest with that concerning brother Edward. Ernest, twenty-one years younger than Edward, was destined originally for the Army, but found himself in the Navy almost by chance, when at the beginning of the Crimean War, the Navy was anxious for recruits. He was then only thirteen. The action he saw then in the Baltic as a midshipman (or 'mate', an obsolete rank even inferior to that of middy) on board the *Odin* was probably as dangerous as anything he experienced subsequently; in particular the attempt to attack the Russian stores and boathouses at a place called Gamla Carleby, during which the boat in which he formed part of the crew came under heavy enemy fire, and twenty-six men were lost, leaving the thirteen year old tyro the senior surviving officer! Ernest's career thenceforward was uniformly successful; he was hardworking and very intelligent, and became a specialist gunnery officer. Perhaps such early experiences of responsibility and command emphasised the martinet in him; his niece Marcia fails to find the wit, gaiety and sweetness of disposition that she attributes in such good measure to the other brothers. She described him as:

> a man of forceful character, always the Naval Captain, dominating his family and his sisters, who regarded him with admiration and respect, and leant upon his advice on all subjects. Underneath this somewhat masterful manner was a sensitive nature depending greatly upon affection and sympathy. The

main influence upon his life in boyhood and youth had been that of his father, of whom he always spoke with great affection.

One is inclined to think these judgements are passed upon the elderly Admiral, whose life had been punctuated by some very severe trials and tragedies, and whose career, like his brother Edward's, accustomed him to habits of rigid discipline and command. In youth, as his surviving letters show, he was lively and affectionate, with the devotion to his family and home which was common to all the clan. He was held in great affection by his brothers and sisters, as Walter's diaries testify, and he was no avuncular ogre to his nieces, Augustus' daughters, who rejoiced in his hospitality when he held the command at Portsmouth.

After his exciting debut in HMS *Odin* in the Gulf of Bothnia, Ernest's naval career proceeded very smoothly and successfully on board *Ganges*, *Topaze* and *Vixen* in different parts of the globe. He earned golden opinions and specialist qualifications as a gunnery officer, and Lord John Hay recorded of him that he had 'very good French; very able man in any sphere of life much above the average…' Many of Ernest's appointments reflected not only his technical knowledge and skill but also his intellectual stature and administrative abilities. For example, in 1866 as Gunnery Officer in HMS *Duncan* he was appointed as a member of the commission sent out to investigate the proceedings of Governor Eyre in quelling a rebellion of black Jamaicans; it had been led by a wealthy mulatto Wesleyan preacher called Gordon, who had been captured, condemned to death and hanged; Eyres had been criticised for his harshness in putting down the rebellion and hanging the ringleaders. Ernest's comments on the subject in one of his home letters were sensible and well-informed.

After his marriage in 1868 to Laura York, the sister of the wife of his brother Morland,[11] he was appointed Assistant Director of the Naval Ordinance, a home appointment based in London. In spring his happy domestic life was interrupted by his appointment as Commander of HMS *Albatross*, which was about to embark on a long tour of duty to South America, which kept him away from home for more than four years. The tour took him round the shores of South America from Rio de Janeiro through the Magellan Straits and up to Panama, with long periods cruising along the coastlines of Chile and Peru, and thence to the north-west shores of the United States, to Vancouver Island and south to California and Mexico.

His naval duties appeared to be relatively light, involving cruising up and down the coast with extended periods at major ports, such as Callao, near Lima, and Panama, Coquimbo, Valparaiso, etc. He intervened effectively in the problems of English merchant ships, particularly in one which involved a crew mutinous against bad treatment by some of their officers; his presence was also effective in quelling local riots and rebellions. He rescued a deposed President of Panama in a cloak-and-dagger operation, and received special commendation for a similar operation in Tumaco, involving a British subject, 'Mr Grimdale' as well as a citizen of the US. The *Albatross* would remain in some of these major ports for some considerable time, long enough for Ernest to establish warm friendships with some of the local or expatriate British families, and indulge his passion for exploring the countryside, and hunting and shooting – the results of the latter activities supplied the crew with much needed fresh meat or fish. Ernest wrote a

---

[11]The occasion recalled with naval precision by Ernest in a letter to Louisa in 1876: 'I have not seen Haverholme since I proposed to Laura in the Wilderness on the 4th of May 1868 at 11.30 a.m. – such is life, what changes have gone on...'

long and detailed journal for his wife of this extended tour, which is of great interest, and describes, for example, the visit to the almost uninhabited island of Juan Fernandez, the island of Robinson Crusoe, where he enjoyed a long and dangerous chase to round up a herd of semi-wild cattle. He described himself riding 'like a wild Indian galloping after a herd of cattle with my lasso whirling over my head... I don't think I have enjoyed anything so much since I came out!' His description of leaving the island is rather a masterpiece, and deserves to be quoted.

It is a lovely island, but it is a most insecure anchorage, quite open to the north, and to my horror about 2 p.m. the wind set in from the north with heavy rain, at 4 o'clock I went on board and hoisted all the boats up and made Bingham get everything ready for sea. I was on deck constantly until 11 p.m. when it came on so bad and such a heavy sea set in that I was afraid she might part her cable and run on shore, and as we were only about thirty yards from a rocky coast nothing could have saved the ship, so at midnight I turned the hands up, weighed and steamed out into a gale of wind and tremendous sea; but that was nothing in comparison of being anchored close to a lee share and no shelter. It was a grand sight on a dark night seeing the foaming surf dashing against the rock-bound coast close to the ship and feeling that nothing but a small iron chain was holding her, the wind roaring and the rain pelting and the steam roaring up the funnel. I could, despite the cold, enjoy it all when steam was up and I felt that by turning a small tele-graph I could set in motion a power stronger than the sea and the wind and force the ship safely out against both. The men knew the danger and worked well and the anchor came flying up and in half-an-hour we were rolling off south before a N.W. gale with lots of sea-room.

Albatross was paid off at Chatham in June 1878 and Ernest's next appointment was as Naval Attaché to the 'European Powers', based in Paris, where his family could be with him. This was a post concerned with Naval Intelligence, and he evidently pleased his superiors by his 'energy and ability', earning particular commendations for work at St Petersburg, and for his negotiations with France and Egypt concerning the Suez Canal.

Later commands at sea found him involved in our conflicts in Egypt and the Sudan against Mahdist attacks. By leaving his ship *Salamis* at Ismailia and claiming his right as a 'commissioner', he joined Sir Garnet Wolseley's staff on the eve of the Battle of Tel-el-Kebir, and shared in the glories and horrors of that victory. He wrote a very detailed account of his experiences for his wife, concluding, 'we had 52 hours away from the ship without taking our clothes off, and a more eventful time I think I never passed in my life…'

Fine sailor though Ernest evidently was, two episodes marred his record, and earned him the nickname 'Ground Rice' from his heartless sister Fanny. When in command of HMS *Iris* in the Mediterranean, he ran his ship aground on the Avola shoal; though there was no loss of life and little damage, the court martial gave him a reprimand. A much more disastrous accident occurred a year or two later when he was in command of HMS *Sultan* in the Mediterranean; coming into harbour in Malta, he ran his ship aground on an uncharted rock, and it sank, though fortunately without loss of life. It was universally believed that no blame could be attached to the Captain, who was relying on faulty charts; but the blow was overwhelming, grief for the loss of his ship combined with chagrin at the damage to his professional pride. He wrote a brief note to his sister Caroline:

> All is over as you will know with my fine command, and all I have to do is to bear it all as bravely as I can and try to save my professional reputation. God will give me strength to do so and for this you can pray. I have many blessings left, now it all looks dark and dreary. The Duke is like a brother. [The Duke of Edinburgh, now Admiral C-in-C of the Mediterranean Fleet.] ...There is as you say no disgrace but it is the hardest trial that can come to a sailor and this I see you understand... The Court-martial is ordered at Portsmouth...

To the surprise of everyone concerned, the court martial found Ernest guilty of an error of judgement and issued a reprimand. The Duke of Edinburgh had been called to give evidence which would have favoured Ernest's case, but he was prevented by illness (and by his Mother!) from testifying on his behalf. The Queen's personal physician, Sir James Reid, wrote:

> The Duke of Edinburgh has been suffering from Maltese fever. The Queen made the most of the illness because the Admiralty wanted to have him examined in a Court of Enquiry over the loss of HMS *Sultan*, and naturally enough the Queen and the Duke

wished to avoid that. Consequently Sir Oscar Clayton, who the Queen says, 'understands him better than anyone else' (which means that he will do whatever he thinks will please) is sent down to Portsmouth to go and meet the Duke at Spithead and report to HM and the Admiralty on his condition and say whether he does not think the Duke unfit for travel to London, or for business of any kind.

Ernest never had another command at sea, but this was by no means the end of his career. During the next years he filled a number of more administrative posts, for example serving on the Committee of the Royal Naval reserve, and in 1891 in command of Special Service at Pembroke. In 1894, now a rear-Admiral, he was sent to the Conference in Paris to represent the Admiralty with regard to British land rights at Port Said. Finally in 1896 he was appointed Admiral-Superintendent at Portsmouth; apart from the opportunity this appointment gave many members of his family to visit him, especially during the Royal Jubilee celebrations of 1897, he superintended the building of three new battleships, *Canopus*, *Carson* and *Formidable*. It was during his time at Portsmouth that Ernest's beloved wife Laura died at the end of 1898. Ernest eventually found consolation in a second marriage, with Fanny, the widow of Lt. Col. Gunning, with whom he spent his long retirement, which began in 1905. Two major sorrows blighted his later years. His second daughter Beatrice (Bea) had married Eric Serrocold, an army officer stationed in Ireland, and in 1906 they were living in Bansha, near Tipperary; they already had one daughter, Elizabeth, and Bea was expecting another child. It was born, a daughter, Ann – *tout va bien* recorded Eric Serrocold cheerfully, but on 10th October Bea died 'of blood-poisoning', leaving the two little girls to the care of their aunt Gwenllion, now married to Walter James, later Lord Northbourne.

An even more crushing blow followed; Ernest's youngest child was a son, Arthur, a very gifted and brilliant young sailor; in 1914, a few months before the outbreak of the First World War, he was drowned in a seaplane accident near Calshot. Marcia Rice's family account continued after describing this tragedy:

> ...after writing of such a sorrow it seems an anticlimax to mention the material disaster that overtook the Admiral in his old age. But it was a great one. Six years after his son's death, in the winter of 1920, Sibertswold House near Dover where Ernest Rice had made his home since his retirement was burnt to the ground. The fire began in one of the attics and nothing could save the house. In the bitter cold of the winter night Admiral Rice personally directed gangs of villagers and miners in saving the furniture and pictures. Among the pictures saved was the Zoffany portrait of Jane Austen.[12]

Fortunately Ernest (now Sir Ernest Rice) was able to rent Dane Court from his nephew Henry Rice, who farmed his land from North Court nearby. His second wife died in 1923; Ernest lived on until 1927, outliving all his brothers and sisters except for Lionel, the youngest member of the family.

---

[12]This portrait, now not thought to be by Zoffany, is still in possession of a member of the Rice family.

15   Lionel

Lionel was the last of Elizabeth's family, and was known as 'Ba', long after that abbreviation of 'Baby' became inappropriate for the tough young man of six feet three inches he became. He shared his height with his brother Cecil, a talent for drawing and painting with his sister Fanny; his cheerful and affectionate disposition he shared with almost all his siblings, as well as the possession of a lively and graphic pen. His wanderlust and rather restless disposition seen to have been singular in the family; most of the other sons came home to roost at Dane Court, and were happy if fate permitted them to settle in its vicinity, Lionel soon moved on, living in Norway, Scotland, Sussex and Witney in his later years.

Lionel was born in 1842, and was sent to the recently founded public school at Cheltenham. As with the other sons, the problem of his future career aroused family concern and discussion. By the time Lionel left school, his father's Parliamentary career was over, and his influential brother-in-law, Lord Winchilsea, was dead, so the patronage necessary for a successful launch into a career in the services may have been hard to find. Emigration to the Colonies was becoming popular; settlements had been established in New Zealand, at Christchurch and Wellington, and in Australia, the discovery of gold in 1840, and the awareness of the country's potential for sheep and other farming, had created a flood of new emigration about the same time. The Rices had friends in Australia, amongst them Sir George and Lady Bowen, who had known Augustus Rice in Corfu; he was now the Governor-General of Queensland; also some people called Scott, settlers who turned out to be less reliable than expected. Edward made available to Lionel some of the money he would expect to inherit, and launched him on his Australian adventure. He left England in October 1865, when he was twenty-one years old. His first surviving letter is dated 28th January 1866, and was written at Bowen, Port Denison, North Queensland. He was *en route* for a point even further north, Rockingham, a place recently established by the pioneer settlers, the Archer brothers, at that time surely on the very extremity of civilisation. His letter was written to one of his Knight cousins at Chawton House, Adela Louisa, Edward Knight's daughter, and describes vividly the extreme discomforts as well as the exotic beauties of the place.

> I have gradually made my way up here from Brisbane [he wrote] in horrid little steamers and seem to have reached the farthest point of civilised country. It has been bad enough coming up from Brisbane, very rough weather, very bad food, and I was always obliged to sleep on deck as I could not get into my berth below, but even that will probably seem pleasant when we start to Rockingham... in a 15 ton schooner. It will probably take about a week to get there, by which time I expect to be nearly dead. We certainly can't give a fair account of the country yet as we got here in the worst time of the year – but I can only say if it is always like this I would sooner be a ploughboy at home than a millionaire at Australia. I don't really always feel like this but just now I am gradually being driven mad by flies, poo-sing which settle in hundreds all over one's head and face, I never could appreciate before the misery of the plague of flies. It must have been feafu' but I don't suppose there were many more than there are here. After dusk mosquitos rage in thousands and

devour your unwary colonist, altogether one's life is not exactly enjoyable, the sun is too dangerous for one to go out all day, and mosquitos too venomous to go out at night. When I can get a chance I always start off into the bush as everything is extraordinary to a new chum as they call us – the 'scrub' is most lovely immense woods of lovely sweet-smelling evergreen, covered with creepers of every colour and variety... there are some creepers with flowers exactly like the passion-flower at home only scarlet mauve and white. I saw all three colours close together. All the birds too are curious enough, white and black cockatoos, parrots of every colour, scarlet, green, etc., black swans, every sort of wild foul [sic] and sea-bird, wax-bills, parroquets etc., astonish and deafen you as you push along in the scrub, but all the novelty and romance is spoilt by one's having 500 flies and mosquitos on your face all the time, and being obliged to look on the ground all the time if you are walking to keep clear of snakes. I killed an immense whip-snake the other day, the most venomous of any, I believe, you die about 4 minutes after the bite... Wood has just come in from 'trying to take a short walk', but sun, flies and mosquitos have effectually stopped him. We are putting up at 'Hart's Metropolitan Hotel' and it is certainly 'Colonial' in every way. Squatters, stockmen etc. lounge in and out and drink all day in large cabbage-tree hats, flannel shirts, booted and spurred, by about ten o'clock they are most of them tipsy, and joined with mosquitos quite prevent one's getting any sleep as they are generally fighting or rushing about in the passages passed [sic] my door. But the land-lord comes from Hythe and last night I had a long talk with him about Sandling, Sneeth, etc. It was so jolly finding someone who knew the name even of home people and places. I don't the least repent coning out here beastly as it is at present, because I know I couldn't do better at home, but still I can't help longing to be at home agin sometimes.

Visits to the Bowens at Government House in Brisbane were very much more comfortable, though to Lionel's disappointment Sir George Bowen was about to leave Australia for an appointment in New Zealand. Lionel was hoping to acquire a property for himself, but was awaiting the passing of a Land Bill which would classify and evaluate the available territory. Meanwhile he was gaining experience and employment working on the stations of other settlers. The friends from whom he expected support had failed him and his friend Wood, in fact they had proved to be dishonest; Wood, with whom he had travelled out, had deposited his small fortune with the Scotts, and this had been swallowed up in the Scott's subsequent bankruptcy, leaving Wood without redress; Lionel felt himself to have been very fortunate not to have lost his nest egg in the same way. 'This is scarcely what I expected from such old friends and neighbours, they have treated me in a blackguard way,' concluded the unfortunate Wood.

Lionel took to the life on the stations with great zest and enthusiasm, the simple living conditions, the rough riding over huge areas of terrain, the companionship of all sorts and conditions of men, and the marvels of the unique flora and fauna; two things he complained of – the absence of members of the female sex, and the universal habit of violent and blasphemous language, which he did his best to eradicate when he became established on his own property. And of course his thoughts turned ever and again to home and Dane Court and the family. As with his brother Augustus, and indeed his mother, when on the subject of Dane Court he waxed poetical. Late in 1867 he wrote to his sister Caroline Cassandra:

> ...the Miss Gores who long to go home and like hearing about it, and I sit on the verandah in the evening and describe Dane Court to them exactly, what the wood is like, and take them with me at 3 o'clock in the morning into the kitchen out at the door and across to our gardens, wetting our feet in the grass and our hands with drops on the rails, but I cannot describe to them the smell of the gardens or the stomp of the rabbits or the stillness of the grotto just before the sun first gilds the top of the fir trees. I wonder if early thrushes still break snail-shells on a root about half-way along the walk to the grotto opposite to that sloping tree covered with ivy. It is not very wonderful to me but it would seem so to them how exactly I know every root, branch and stone about home. They cannot appreciate the stillness of the wood at night when one can hear acorns dropping and a dog bark at Betteshanger, and a cart trot along to Eastry, there is no sich thing out here, where frogs and crickets and beasts shriek and croak and burr and cohii and whirr all night. Fancy! Cam, I was walking after church in the gardens at Brisbane with Lady Bowen and some

others when I heard a blackbird make the noise they do when you frighten them out of a laurestinus. I was quite aghast with rouge and rushed off and discovered two real blackbirds in a wire aviary, they were going to roost and were so like the terrace walk. I took all the ladies to see them. Lady B. said it rouged her too, and tried to explain to the others what rouge meant but could not, well. Sir George insists always on telling everybody about all of us at home, and stories of Augustus, etc. He always begins by saying, 'You must know, Miss – that young Rice has lots of tall handsome brothers at home all in the Army except one who when I knew him at Oxford was the greatest swell of any, a tremendous swell,' etc. etc.; Then he goes on to Augustus at Corfu...

A letter to Fanny about the same date recalls happy times with her family at Haverholme:

...Cadge, how it rouges me writing to you, Fanny, how well I remember the last time I was at Haverholme... I little thought then I was saying goodbye for good, what a lovely summer I had there. It is very sad thinking those days can never come again or any like them for me but it does not make me the least mis, thankee... but what I hate as much as anything about it is, that your children will be grown-up, more or less. Murray and Henry tall collared ponces in coats and the last thing in neck-ties and waistcoats, Evelyn I daresay bestriding or at best riding a tall gaunt horse in Rotten Row in hat and boots and Harold instead of appearing at prayers with a neat velvet frock and bare feet, legs I mean, will come assing in, in trousers and boots with large teeth and hair cut short, as such I shall look forward to meeting them with great pleasure. I don't the least know when there is a chance of my ever coming home again, as long as I have good health, for supposing, as I hope to do, I start for myself in a few months with a cattle-station, I never should be able to leave it without paying a man £200 a year to manage it whilst I was away...

Lionel's letters are also full of descriptions of life and conditions on the stations, of the aborigines – as might be expected, superficial, but not unappreciative of their physique, their skills and their humour – the rigours of mustering the cattle, and the fascination of the flora and fauna of this exotic country.

On the evidence available it is not possible to trace all Lionel's early movements in Queensland with any accuracy, but at first, and probably for quite a long time, he worked on the stations of other earlier settlers. Most important to Lionel, and indeed very important in the early history of the settlement of Queensland, were the Archers of Gracemore, where he lived and worked around 1866–7. Two of the brothers – there were nine of them, rivalling the Rice clan – had discovered and named the River Fitzroy in 1853, in North Queensland, and had established a station there, on the edge of a lake, eventually calling it Gracemore after the name of the wife of Thomas Archer. They later established the town of Rockhampton, and particularly with the discovery of gold in the neighbourhood in 1858, the area became very prosperous.

The Archers were a Scottish family which had settled in Norway, and subsequently some of the brothers returned to that country. It is most likely that this was the reason why later in life Lionel and his wife bought a property in Norway and spent many happy years there. In Queensland, Lionel was one of many young men of the category described by an Australian writer (C.R. Moore, *Whips and Swizzlers* from *Lectures on North Queensland History*, James Cook University, 1975):

> The plantation owners and managers were mostly wealthy well-educated English or Scots minor aristocracy, middle gentry, and middle bourgeoise [sic] the third sons of country squires who could hope for no future in England...native-born Australians were a minority among the plantation owners.

In a list of 'Mackay's aristocracy' the author mentions General Sir Reginald Pole-Carew, a member of the Devon family so friendly with the Rice brothers, and Henry Finch-Hatton – 'perhaps the most famous of all who had property in the Pioneer valley and was often visited by his aristocratic friends and relations.' The Queensland records tend to confuse Henry and Harold Finch-Hatton, the two younger sons of Fanny Winchilsea, and indeed to regard them as one individual; both joined their uncle Lionel in the late 1870s and with him bought the station at Mount Spencer on the Pioneer River, like Gracemore, on the edge of a fine lake. It is no doubt because of this joint ownership that it is the Finch-Hatton name rather than that of Lionel Rice which seems to appear in such historical documents as exist. Neither brother settled in Australia, though Harold spent enough time in the country (eight or nine years altogether) to take part vigorously in local politics and to write his book *Advance Australia!* As C.R. Moore wrote, 'Almost without exception these expatriate Britons viewed their squatting ventures as short-term ventures. They had strong family bonds at home but economic demands or primogeniture forced them out to the colonies...' Lionel and other settlers called themselves 'squatters', a term originally applied to men who settled illegally on Crown land in Queensland and whom it was found impossible to dislodge, but which came to mean those who owned pastoral grazing property, less improperly acquired.

Lionel was eventually able to afford the occasional passage home; in the summer of 1875, he was home for some months, in the course of which he married Eleanor Murray, a Scottish girl of ample fortune, only a very short time before his older brother Augustus married his cousin Adela Mary Margaretta Knight. Lionel's marriage was to be childless, but it was a long and happy one, and both survived to celebrate their golden wedding in 1925. Lionel returned to Australia with his bride, and it was about at this time that his young nephew Henry Finch-Hatton joined him, and set up in partnership with him on the station they had acquired near Mackay. It was called Mount Spencer, and consisted of three 'runs', Mount Spencer, Haslewood and Blue Mountain, with about 15,000 head of cattle. Harold, the third Winchilsea son, joined them later, and in his book *Advance Australia!* (W.H. Allen and Co., London, 1885) he described in entertaining style his long and tedious journey and his arrival at last at the coastal town of Mackay, where he was met by his brother. The town he depicted as deserted, derelict, and without civilised amenities of any sort; his description of the wide empty street, paved with dust or mud according to the season, and the uncouth and drunken liveliness of the 'hotel' with its communal dinners, are reminiscent of an early 'Wild West' film.

The stations were a different story. Harold described Mount Spencer in some detail, as a place of great natural beauty.

> The view from Mount Spencer is magnificent and certainly beats anything I ever saw in Australia. The station stands on a low broad ridge, which was originally timbered like the surrounding bush, but the trees have all been cleared away, and stumps burnt out, and the holes filled in, so that the ground is now a smooth expanse of short green turf, sloping gently down to the edge of a large lagoon, about 300 yards away. The lagoon itself is about a mile and a half long, and about a mile across, the centre covered with water-lilies, and the edges fringed with a thick wide belt of rushes. On the far side from the station a forest of huge gum trees follows the winding shores of the lagoon, its outline broken by one or two little promontories running out into the water, and above the forest, like an amphitheatre, rise the mountains of the coast, running back in broken rocky spurs to Blue Mountain, a vast densely wooded range, 3,000 feet high and 14 miles away...

The lagoon was the haunt of countless waterfowl, including egrets and pelicans, and Lionel kept that part of the lagoon which faced the house as a sanctuary. He was an enthusiastic poultry-breeder, and had some very rare specimens. Harold listed the members of Lionel's menagerie:

> Rice was immensely fond of his chickens and his pigeons, never went home to England

without bringing back a fresh supply, and some of the birds which he raised on the station were very high-class specimens indeed. Besides all these he had a menagerie of tame birds and beasts of all kinds. When I got there the collection contained an eagle-hawk, 3 crested falcons, 7 wood-ducks, 5 whistlers, a magpie, 3 teal, a kangaroo, a wallaroo, a native bear, 5 flying squirrels, 3 spur-winged plovers, and last but not least, the infernal carpet-snake which I found in my bed...

The house, Harold reported, was a comfortable two-storey wooden building on seven-foot piles, well-furnished and embellished with creepers and geraniums; surrounded by huts and outbuildings, in one of which, primitively equipped, Harold slept, once he had removed Lionel's pet carpet snake from his bed to its proper quarters in a barrel. Lionel and Henry Finch-Hatton ran the station with two stockmen and three or four black boys, together managing 12 to 20,000 head of cattle. Harold described a muster or round-up of cattle, which, with the vast areas of territory, most of it rough bush, and the semi-wild cattle, was an arduous and quite dangerous business, demanding great skill and horsemanship. Lionel himself has left a long account of a muster, which he illustrated with pen and ink drawings; the station he described was one he was working on during an earlier period, possibly the Archer station at Gracemore. The work is lively and dramatic and full of humour and sheer enjoyment, but much too long to reproduce here.

Lionel and his wife were home again at the time of his father's death in 1878, but returned to Australia early in the following year. Two letters survive from his mother from this period, very much the customary pattern, which was what the absent son so much desired to hear, trivia about Dane Court and its occupants, and family news. She would go for:

> little drives in the Pony carriage when I can, and take small walks down the Long meadow hedge and watch for the young thrushes that it is full of and listen to the nightingales and black caps and pick a few cowslips and gaze at the cows and think of past days...

Elizabeth's comments on friends and neighbours still tended to be caustic, though no doubt were meant to be interpreted through the medium of a long-term affectionate relationship: 'Miss York is staying – how frightful she is...' or 'Montague Oxenden... called here a day or two ago... the end of his life is gilded by the Duke of Edinburgh having of his own accord attended his daughter's wedding – he can talk of little else,' or 'William Hammond lives on in solitary grandeur, we see very little of him, he took a great fancy to Laura when they first settled at Street End [Laura, wife of Ernest] but now he is tired of her and takes up with a pretty Mrs Mackenzie a Canadian whose husband keeps the hounds.' She was mildly critical of Edward, whose appointment at Malta had terminated – 'no news of any appointment for him at present... E. does not choose to take the trouble of showing himself or asking for anything so he gets nothing... Lord Northbrook the First Lord asked Ernest the other day if E. had not retired!...' Edward in fact shortly afterwards became Superintendent of the Dock-yards at Sheerness; he was the Admiralty choice, whereas the Queen was determined that Prince Ernest of Leiningen, George Rice's erstwhile friend and protégé should have the appointment. She set off for a holiday on the continent without signing the appropriate document, and had to be pursued to France to be tactfully bullied to comply. The Prince bore no grudge against Edward, and in fact succeeded him in the post at a later date, agreeing with him in a later letter that it was a good appointment but a ghastly place to be posted to! Edward meanwhile was at this time happily preoccupied with making alterations at Dane Court, which Elizabeth described without complaint, although the house was full of workmen.

Lionel and his wife returned to England finally in about 1890. While he never made a fortune, and evidently experienced some vicissitudes in the success of his farming career and perhaps in speculations in goldmining shares and other ventures, they left behind them with much regret a very beautiful and prosperous property. Their long retirement was spent partly in Norway, where they built a house and where he could indulge his passions for fishing, birdwatching and sketching. In about 1909 the house in Norway was destroyed by fire, and in a letter to Louisa, Lionel expressed his sorrow. He railed too against the general degeneracy of contemporary politics, 'advanced liberalism', and the rascality of people like Lloyd George and Winston Churchill! Like Cecil, he must have felt the world was leaving him behind, 'rollin' down the 'ill!' Cheerfulness prevailed however, as it always did, in spite of everything – 'I am better, thank-you,' he wrote, 'in fact to all intents and purposes well, but turble liable, but only as to my cough.'

The latest letter from Lionel was again to his sister Louisa, written from Sandgate some time between 1910 and 1916, when Louisa died. It continued to manifest the cheerful optimism and gaiety which characterise all the earlier ones.

> ...I am much honoured and delighted to get a
> letter from you... I'm glad I seem lively to you

and do you mean alive, I am as cheerful as may be, tho' I am poorer than Adam (tho' I have more clothes) and my cough is that of a sheep in an autumn turnip field. I have not been out yet but intended to go today but it is now clouded over and the wind is a wind of bitterness they tell me so I shall cough on cheerfully here; we go to our own house tomorrow and though luxuriously comfortable and most kindly treated, and begged to stay here, I want to get back to my own burrow and so does E. Yes, our gardener is quite bad enough to be helped in fact to have one leg taken off and another seriously hurt is looked upon here as quite a bad accident! but he also I hear is cheerful and lively, friends here have subscribed over 100 guineas to help him towards a new leg... Who is Mr Bevan that Cam goes to tea with?... didn't some old Bevan with the memory of 3 wives once propose to Cam?... affectionate messages to you both, yes, it is really almost unthinkable that there are only 5 remaining, you say only 4, underlined, but please do not forget your most affectionate Lionel K. Ba.

Elizabeth Rice Envoi

A portrait of Elizabeth Rice was written by one of her older nieces and recorded by Marcia Rice, the other niece who wrote a brief account of the family of Edward and Elizabeth; it is enshrined like a precious miniature in the family archives garlanded with flowers and fragrant with the dusty perfume of potpourri. The writer was Lady Evelyn Templetown, the daughter of Fanny Winchilsea, and she called her essay *Beautiful Old Ladies*. It is worth quoting in spite of its saccharine tone because it gives a description of Dane Court as well as of its mistress:

> My grandmother was the most beautiful old lady I have ever seen; one whose very name recalls a vision so rare and delicately sweet that one despairs of putting it into words; a vision that brings with it the faint perfume of cedar and sandalwood, of bergamot and summer flowers!
>
> The background of this vision is an old English home, white-walled, with steep brown-tiled roofs and tall white chimneys, at the foot of the low hills crowned with woods where bluebells and primroses made a glory in the Spring and the nightingales filled the summer nights with melody.
>
> Splendid old trees, elm, oak, beech and lime surrounded the house and threw their

long shadows across the deep rich meadows in the golden sunset, and sheltered from the mid-day heat the herd of Jersey cows and the many little Southdown sheep which passed their lives in peace and plenty.

An old home full of lovely old Chippendale furniture, beautiful pictures and old china, all of them so entirely a necessary part of the home that they were for the most part almost unnoticed.

There was a 'breakfast Room' and a 'Cedar Recess', a Powdering Closet and a wide shallow staircase with twisted balusters of black oak; little flights of stairs in every direction leading to long narrow passages and wide landings and sweet old-fashioned bedrooms with four-post beds, blazing fires in old hob grates where copper kettles sang their dutiful song. Quaint old prints on the walls, wide sofas and welcoming armchairs covered with tiny patterned chintzes.

Downstairs the drawing room (parlour it was called not so long ago) had small paned high windows with deep low window-seats, the windows always thrown wide open in summer, and protected from the sun by striped red and white awnings, and through them floated the perfume of heliotrope and rose, scented geranium and sweet verbena, the lazy cawing of rooks in the tall elm trees and the sweet, sweet song of blackbird and thrush; lovely pictures on the walls; beautiful old china, the faint rich smell of potpourri from old vases and bowls, old-fashioned chintz covers and curtains, and through the door which almost always stood open to the library, the scent of hot-house flowers from the conservatory beyond, and the song of many birds whose carefully tended cages hung on its walls: a fit setting for a beautiful old lady!

But who shall find words that will describe her and do justice to the unconscious fascination she exerted over anyone who had to do with her? I can see her now, walking about her dressing-room with swift light steps, or sitting in her own particular armchair; her beautiful hands with their old-fashioned diamond, pearl and turquoise rings, busy with some soft piece of knitting destined for one of her many children or grand-children, or tending her flowers in the conservatory, and the beautiful golden canaries which lived there and had their nests and brought up families of little golden children year after year under her careful management; for whatever she did was perfectly done; and the management of her house was always a wonder to me! No one, not even her own children, knew when her housekeeping was done, and yet what house was ever run as that one was? The orderly quiet comfort of it, behind which, if one had thought of it, one would have recognised the firm unseen hand; the servants grown old in the service of the 'Master and Mistress' whose interests were identical with their own, the perfection of every detail and the utter absence of apparent effort to attain it!

What did my beautiful lady wear? Soft old brocades and silks, finest of lawn and lace yellowed by age, soft Indian shawls, a cap of delicate old lace and coloured ribbon on the soft brown hair, more brown than grey to the last day of her long life.

Beautiful in her youth, she was yet more beautiful in her old age, high-bred, gracious and witty with an ever-young interest in all that went on around her, a keen sense of humour and a smile which an adoring grandson compared to the light of a thousand lamps, there was still something more, a feeling when one was with her that one was ever on the verge of great discoveries, and that behind the delicate veil of a reticence unknown to this generation there were depths of character still ungauged, but, as one felt, based on and pervaded by a religion, about which she did not talk but which brought her through every trial and sorrow, calm and undismayed.

Small wonder that such a beautiful old lady was worshipped alike by husband, children, friends and relations and that even to her grandchildren, to claim her attention and to get her to themselves if only for a few minutes, was a thing to covet and scheme for! Small wonder that her memory is ever green and that loving hearts look forward to the time when they will see her again in the land that is very far off.

This sentimental Victorian version of Elizabeth is only part of the picture. Elizabeth's life in many ways resembled that of her mother, although she had the good fortune to live long enough to see all her surviving children well established. In many ways her character and disposition were similar; but in certain respects their personalities were very different. It is interesting to compare the letter which Elizabeth Austen wrote to Lizzie on 8th September 1807 from Chawton House with one Lizzie herself wrote from Chawton House to her daughter Louisa in 1831. In 1807 Elizabeth and Edward had taken Fanny and the two older boys, Edward and William, for a visit to Chawton House, leaving Lizzie and the rest of the children at Godmersham. Cassandra Jane, the tenth child, was then a baby, born in November the previous year, Elizabeth was seven; the family would be completed in October of the following year with the birth of John Brook, whose birth would result in the death of Elizabeth Austen, at the age of thirty-five.

> I was quite delighted with your letter my sweetest dear little Lizzie [she wrote] and as I daresay you are every day in hopes that Russell will bring you an answer I will not put off writing, as I should be very sorry to disappoint you. You cannot think how I much I miss you all the house is quite dull and melancholy, and it appears already a long time since I have seen any of you. My little darling Cassandra, I am afraid she will forget me, I hope you talk to her of Mama sometimes that she may be accustomed to the sound, sweet Angel! how I long to kiss her fat soft neck and her sweet little lips. I am very glad she has cut another tooth, and I hope she will have four by the time I return home, and not look quite so pale as she did. How happy you must have been riding out with your Uncle John [probably Elizabeth's brother John Bridges] I should have liked to have seen you very much, I suppose you did not venture to trot or canter, but you will another time, so poor little May was

afraid! I am not much surprised at it, as it was the first time. I remember feeling very odd when I found myself on horseback. I felt so far from the ground. The weather is very much altered since we left home. It is grown quite cold, we have talked of having a fire several times, but we have not yet. I don't like beginning so early, because I think it impossible to leave them off again, this house is very cold and dreary, but it would be very comfortable if it was well filled with children, their playing and prattling would enliven us very much. We all breakfast together at half-past nine o'clock, your brothers then go out and amuse themselves generally with a nice little green chaise which Edward gets into and William stands up behind, then they guide it down the hills as fast as they can, and enjoy it extremely, they have got a trap, Bat and Ball likewise. Wm. comes in about 12 and does a few lessons, afterwards he takes a walk with Fanny and me, whilst Papa and Edward ride, we dine at ½ past 4, walk in the evening, drink tea at 8 or before, and your brothers generally go to bed soon after, not knowing what to do besides. I thought you would like to know how we pass our time, we shall soon have a little variety, for today your Grandmamma, and your Aunts Cassandra and Jane come to us (from Southampton) which we shall like very much and tomorrow Uncle and Aunt James Austen, and little Edward, who will be a charming companion for William, he is to ride here on a donkey, it is about 14 miles, which is a long ride for him, little Caroline is to stay at home, which I regret very much, for she would be a nice little plaything. I am afraid, my darling, you will not be much amused by this letter, for I am not in spirits to be entertaining. If you cannot read it, you must ask Marianne to help you, I know she is a clever little thing in reading letters, you must give her a great many loves and kisses from me, likewise my little angels, Charles, Louisa and Cassandra. Oh, how I wish you were all here, that I might kiss you myself, dear sweet little loves... Papa, Fanny and your brothers send their kindest loves to you all, believe me, my dearest Lizzie, yr. fond and affectionate E.A.

Louisa was also seven years old and already had a nursery-full of little siblings, just as Lizzie had in 1807. Even the nurse left in charge was the same, the invaluable Sackree, or Setree. Elizabeth and Edward Rice had come to Chawton from Dane Court with the three oldest boys, Edward, Henry and Morland, the two latter to be deposited at school, while the others continued a visit to Elizabeth's oldest brother Edward Knight junior and his family – his first wife Mary Dorothea and the first three of their children, Lewkenor, Wyndham and baby Annabella.

'My dear little Lou,' she wrote,

As I promised to write next to you, I hope Miss Setree will excuse my answering her letter which I received this morning and that she will read this to you instead. Pray thank her for the good account she sent me of you all, and don't let me catch you being ill again when I am away, or else I shall never come back. By the time you get this letter I hope

Cozens will be at Dane Court to take care of you and prevent any more alarms in attempting the house, but I do not understand how if the windows were all fastened at night one could have been found open in the morning. I think Mary must have forgotten to fasten it, or it could not have been found open without breaking the glass, ask Miss Setree to mention how it was the next time she writes. We took Henry and Morland [aged ten and eight] to school last Thursday and left them both crying, poor little boys with Mr and Mrs Earle standing by them ready to whip them as soon as we were gone. Aunt May had an immense plum cake made for them which I daresay they found a great comfort and Papa bought each of them a bat and a ball and a humming top at Maidstone and Grandpapa gave them five shillings apiece. Henry rode Edward's pony several times with Grandpapa and one day the pony jumped and kicked a little and over went Henry on his head, he thought he was nearly killed I believe but he was hardly at all hurt. Whilst I think of it, tell Charlotte that she may send for some Irish and Flannel to Dover but she must not leave the price to Mrs Richards as she is a very extravagant woman – the Irish should not exceed 22d or 2 shillings a yard and the flannel about the same or 10d. I hope to bring home 6 frocks for the darling little Cecil; Aunt Mary's baby is a sweet little pretty thing, she cut her first tooth yesterday, Lewknor and Wyndham are very nice little boys… and come every day to ask me to tell them about Thomas and the Pigeons which is a story I told them the day after I came. Aunt Mary has got a nest of young bullfinches which the Gardener found in her garden and she keeps them in a cage in the drawing-room, they grow very much and are hideously ugly. I hope my two layers will be done moulting and be grown quite beautiful by the time I see them again which will be in a very little more than a fortnight. Charlotte may have the nursery and the passage whitewashed and whilst it is doing if the smell is disagreeable she had better move to the Lilac room, but she must be very careful of the bed and curtains not to let them get stained. The little boys have got very nice gardens and 5 or 6 rabbits and a dormouse and Aunt Mary has got quantities of Ducks, Turkies, chickens and canary birds so that the whole place seems alive with them. Edward is gone down into the Hall to draw Lewknor and Wyndham about in a little Carriage, it is a wet evening and they cannot get out. I must now leave off my dearest Louisa – kiss all your brothers and sisters for me and then ask Fanny to kiss you – I hope you are all very good and very happy and remember me very kindly to Miss Setree and believe me your very affect. Mama E. Rice

Edward sends his love to you all and longs to be at home. Tell Miss Setree that I shall not hope to hear from her again till Tuesday 16th if you all continue well.

Young Elizabeth Rice, with her mock scolding and her cheerful accounts of her little boys' sufferings, writes a much perkier letter than her mother at the same age; and perkiness, to judge from Jane Austen's letters, is more an Austen characteristic than a Bridges one. Elizabeth Bridges – that is, Elizabeth Rice's mother, who with her sisters, attended the very smartest girls' school in London, was probably more well-bred than well-educated as we understand the term, and we are told that she was not a woman of any intellectual pretensions.[1] Both mother and daughter in their lives shared the same happiness and fulfilment in husband, home and family; but all her life Elizabeth Rice retained an ironic attitude towards people and situations, and was able to express her opinions with a slightly caustic wit which nevertheless was cheerful and good-humoured. She had a lively turn of phrase and a strong pictorial sense. Her letters are full of small vivid pictures which bring the house and its inhabitants to life – Cecil leaping with his long legs over the flower beds with his dogs in an excess of exuberance, Ba walking about 'with... a stiff leg bandaged up tight in my garden with a very small Tabby kitten in his arms and looking white as wax...'; or a presumptuous employee 'walking about with a hat instead of a cap on and looking sharply from side to side as if he saw something that wanted attending to', and another, William, 'creeps about with a stick and looks like a withered old bit of lemon peel...' In 1882, when she was fit for little more than sitting indoors watching what went on outside her windows, she reported to Walter '...there are such lots of mushrooms here! ...Bayne saunters elegantly out in a jacket and cane

---

[1] The school attended by the Bridges girls was in Queen's Square, Bloomsbury; it laid stress on social graces and elegant accomplishments, and the academic teaching was rudimentary. This evidently suited Elizabeth Bridge's natural inclinations – Anna Austen wrote that her aunt was 'a very lovely woman... though not, I imagine, of much natural talent.' She added that, a little talent went a long way with the Goodnestone Bridges of that period, and much must have gone a long way too far. Lefroy family mss. and Deirdre Le Faye and R.A. Austen-Leigh, *Jane Austen, A Family Record*, British Library, 1989.

and 2 dogs and a basket every afternoon and brings in lots…' Another glimpse from her window gave her a summery rural picture – 'the Cows are whisking their tails at the top of the 40 acres today for a treat, presided over by the ragged Coachman's boy spudding thistles.' A neighbour came under her amused scrutiny – '…Lady Guilford called yesterday… dressed à quatre Épingles – she is a little altered, older plainer and more twisty about when she talks which I suppose is the fashion, as well as a tight brown cloth jacket, grey mixy skirt, and a double fringe of short hair at the top of her face, all very ugly…' Visitors were not always welcome! She records escaping from a visit from William Hammond 'with a waggon-load of guests', and reported 'the James's are just come home – she threatens to come and see me soon, I hope she won't.' Sometimes house guests stayed too long, did not understand the house rules regarding the proper length of a visit; she hoped 'the Edwards… will not want to stay over their time, they don't seen to have a notion of being in anybody's way or of going before their self-appointed 2 months which with their family and our constant housefull is one month too much…' It is not possible to identify which the 'Edwards' are, probably not her son, as their one little boy could hardly be described as 'their family', maybe her brother Edward and some of his huge family.

Her rare mentions of visits to neighbours yield a small harvest of observations, some of them not meant to be taken too seriously – 'If Mrs Cadman Jones were more beautiful than 40 angels I could not be interested in her; and her husband ought to have been ashamed of asking anybody to share such a name, if he ever arrives at a seat on the Woolsack even, I shall think less than nothing of him, he may depend upon it!' Her comment on a boastful young warrior is more scathing – 'John de Courcy [is] safely home – he pretends to have been in great danger from the

Bedouins but was not in the least in the world as his most foolish account of it plainly denotes – those sort of people always seen to get safely along so I daresay his life is of some use to somebody.' Her remarks on a visit to Sandling, the home of the Deedes, remind one irresistibly of scenes in her Aunt Jane's novels where ladies are gathered in the drawing room 'working', talking, and making music, and observing each other shrewdly and critically – 'they are very civil and pleasant and unlike ourselves... a small hook-nosed daughter dined here yesterday, and a frightful German governess sang very loud in the evening, the Girls sang by turns and we three Mrs's worked and talked... Miss is nice-ish-looking, a very good figure, plainish face, little Miss Branston is plain and like a cub fox...'

Relations and friends are not immune from her occasional shafts; Henrietta Knight, Wyndham's 'Hottentot' bride, 'is so frightful I can hardly bear to look at her, she is become fat and looks sixty', and 'Isa K.' (probably her niece Louisa Knatchbull) is reported at Haverholme 'mooning about with vinegar aspect and oily tongue'. Of her own children, Edward is the recipient of mild criticism from time to time – some comments have already been quoted, his 'man-of-war' moods and his refusal to seek appointment. After the death of her husband, she was very dependent upon Edward's help and advice, and very grateful for it, but commented after one visit, 'Edward and Ceci went away yesterday, he got thro' a great deal of business and I believe was satisfied on the whole tho' he thinks at least he says of course he is going to be ruined as people always do when they have got much richer than they ever were before...'

Mostly though Elizabeth is sympathetic about her children and her grandchildren, even while she perceives that they are not perfect – 'poor little Floss,' she commented, after the visit from the Deedes family, Mrs Deedes so contented and complacent and Lou with her 'rough arms and red cheeks' – 'plain as she is I think her soft white skin and peaceful ways are preferable to upright, stiff, dimpled Lou Deedes.' Caroline, who was often a problem with her moodiness, is 'thin and pale and weak and downcast and she is a dear good little girl and I hope will be happier some day...' Granddaughter Blanche, Marianne's oldest daughter, was a disappointment to neighbour William Hammond – he 'was very much disappointed with Blanche, he said to May, "I should not have known Blanche in the least, she is not the least what I thought she would be, she has not even got your voice."' She certainly does not do her real nice self justice by her abrupt voice and manner, and too much speaking and as she is not pretty strangers have nothing to fall back upon...' Usually grandchildren were very welcome guests, especially as Louisa could be relied upon to care for them and love them. Basil Wright, Florence's son, was a universal favourite – 'we are really very glad to have the dear little fell and will do our best to finish spoiling him, not a morsel shall he have to eat of anything at all good.' Cecil's three oldest children paid a visit to Dane Court in 1874 – 'we have got Cecil's 3 eldest children here, nice little things, not at all pretty, all too much like Fan – they are quite untrained and very noisy, but improving fast and getting tractable – if my head could bear it I would engage in a fortnight to make them what they ought to be...'

It cannot be denied that Elizabeth was what we would call a snob, though this characteristic must be taken in the context of the times, when a consciousness of class distinctions was universal and much more easily defined than now; just as the attitude of her sons to the native inhabitants of India or Africa – even the former sometimes referred to as 'niggers'! – and to Orientals and even 'Yankees' was distinctly Imperialistic. She could judge to a nicety the fine line which divided ladylike or gentlemanly behaviour from behaviour less refined – but derived entertainment from the latter nonetheless. She disliked vulgar ostentation – hence her condemnation of the Portals and their rubies and red velvet. Perhaps this partly accounts for her dislike of weddings which were beginning to be much more lavish than in her younger days. She described one in Dover in about 1860:

> the Wrights had a very fine wedding, Lou and Cha [Charlotte Russell] saw the bride and groom tear off under a stream of old shoes (I *cannot* conceive the use of that vulgar absurdity) in a Carriage and 4 greys, scarlet post boys and white favours – fancy the folly of 4 horses to go from 10 Waterloo Crescent...

She continued in the same vein:

> the girls were invited with some pomp to a musical party at General Russell's last Friday, so they went in their best and more becoming suits and found 20 other ladies and not a single gentleman – imagine their rage – they came back in an hour, furious. Miss Turner, the Houston Governess, officiously introduced Miss H to Cha – this was the climax – people that we do not even visit!

She could laugh at herself too – she wrote to a daughter 'what a nice dinner-party you had, all over Lords!' and to a son, 'I am glad Mr White is found out to be vulgar – Yankees must be...'

Elizabeth's enjoyment of the various manifestations of nature around her, both cultivated and wild, pervade her letters in repeated descriptions of the trees and flowers, birds and animals, sweet airs and perfumes around her home. Her love of fine scenery did not include the immediate environment of Dane Court and its neighbourhood, attached though she became to the place.

> In Godmersham days [she wrote] it was always with the greatest difficulty that I could endure the contrast between it and Dane Court and it is only since those days have ended for me that I have been able to see any beauty in this place. ...there are moments when I repine at the lot that has been mine, to live in a hideous country when I love beautiful scenery to an unknown degree.

The climate she was never reconciled to, attributing to it many of her and her family's rheumatic and chesty ailments 'the enervating damp of this worthy old Birds nest at the bottom of a Well,' she described it. Even nearby Walmer or Dover were vast improvements and her visits there always invigorated her. Sometimes her accounts of her enjoyment in the scenery are quite ecstatic. She wrote from Dover to Walter,

> Saturday was the most beautiful of days and Papa and I drove up to the top of Folkstone hill and I got out and walked along the top of the cliffs in an ecstasy of delight, first of all because I trod on grass instead of pavement, and next because I never saw any view so beautiful, such an immense stretch of sea from the South Foreland to Dungeness nearly, 100s of ships that the N. wind had brought out of the Downs, the Pier and the Church of Folkstone

looming out beyond the enormously high cliff and the immense depth from where I stood to the sea with the railway looking like a little gravel walk careering through the broken ground, I walked on tipsy with delight for three-quarters of a mile the carriage slowly following – I can't think what people mean by living in Dover when there is such a lovely place within 5 miles of them and I quite detested it when we sneaked humbly back into Biggin St and despised everybody I saw…

Similarly, when Lou was travelling in France and Switzerland with Ernest and Walter, she commiserated with Lou's regret on leaving Hyères:

one gets to like any place one has lived some weeks in, and especially if new people have gilded it, but now that you are gone I hope you will go mad with joy as I should and did at seeing the glorious Alps, I like their short name so – it sounds so grand… I cannot think how anybody can long to be here when they have got the Alps! – and the lake Geneva to look at – it would be meat and drink to me and Bed and Board!

In the course of her relatively comfortable and affluent life, Elizabeth had her share of trials and bitter bereavements, and certainly the death of her three sons was the most grievous. But the event of all others that shocked and wounded her, and caused her anger in equal parts with sorrow, was the loss of her beloved Godmersham. After her father died in 1853, her brother Edward Knight II decided to make his permanent home at Chawton House, and eventually Godmersham was let to tenants. In 1874 it was sold, to Elizabeth's disgust and grief. One of the family photograph albums had on its first page a picture of Godmersham in solitary splendour; this has been ripped out, leaving nothing but a decorated border. She could not bear to be reminded of that 'once happy and always lovely place'. Her brother's decision in 1874 to sell Godmersham was probably taken for financial reasons, and was associated with disagreements of some sort between Edward and his two families, the children of Dorothea Knatchbull and those of his surviving wife, Adela Portal. Little is known of the cause of these disagreements, but Elizabeth was antagonistic towards the older family, and it was Montague, the oldest son of the second family, who eventually inherited the Chawton property. On 25th July, 1874, Elizabeth wrote to Lou, who was at Chawton House:

> I am thinking so much of all the dreadful sale which even now seems impossible for Uncle Edward ever to have done, that I cannot help writing about it to somebody who feels it and cares about it which alas he cannot do or he never could have done it. I quite dread to hear who has bought it, don't say this, but if it should be a Jew or a man of low birth and bad character the disgrace will be complete indeed. I can hardly think of anything else and till it was done I could not help having a faint hope that something might happen to prevent it. I daresay everything goes on at Chawton exactly the same as if this cruel blow had not been struck and to outward observance no one is the least more sad or less happy – why should they be... I am glad I am not at Chawton I do not think that I could behave with the affec-

tion towards Uncle Edward that I always have had for him especially, he has done such a very wrong and totally unjustifiable thing. I never seem to have realised it so completely until now that it is as I suppose completed, it is a relief to me to write some of my mises out, and I hope I shall soon feel less angry and more rightly as to the vanity of Earthly things – still such a thing as this must be felt and never can be forgotten.

On 29th July she wrote again to Chawton:

Your letters are such a comfort and pleasure to me. I like so to hear about everything and everybody at Chawton sad as I am and always must be – of course Godmersham is never out of my head but I try to think how little it ought to signify to me now and the great happiness it has been. What you say of Brodnax [son of Edward and Dorothea] is no doubt a fair sample of what they all are and always have been and unless it is put out of Uncle Edward's power to comply with their shameful demands upon him he will soon waste the money he has now got – I hope most sincerely that Mr Portal and Gusty if it rests with them will tie it all up – Morland is very anxious for that and so is Papa… My head is shaky and noisy owing to tears and gout, but it is better than it was and I do not mean to cry any more if I can help it – you justly say how much worse illness etc. would be, and I feel that all the time we are spared that sorrow we ought not to sorrow overmuch for anything else… I am glad Monty is so nice – I hope he will have courage to resist his brother's impudence but he will have much to bear I am afraid… Beast Brodnax – I hate the thought of him!

Caroline Cassandra wrote to Louisa too from Dane Court:

You and Gusty both say very good things about Godmersham. I hoped Mama had got over it more – I mean she felt hearing of the sale more than I hoped she would – but still it would have been wonderful if she hadn't; now I think she is better again and it is very nice for her having Morny and Walter and Ba here, and Walter has just driven her out in the pony-carriage before luncheon; on the whole one may be thankful that it is I trust doing her no more harm.

Elizabeth herself added a postscript:

…don't distress yourself about my sorrow for Godmersham it will not do me any harm now and my head is better and I go on liking my drives and planning work… Uncle E. is too dreadful to think of – not care for the pictures and books…

In the following summer the unwanted furniture and effects were put up to auction, and an employee on the estate, J.F. Harvey, wrote to Edward Royds Rice on the subject:

May 4th 1875

Dear Sir,

I mentioned to the auctioneer that I should like to take the clock and Dressing Table out of the Sale as I felt Mr Knight would have been quite willing for you to have them, but he said as they were in the catalogue I had better buy them as persons attending the sale might possibly object to any article being withdrawn so I paid for them two pounds nine shillings, I could not find the key which winds the clock up, and I believe it will require some putting in order as it has not been used for some time.

The sale of the Estate is regarded by myself and I may say by every tenant and Labourer on the property with deep regret, a feeling in which I am sure yourself and Mrs Rice deeply sympathise, I shall leave at Michaelmas and close my connection with Godmersham in which for the long period of 43 years I have received both from Mr Knight and his Father great kindness and friendly consideration, and which I shall through the remainder of my life remember with grateful though not unmixed with sad recollections. I often have the opportunity of enquiring about you from my friend Wilks and am glad to hear you continue to enjoy good health, with the usual infirmities which accompany old age, if I remember right you are about eighty five...

Even in old age Elizabeth never referred to Godmersham without regret, '...that bit about Godmersham' she wrote to Lou in reply to one of her letters, 'cast a gloomy glitter over all, how I wish I had heard all Edward said – 'he must have been a bad man' – I don't think he did say – I am afraid I wish that I could look into futurity and see whether it gets back into the Knight family again...'

As Calais was engraved on the heart of Mary Tudor so Godmersham was certainly engraved on hers.

Yet her heart, however engraved, was in the final analysis, given to her family. 'You each one has its place,' she wrote to Edward after her husband died, 'which no other can fill up, and I do miss your dearest face and cheerful voice very very much.' She wrote to Caroline Cassandra a few months after Edward Royds Rice died.

> I have had a pretty nice Sunday tho' full of sorrowful thoughts and memories which the Green room gives more than almost any other. I used to watch for the first sight of the dear old grey pony's head coming down the green road, *his* road from Church and if I *had* seen him today with George by him and Gusty it could hardly have been plainer and more real than it was – I have read that part of the sermon that you refer to and there is the greatest comfort in it if we can but believe so as to realise it that he is conscious of rest and happiness now, I try to do so and I hope do, but 'Darkness and Sorrow encompass the Tomb' and there are times when one cannot get beyond it...

This passage exemplifies two of the characteristics most conspicuous in her letters – her pictorial imagination, and the unsentimental honesty of mind which rejects the solace of conventional religiosity. Like her Aunt Jane, this is a woman one would have liked to know.

Selected Bibliography

Chapman, R.W. [ed.], *The Novels of Jane Austen* in six volumes, third edition; OUP, 1933

Chapman, R.W. [ed.], *The Letters of Jane Austen,* second edition; OUP, 1952

Lane, Maggie, *Jane Austen's England*, Hale, 1986

Lane, Maggie, *Jane Austen's Family*, Hale, 1986

Honan, Park, *Jane Austen, Her Life*, Weidenfeld and Nicolson, 1987

Austen-Leigh, W. and R.A., *Jane Austen: A Family Record*, 1913. Also revised and enlarged by D. le Faye, British Museum, 1959

Austen-Leigh, James Edward, *Memoir of Jane Austen,* Century Hutchinson, 1987

Southam, Brian, *The Critical Heritage*, vols. I and II, Routledge and Keegan Paul, 1987

Reminiscences: Caroline Mary Craven Austen, JAS, 1986

Rice, Marcia, *The Rices of Dane Court*, (unpublished)

Lefroy Family Papers

Dick, Diana, *Yesterday's Babies*, Bodley Head, 1987

Knatchbull Papers, Kent Archive Office, Maidstone

Wilson, Margaret, *Almost Another Sister*, Kent C.C., Arts and Libraries

Osmaston, Henry, *Foresters and Imperial Servants: The Osmaston Family; Commonwealth Forestry Review*, March 1989

Priestley, J.B., *Victoria's Heyday*, Heinemann, 1972

Morris, J., *Pax Britannica* trilogy, 1973